Reclaiming Latin America

RECLAIMING LATIN AMERICA
experiments in radical social democracy

edited by Geraldine Lievesley
& Steve Ludlam

Zed Books
LONDON | NEW YORK

Reclaiming Latin America: experiments in radical social democracy was first published in 2009 by Zed Books Ltd, 7 Cynthia Street, London N1 9JF, UK and Room 400, 175 Fifth Avenue, New York, NY 10010, USA

www.zedbooks.co.uk

Editorial copyright © Geraldine Lievesley & Steve Ludlam 2009
Copyright in the collection © Zed Books 2009

The rights of Geraldine Lievesley and Steve Ludlam to be identified as the editors of this work have been asserted by them in accordance with the Copyright, Designs and Patents Act, 1988

Set in OurType Arnhem and Futura Bold by Ewan Smith, London
Index: ed.emery@thefreeuniversity.net
Cover designed by Andrew Corbett
Printed and bound in the UK by the MPG Books Group

Distributed in the USA exclusively by Palgrave Macmillan, a division of St Martin's Press, LLC, 175 Fifth Avenue, New York, NY 10010, USA

A catalogue record for this book is available from the British Library
Library of Congress Cataloging in Publication Data available

ISBN 978 1 84813 182 8 hb
ISBN 978 1 84813 183 5 pb
ISBN 978 1 84813 184 2 eb

Contents

Tables and box

Acknowledgements

As this book has made progress, we have had much-appreciated support and encouragement from Ellen Hallsworth at Zed Books. The chapter authors have been patient with us, and sometimes vice versa. We thank them all, and each other. We also thank the following for facilitating discussion of the book's contents at different stages: Nina Fishman of the Rethinking Social Democracy project, Sylvia McColm and Margaret Holder of the Political Economy Research Centre, University of Sheffield, the Labour Movements Specialist Group of the UK Political Studies Association, and the UK Society for Latin America Studies. We both owe many debts to friends and colleagues in Britain and in Latin America, too numerous to mention. Steve wishes to thank, especially, his brave friend Juan Miranda Inalef, who came to Sheffield straight from one of Pinochet's jails, with Edith, Catalina and Cristian, and introduced him to the realities of life on the left in Latin America; and who, with Teresa Orosa in Havana more than twenty years later, introduced him to the achievements and complexities of the Cuban revolution. Geraldine once again wishes to thank David, Claire and Kate. Steve wants to thank Julia, Joe and Thomas for putting up with his physical and mental absences as this book came together.

Geraldine Lievesley and Steve Ludlam

Acronyms

AD	Acción Democrática, Democratic Action (Venezuela)
ADN	Acción Democrática Nacionalista, Democratic Nationalist Action (Bolivia)
ALBA	Alternativa Bolivariana para los Pueblos de Nuestra América, Bolivarian Alternative for the Peoples of the Americas
ALCA	Área de Libre Comercio de las Américas (see FTAA)
ALN	Alianza Liberal de Nicaragua, Nicaraguan Liberal Alliance
APEOC	Sindicato dos Professores do Estabelecimento Oficial do Ceará, Union of Teachers in Official Establishments of Ceará (Brazil)
APPO	Asamblea Popular de los Pueblos de Oaxaca, Popular Assembly of the Peoples of Oaxaca
CARICOM	Caribbean Community
CD	Coordinadora Democrática, Democratic Coordination (Venezuela)
COB	Central Obrera Boliviana, Bolivian Workers' Confederation
CONAIE	Confederación de Nacionalidades Indígenas de Ecuador, Confederation of Indigenous Nationalities of Ecuador
CONAMAQ	Confederación Nacional de Markas y Ayllus de Q'ollasuyo, National Confederation of Markas and Ayllus of Q'ollasuyo (Bolivia)
Condepa	Conciencia de Patria, Conscience of the Fatherland (Bolivia)
CONPES	Comité Nacional de Planificación Económica y Social, National Committee for Economic and Social Planning (Nicaragua)
COPEI	Comité de Organización Política Electoral Independiente (Committee for Independent Political Electoral Organization), Venezuelan Social Christian Party
CPC	Consejos de Poder Ciudadano, Councils of Citizen Power (Nicaragua)
CPERS	Centro dos Professores do Estado do Rio Grande do Sul–Sindicato dos Trabalhadores em Educação, Rio Grande do Sul State Teachers' Centre–Workers in Education Union (Brazil)
CSUTCB	Confederación Social Unica de Trabajadores Campesinos de Bolivia, Confederation of Bolivian Agricultural Workers
CTC	Central de Trabajadores de Cuba, Cuban Workers' Centre

CTV	Confederación de Trabajadores de Venezuela, Confederation of Venezuelan Workers
EPR	Ejército Popular y Revolucionario, Popular Revolutionary Army (Mexico)
EZLN	Ejército Zapatista de Liberación Nacional, Zapatista National Liberation Army (Mexico)
FA	Frente Amplio, Broad Front (Uruguay)
FARC	Fuerzas Armadas Revolucionarias Colombianas, Colombian Revolutionary Armed Forces
FEJUVE	Federación de Juntas Vecinales, Federation of Neighbourhood Councils (El Alto, Bolivia)
FMLN	Frente Farabundo Martí de Liberación Nacional, Farabundo Martí National Liberation Front (El Salvador)
FSBT	Frente Socialista Bolivariana de Trabajadores, Bolivarian Socialist Workers' Front
FSLN	Frente Sandinista de Liberación Nacional, Sandinista National Liberation Front (Nicaragua)
FSTMB	Federación Sindical de Trabajadores Mineros de Bolivia, Federal Union of Bolivian Mineworkers
FTAA	Free Trade Area of the Americas
FUNDEB	Fundo de Manutenção e Desenvolvimento da Educação Básica, Basic Education Maintenance and Development Fund (Brazil)
FUNDEF	Fundo de Manutenção e Desenvolvimento do Ensino Fundamental e de Valorização do Magistério, Elementary School Maintenance and Development Fund and Professorship Valorization (Brazil)
IFI	international financial institution
IIRSA	Iniciativa para a Integração Regional da Infraestrutura Sul-Americana, Initiative for the Regional Integration of South American Infrastructure
IMF	International Monetary Fund
INCRA	Instituto Nacional de Colonização e Reforma Agrária, National Institute of Colonization and Agrarian Reform (Brazil)
MAS	Movimiento al Socialismo, Movement towards Socialism (Bolivia)
Mercosur	Mercado Común del Sur, Common Market of the South (Mercosul in Portuguese version)
MIP	Movimiento Indígena Pachakuti, Pachakuti Indigenous Movement (Bolivia)
MIR	Movimiento de la Izquierda Revolucionario, Movement of the Revolutionary Left (Bolivia)
MNR	Movimiento Nacionalista Revolucionario, Revolutionary Nationalist Movement (Bolivia)

Acronyms

MRS	Movimiento de Renovación Sandinista, Sandinista Renovation Movement (Nicaragua)
MST	Movimento dos Trabalhadores Rurais Sem Terra, Landless Workers' Movement (Brazil)
MTA	Mesas Técnicas de Agua, Water Committees (Venezuela)
MVR	Movimiento V [Quinta] República, Fifth Republic Movement (Venezuela)
NAFTA	North American Free Trade Agreement
NED	National Endowment for Democracy (United States)
OPEC	Organization of Petroleum Exporting Countries
PAC	Projeto de Acceleração do Crescimento, Acclerated Growth Project (Brazil)
PAN	Partido Acción Nacional, National Action Party (Mexico)
PAS	Plano Amazônia Sustentável, Sustainable Amazonia Plan (Brazil)
PBS	Pensión Básica Solidaria, Basic Solidarity Pension (Chile)
PCC	Partido Comunista Chileno, Chilean Communist Party
PCC	Partido Comunista de Cuba, Communist Party of Cuba
PCP	Partido Comunista Peruano, Peruvian Communist Party
PCV	Partido Comunista de Venezuela, Venezuelan Communist Party
PDC	Partido Demócrata Cristiano, Christian Democrat Party (Chile)
PDR	Partido de la Revolución Democrática, Party of the Democratic Revolution (Mexico)
PDT	Partido Democrático Trabalhista, Democratic Workers' Party (Brazil)
PDVSA	Petróleos de Venezuela, S.A., Venezuelan Oil Corporation
PFL	Partido da Frente Liberal, Liberal Front Party (Brazil)
PJ	Partido Justicialista, Justicialist Party (Argentina)
PLC	Partido Liberal Constitucional, Liberal Constitutional Party (Nicaragua)
PMDB	Partido do Movimento Democrático Brasileiro, Brazilian Democratic Movement Party
PPT	Patria para Todos, Country for All (Venezuela)
PRD	Partido de la Revolución Democrático, Party of the Democratic Revolution (Mexico)
PRI	Partido Revolucionario Institucional, Revolutionary Institutional Party (Mexico)
PRONAF	Programa Nacional de Apoio à Agricultura Familiar, National Programme for the Support of Family Agriculture (Brazil)
PSB	Partido Socialista Brasileiro, Brazilian Socialist Party

PSC	Partido Socialista Chileno, Chilean Socialist Party
PSDB	Partido da Social Democracia Brasileira, Brazilian Social Democracy Party
PT	Partido dos Trabalhadores, Workers' Party (Brazil)
RN	Renovación Nacional, National Renovation (Chile)
SAEB	Sistema de Avaliação Basica, Basic Evaluation System (Brazil)
SE	Secretaria da Educação, Rio Grande do Sul State Education Secretariat (Brazil)
SEDUC	Secretaria da Educação Básica, Ceará State Basic Education Secretariat (Brazil)
SERNAM	Servicio Nacional de Mujeres, National Women's Service (Chile)
Sindiute	Sindicato Único dos Trabalhadores em Educação do Ceará, Ceará Education Workers' Union (Brazil)
SPAECE	Sistema Permanente de Avaliação da Educação Básica do Ceará, Ceará Permanent System of Basic Education Evaluation (Brazil)
UCS	Unión Civica Solidaridad, Civic Solidarity Union (Bolivia)
UDI	Unión Democrática Independiente, Independent Democratic Union (Chile)
UNASUR	Unión de Naciones Suramericanas, Union of South American Nations (UNASUL in Portuguese version)
UP	Unidad Popular, Popular Unity (Chile)
URNG	Unidad Revolucionaria Nacional Guatemalteca, Guatemalan National Revolutionary Unity
YPFB	Yacimientos Petrolíferos Fiscales de Bolivia, Bolivian State Oilfields

Introduction: a 'pink tide'?

GERALDINE LIEVESLEY
AND STEVE LUDLAM

Poverty is more destructive than any weapon of mass destruction
(Luiz Inácio Lula da Silva, President of Brazil, cited in Correa Flores
2005: 14)

Hugh O'Shaughnessy, the veteran Latin America writer and campaigner, opened his 2007 Annual Lecture to the UK Society for Latin American Studies with Wordsworth's immortal words on the French Revolution, 'Bliss was it in that dawn to be alive, but to be young was very heaven' (O'Shaughnessy 2007). O'Shaughnessy's insistence that the continent was infected with hope and progress is easily visualized from media images of a humiliated President Bush at the Mar del Plata Summit of the Americas in 2005, where his neoliberal Free Trade Area of the Americas treaty was finally buried by Latin America's new leaders; of Michelle Bachelet and Cristina Fernández, two new presidents, political activists and mothers who had defied the dictatorships of Chile and Argentina; of Fidel Castro, Hugo Chávez and Evo Morales, shoulder to shoulder in Havana's Plaza de la Revolución in 2006. And far from the high offices, the images of Latin America's historically excluded peoples flooding the political stage: blockading the capital city and reversing the privatization of water in Bolivia; blocking roads in Argentina until its external debt was rescheduled; descending from the *barrios* of Caracas and surrounding the Palacio de Miraflores, chanting 'Chávez! Chávez!' until the coup-makers fled and their president was returned unharmed.

Bliss indeed! Yet confronted by the image of an electoral 'pink tide' engulfing Latin America, which entered journalistic currency after the victory of Tabaré Vázquez in Uruguay in 2004, students of left-wing politics need to interpret events and report cautiously. This is not to deny that events are exciting for socialists and, we would argue, for social democrats (we discuss the distinction in our concluding chapter). For the left, recent developments represent the most inspiring changes anywhere in the world, not least after witnessing the fate of fellow progressives in Latin America in the dark years of Operation Condor's extermination programme (Dinges 2004; Calloni 2005). Similarly inspiring has been the relative impotence of a neoconservative US administration. Stuffed with some of the most notorious militarized diplomats active in Central America in the Reagan era, it faced the reclaiming of *Nuestra América*, the 'Our America' invoked by Cuba's national hero José Martí in the eponymous 1891 essay, written in the USA and proclaiming

> The pressing need of Our America is to show that it is one in spirit and intent, swift conquerors of a suffocating past, stained only by the enriching blood drawn from the scars left upon us by our masters. The scorn of our formidable neighbour, who does not know us, is Our America's greatest danger. (Cited in Schnookal and Muñiz 1999: 119)

Nor should analytical caution mean any less anger at the brutal exploitation of the poor, the racism and the abuse of women that followed the crushing of the left of the 1960s and 1970s. Nor is caution motivated by pessimism about the potential for positive change. We should, however, guard against blurring the complexities of these political phenomena, and, conversely, against the often poisonous partisanship of media coverage of Latin American politics.

In this introductory chapter, we therefore draw attention to aspects of scholarly and everyday analysis that readers should confront critically. We analyse some of the political trends that have produced the electoral shift to the left, that is to say towards candidates and parties committed either to greater equality, including, crucially, material equality, or to greater political control over the economy, or to both. This chapter thus starts by examining the electoral events of the 'pink tide', warning against oversimplification. It then discusses a key element of the politics of the left-wing presidencies: a 'new continentalism'. This new regional integration involves a distancing from US diplomacy, and from the 'Washington Consensus', which promoted neoliberal policies of dismantling and privatizing state services and industries and of opening economies to the full force of international competition. There follows a discussion of factors that have enabled the electoral tide to turn leftwards, including disappointment with democratization and neoliberalism, especially in terms of poverty and gender and racial exclusion. The chapter then considers how the left regrouped after earlier failures and repression, how it related to the social movements that mushroomed in the 1990s, and how left-wing governments have addressed the demands of these movements, not least in the area of women's rights. Before briefly discussing the content of the book, this chapter sounds a critical warning about the way analysts have sometimes characterized the contemporary left in Latin America.

The temptation of oversimplification

Not only journalistic and right-wing accounts, but also some left-wing analyses which over-romanticize developments, have presented the 'pink tide' as if the whole continent were marching leftwards in close order. This is mistaken. There remain, obviously, powerful right-wing governments in Latin America, strongly committed to neoliberalism and military pacts with the USA: notably Colombia, Mexico and several Central American states (see Lievesley below). Some remain violently authoritarian, and have imposed neoliberalism by armed force, notably in Colombia (Stokes 2006; Novelli 2007). Further, perception here is partly a matter of periodization. One recent left-wing account cautiously counts twenty-eight left-wing challenges in presidential elections between 1988 and January 2006, which produced only nine victories. Of those, four, twice each in Panama and Chile, led to centre- or centre-right-dominated coalitions, leaving just five outright left victories, in Venezuela (twice), Brazil, Uruguay and Bolivia (Regalado 2007: 223-4). If we move the timeline, however, and start with Hugo Chávez's first win in 1998, we can add to Regalado's list four more left-wing victories later in 2006, and two more enormously symbolic victories: in 2007, when Colom became Guatemala's first left-wing president since Jacobo Arbenz was overthrown by the CIA's military coup of 1954; and in 2008, Lugo's victory in Paraguay, which ended half a century of Partido Colorado rule, most of it under military dictatorship. In the period since Regalado wrote, though, the left also suffered, in 2006, the disputed defeat of Lopéz Obrador in Mexico; the narrow defeat of Solis, regarded as to the left of the victor Arias in Costa Rica; and the defeat of Huamala in Peru. The 'pink tide' is thus not as high as is sometimes suggested, but the results captured in Table 1 nevertheless demonstrate why the metaphor has taken hold.

Although many of these electoral victors have strong majorities, some could be removed in a relatively small swing. To push the metaphor, electoral tides go out as well as come in. Nor should the strength of the left-wing current in this presidential tide be overstated. The left-led governments have different ambitions and are subject to different political and economic constraints. Their presidential majorities may not be reproduced in their legislatures, nor among powerful provincial executives or mayoralties in great cities. Their histories are also different. Regalado, for example, regards the Kirchner and by extension Fernández victories, in Argentina, as those of a traditional, not a left-wing, party. Others include these results in their tide tables, while remaining sceptical about a 'pink tide' (Robinson 2007: 144). Some left leaders have been elected, as noted above, at the head of coalitions in which the left is in a minority.

TABLE 0.1 Latin America's 'pink tide' of presidential election winners since 1998, vote share in the final round, and lead over nearest rival (%, rounded)

Year	Country	Presidential election winner	Vote share	Lead
1998	Venezuela[1]	Hugo Rafael Chávez Frías	56	16
2000	Chile	Ricardo Froilán Lagos Escobar[2]	51	3
2001	Venezuela[1]	Hugo Rafael Chávez Frías	60	22
2002	Brazil	Luiz Inácio Lula da Silva	61	22
2003	Argentina	Néstor Carlos Kirchner Ostoić[3]	22	-2
2004	Panama	Martín Erasto Torrijos Espino	47	17
2004	Uruguay	Tabaré Ramón Vázquez Rosas[2]	52	16
2005	Bolivia[1]	Juan Evo Morales Ayma	54	25
2005	Chile	Verónica Michelle Bachelet Jeria[2]	53	7
2006	Brazil	Luiz Inácio Lula da Silva	61	22
2006	Costa Rica	Óscar Rafael de Jesús Arias Sánchez[2]	41	2
2006	Ecuador[1]	Rafael Vicente Correa Delgado	57	13
2006	Nicaragua[1]	José Daniel Ortega Saavedra[2]	38	11
2006	Venezuela[1]	Hugo Rafael Chávez Frías	63	26
2007	Argentina	Cristina Elisabet Fernández de Kirchner	45	22
2007	Guatemala	Álvaro Colom Caballeros	53	6
2008	Paraguay	Fernando Armindo Lugo Méndez	42	12
2008	Bolivia	Juan Evo Morales Ayma	68	-[4]

Notes: 1. ALBA member state, or observer state in the case of Ecuador. 2. Member of party affiliated to social democratic Socialist International; in Chile and Uruguay the parties were part of a wider electoral coalition. 3. After incumbent president Carlos Menem withdrew, having won only 2 per cent more than Kirchner, no second round took place. 4. Recall referendum prompted by incumbent president Evo Morales.

The Chilean Socialist Party is such a party, though its commitment to neoliberalism makes it a special case anyway (see Silva below). Election winners, as the Chilean socialists discovered so tragically in the 1970s, can be destabilized by internal opposition and external intervention: as in Bolivia during the struggle over the constituent assembly in 2007 and the autonomy referendums in 2008; by US allies such as Colombia creating border incidents and accusing neighbouring states of supporting Colombian guerrillas; and in the Venezuelan case, in the coup in 2002, the economic sabotage and the media 'dirty war' orchestrated by local 'oligarchs' and by US agencies (Golinger 2005, 2006).

Furthermore, beyond the superficial variations in electoral performance, there are numerous dimensions of politics at the national level that might be considered in judging the robustness of the 'pink tide' analogy. Aspects that are discussed in the chapters that follow, for example, include the impact of recent political history (see Silva, Close, below); the nature and degree of state intervention in the economy, including forms of social ownership (see Vivares et al., Crabtree, Branford, and Silva below); policies for reforming governance and democracy (see Motta below); the scale and content of welfare programmes (see Burton below); the degree of egalitarianism, especially in terms of income and wealth differentials; and regional and international policy stances (see Dominguez below). In the specific historical circumstances of Latin America, another core issue is that of 'truth and reconciliation', and punishing murders and violations under the dictatorships. Of course, as ever in left-wing politics, differences between aspirations, promises and delivery are always a rich seam of material for critical analysis. Some adopt radical positions just to obtain electoral advantage with no serious intention of implementation. Others may want to implement radical policies, but find they lack the power in the face of internal or external constraints. For example, the Bolivian vice-president wrote shortly before taking office that Bolivia was entering a 'revolutionary epoch' in which electoral and insurrectionary political methods would be 'complementary' (García Linera 2007: 85). Such statements are easily contrasted with more cautious and heavily contested policy developments in Bolivia (Petras 2007b). García Linera's own published view can be cited, of Bolivia's revolution as a state programme for capitalist development rather than a socialist revolution (in Dunkerley 2007). And in Brazil's case, the stark contrast is frequently noted between the expectations surrounding Lula, and what has so far been achieved in office (see Branford below). As the history of socialist and social democratic governments in Europe has surely taught us, the best of intentions have been routinely undermined, above all by the power of strong and hostile capitalist states and economies. Such is the fate of the reforming left, and those riding the 'pink tide' are no exception (see Lievesley below). Futhermore, different degrees of radicalism can also exist within one state in successive administrations, the most prominent example being the evolution of Bolivarianism into Twenty-first-century Socialism in Venezuela during Chávez's three terms (see Buxton below).

A 'new continentalism'?

An important aspect of the 'pink tide' image is the perception of shifts towards a more independent foreign policy. This shift includes stances on the US 'war on terror', on relations with Cuba, and in general the adoption of a more explicit anti-imperialist discourse. It also includes positions on free trade globalization, Latin American economic integration, social welfare, and related proclamations of an alternative political economy. Part of the perception of a 'pink tide' thus derives from the linked perception of a 'new continentalism' that derailed the US-promoted Free Trade for the Americas (FTAA) policy (see Leogrande 2007). The Bolivarian Alternative for the People of the Americas (Alternativa Bolivariana para los Pueblos de Nuestra América, ALBA in its Spanish acronym) was first floated by Chávez in 2001 as an alternative to the FTAA (ALCA in its Spanish acronym). Introducing a book on ALBA, the secretary-general of the Latin American parliament, referring to the nineteenth-century US Monroe Doctrine, which designated the Americas as a US sphere of influence, described two alternative visions, the *Monroísmo* of the North versus the *Bolivarismo* of the South (Correa Flores 2005: 4). ALBA's purpose is described as a direct challenge to neoliberalism, offering instead regional integration prioritizing, among other things, 'the fight against poverty and social exclusion', the end of 'unequal exchange' in international relations, and a revival of state intervention and political participation, especially by indigenous peoples (ALBA n.d.: 4–5). Since its first accord between Cuba and Venezuela in late 2004, ALBA has been joined by Bolivia in 2006, Nicaragua in 2007, and Dominica and Honduras in 2008, with others having observer status. At the 2008 ALBA summit representatives were also present from Antigua and Barbuda, St Vincent and the Grenadines, Ecuador, San Cristóbal and Nieves, Haiti and Uruguay. ALBA is already producing agreements for a variety of economic links, including trade and barter deals. Progress was marked in energy integration in 2005, with Petrosur formed by Venezuela, Brazil and Argentina, and Petrocaribe formed by Venezuela with Cuba, the Dominican Republic and twelve of the fifteen member states of the Caribbean Community (CARICOM). Petrocaribe offers oil at preferential rates, with 40 per cent financing on twenty-five-year terms, with barter repayment possible. It was after joining Petrocaribe that Honduras became an ALBA member. And it is worth noting, as a sign of the wider regionalist sentiment that can cut across left–right dimensions, that the Honduran president, José Manuel Zelaya Rosales, is far from being part of any 'pink' tide. He leads the National Liberal party, the less conservative of the two long-standing parties in a political system in which the left-wing candidates won only 2.5 per cent of the vote at the 2005 presidential election. Finance and investment initiatives have followed Petrocaribe, including the Banco del Sur launched in 2007 by Venezuela, Bolivia, Argentina, Ecuador, Brazil and Paraguay, and the Banco del ALBA, launched by Bolivia, Cuba, Nicaragua and Venezuela in 2008. These may take on new significance in the wake of the world banking crisis of 2008. In 2005 TeleSur, the Caracas-based regional TV channel owned by Venezuela, Argentina, Cuba, Uruguay,

Bolivia, Ecuador and Nicaragua, was launched with a mission to serve *nuestra América* and counter CNN. Additionally, ALBA has promoted the tremendous social 'missions' in health and education, combining Cuban human capital with Venezuelan finance. These have now restored sight to over a million poor people in Latin America and the Caribbean, created a free primary healthcare system in Venezuela's *barrios*, and rescued 1.4 million Venezuelans from illiteracy. At a conference in Havana in 2005, Chávez and Fidel Castro declared an ambition to eradicate illiteracy in the whole continent. Cuba's new alliances may, furthermore, require a reconsideration of its 'exceptionalism' within Latin America (see Ludlam below). The decision of nine Central American states in 2008 to boost their integration in Proyecto Mesoamérica (Project Central America) also has the potential to further involve Cuba, given that one of the project's aims is an integrated health system and purchasing of vaccines, both areas of Cuban expertise. Here again optimism is justified, but caution is needed. Some historic territorial disputes between key states remain (see Crabtree below). Further, despite ALBA statements proclaiming a new alternative to global capitalism, what have so far emerged are mainly trade deals, ambitious welfare programmes and greater financial independence from US-controlled investment institutions, rather than a fundamental transformation of their capitalist economies, although there is evidence of at least a parallel socialist sector now being promoted in Venezuela (see Buxton below).

The members of Mercosur, created as a common market in 1991 by Argentina, Brazil, Paraguay and Uruguay, are no strangers to regionalist integration, of course, and the founding treaty, while overwhelmingly commercial, also made reference to social justice. Bolivia, Chile, Colombia, Ecuador and Peru are associate Mercosur members, and Venezuela joined as a full member in 2006. Core Mercosur states have also, for example in the 2003 Buenos Aires Consensus signed by Lula and Kirchner, promised a leftist alternative in the region, if less openly hostile to the USA and the US economy, which is so densely linked to their economies (IRC 2003). Free-trading capital has had little to fear in most Mercosur states, where projects of competitive national capitalism are prominent, and internal government debt is often greater than politically sensitive external debt (see Branford, also Vivares et al., Silva below). Nevertheless, in 2002 Chile's application to become a full Mercosur member was suspended after it signed a bilateral free trade agreement with the USA. The South American Community of Nations announced in Cuzco, Peru, in 2004 aimed to combine into one free trade area Mercosur, the Andean Community, and Chile, Surinam and Guyana. In 2008 these twelve states,

Argentina, Bolivia, Brazil, Chile, Colombia, Ecuador, Guyana, Paraguay, Peru, Suriname, Uruguay and Venezuela, signed a treaty creating the Union of South American Nations (Unasur in its Spanish acronym, Unasul in Portuguese). Unasur illustrates both the deepening of social ambition, and the Latin Americanization of regional politics (see Dominguez below). The treaty opens with a direct reference to 'those who fought for the emancipation and unity of South America' and states that its objective is integration 'with a view to eliminating socio-economic inequality' and strengthened national sovereignty (Unasur 2008). Cammack's analysis of the new political economy of the region warns that it may be necessary to distinguish between social objectives on the one hand, and on the other a potentially contradictory objective of increasing the region's competitive advantage in the global capitalist economy. Nevertheless, the prioritizing of social objectives in all the main regional groupings is certainly further evidence of the social forces propelling the 'pink tide' (Cammack 2004; and see Branford below).

Low-intensity representation

The focus on national electoral results implied by the 'pink tide' analogy also conceals other trends in Latin American politics that deserve critical analysis, trends that help explain how the 'pink tide' swelled in the first place. For one thing, in a continent with strong federalist and localist traditions, the electoral impact of the left at sub-national levels needs to be noted (see Guarneros-Meza, Burton, Motta, Close below; Panizza 2005; Baiocchi 2003). Indeed, among the strongest attractions of Latin America for the European left, prior to Chávez's election, were the armed autonomism of the Zapatistas, and the potential of local budgetary participation in Porto Alegre in Brazil (Baierle 2002). Further, as Motta argues against Panizza's focus on parties, to exclude social movements from analysis of the left in Latin America is to limit the field of view unacceptably (Motta 2006). The criticism of the focus on national electoralism can be linked to the wider critique of 'really existing democracy', a critique that, along with economic distress, has underpinned the rise of militant social movements. The limits to 'third wave' democracy in Latin America are viewed, on the one hand, in terms of the low-intensity representation offered by 'polyarchic', professional party competition (Robinson 1995; Pearce 2004). The literature identifies 'pacted democracies' where procedural democracy outweighs substantive democracy (Lievesley 1999), under-institutionalized 'delegative democracies' (O'Donnell 1994), and 'demobilizing democracies' (Harnecker 2007a). On the other hand, the limits on democracy have been analysed in terms of the impacts of globalized and neoliberal capitalism (Grugel 2003; Boron 2005). Most obviously the impact of neoliberalism produced two decades of rising poverty and inequality, dashing expectations that democracy would bring material security. As one specialist recently put it, after a quarter of a century of democratization, 'the quality of democracy in the region remains low', social exclusion and poverty, corruption, violence and authoritarianism persist, and 'Economic growth, where it has taken place, has gone hand in hand with increases in inequities between rich and poor in ways that are not dissimilar to the earlier periods of authoritarianism' (Grugel 2007: 243).

In bald terms, the proportion of the population of Latin America living in poverty grew from 40.5 per cent (136 million people) in 1980 to 48.3 per cent in 1990 (200 million people), and in 2002 was still higher than in 1980 at 44.0 per cent (222 million people) (ECLAC 2007). Successive reports by the UN Economic Commission for Latin America and the Caribbean attest to the scale of this phenomenon (see www.eclac.org). It is this poverty, linked with social and racial exclusion, abuse of women and other civil injustices, underlying the discontent with 'third wave' democracy, which has so exercised the UN Development Programme, whose studies revealed that 45 per cent of Latin Americans would support a non-democratic regime if it solved their economic problems (UNDP 2004a: 132). Of those in the UNDP study who were pro-democracy, 46 per cent nevertheless said they thought that economic development was more important than democracy, compared to only 33 per cent who took the opposite view (UNDP 2004a: 201). Even the international financial institutions that drove through the neoliberal programme have adopted a 'post-Washington Consensus' posture that incorporates reference to poverty reduction (Panizza 2005).

A linked and politically important effect of neoliberal restructuring has been a significant recomposition of social classes in Latin America. The two most significant effects, according to one extensive study, have been the massive reduction in the public sector workforce, and the similarly massive informalization of the labour market (Portes and Hoffman 2003). This has been linked to an intensive strategy of raising competitiveness, and is seen as marking a new phase of capitalist imperialism in the continent (Cammack 2004). Portes and Hoffman note the political consequence: a rise in new forms of political mobilization. The result in some states, notably in the Andean region, has been a double crisis of both political representation and of political economy. In Venezuela this crisis produced a state massacre of street protesters, the *Caracazo* of 1989, and later brought down the classic Latin American 'pacted democracy', the

9

two-party *Punto Fijo* pact (see Buxton 2005 and below; McCaughlan 2004). The explosion of extra-parliamentary politics was similarly dramatic in Ecuador in 2000 and Argentina in 2001 (see Vivares et al. below; Petras and Veltmeyer 2005). An 'indigenization' of politics was soon under way (see Dominguez below). In Bolivia, two governments were brought down by the social movements, and the first indigenous president propelled into office (see Crabtree below; Albro 2005; Lazar 2006). In Brazil, the landless movement became a major political phenomenon (see Branford below; Branford and Rocha 2002; Stédile 2004). And of course in Mexico the Zapatista uprising not only established an indigenous commune in Chiapas, but also gave a well-networked inspiration to the world's anti-globalization movements (Paulson 2000). The range of Latin American organizations assembled in the 2005 World Social Forum in Porto Alegre, Brazil, was one vivid sign of the energy and international impact of the new popular movements. As one Brazilian writer noted recently,

> Eleven Latin American presidents have been ejected before the end of their mandates over the last fifteen years, not by the traditional process of US-backed military coup, but through the action of popular movements against the neoliberal policies of their governments. The one old-style coup attempt of the period, against Chávez in 2002, was defeated. (Sader 2005: 59)

Realignment on the left

The rise of social movements, and the surge of left-wing electoral success, have their roots in earlier failures of left-wing politics, and in the violent repression of the left in mid-twentieth-century Latin America. James Petras has identified three left-wing political waves. First, the wave of the 1960s and into the 1970s, the 'new left' of *fidelistas* (after Cuba's Fidel Castro) and others to the left of the Moscow commun-ist parties; a second wave of opposition movements, mostly electoral, under the 'authoritarian' regimes and during neoliberalization; and a third wave of extra-parliamentary social movements that emerged in the 1990s (Petras 1997). It was this last wave which helped launch the 'pink tide' leaders into office. The Cuban revolution had ignited a wave of guerrilla struggles in the 1960s. Many followed the narrow strategy of Regis Debray's interpretation of guerrilla *foquismo*, believing they could reproduce the Cuban process (Debray 1967; Rodríguez Elizondo 1990). Governments responded with massive repression, one of whose victims was Latin America's most revered revolutionary, Che Guevara. This experience forced a rethink among a generation of left-wing activists (see Silva below). As the military-to-civilian transitions began after 1980, and hitherto consolidated civilian political systems such as those of Venezuela and Mexico fragmented, many left-wingers forswore revolution and committed themselves to electoral politics. There were notable exceptions, particularly Sendero Luminoso (Shining Path) in Peru and the FARC (Fuerzas Armadas Revolucionarias Colombianas, Colombian Revolutionary Armed Forces), who continued to pursue the overthrow of the capitalist state. Roberto Barros castigated these 'intransigents' for what he termed 'authoritarian Marxism' (and see Dominguez below). By 2008, even Chávez, while actively negotiating hostage releases with the FARC, was insisting that guerrilla strategy was a thing of the past. Barros was, though, also highly sceptical of the new 'revisionist' left of the second wave, many of whom appeared to have jettisoned socialism altogether, believing they could navigate the waters of liberal democracy and neoliberal capitalism without being domesticated or destroyed by them (Barros 1986). This view was shared by Petras, who argued that the revisionists had strengthened neoliberalism by accepting the boundaries the latter imposed upon political debate and policy formulation (Petras 1988).

The engagement of much of the left in electoral politics, depicted by Ellner optimistically as 'breaking out of its traditional ghetto' and becoming a 'major protagonist in politics', was never going to be a smooth process (Ellner 1993: 2). In some cases, for example Bolivia, labour movement militancy was converted into social movement activism (see Crabtree below). And in Venezuela the left has rediscovered the labour movement (see Buxton below). But generally, cut adrift from the familiar terminology of class struggle and the dictatorship of the proletariat, socialists now had to grapple with the rules of liberal democratic games, with resistance by authoritarian enclaves within the state (including the military), and with the concept of citizenship. To create Petras's third wave, they had to create new relationships with social forces whose political importance they had previously denigrated or ignored, such as peasants, shanty town inhabitants and women (for a discussion, see Pérez Lara 2005). Such relationships had to be formed just when the left's traditional constituency, the unionized, industrial working class, was being dispersed by neoliberal restructuring and privatization (see Taylor 2006; and Silva below). For many on the left, the turn to electoral politics, hailed as a dramatic breakthrough, instead produced disorientation, compounded by a failure to offer a coherent challenge to neoliberal hegemony. This was especially the case for older social democratic parties, many of which have virtually disappeared. The Socialist International listed nineteen affiliates in Latin America in 2008, but in only five of the twenty-one Latin America states were such parties in office (Table 1). In two cases, Chile with three affiliates, Uruguay with two, the parties were minorities in coalitions with parties to their right.

Many individuals and parties retained characteristics that beset them historically, notably an inability or a reluctance to forge amicable relationships with popular movements (see Lievesley below). The latter movements, as noted above, organized crucial opposition to military and authoritarian regimes, and to the ravages of neoliberalism (Stahler-Sholk et al. 2007). This third wave, in Petras's terms, would also create the momentum behind the election of left-wing candidates to municipal and then national government. Petras, though, while warning against exaggeration, has argued that the wave of social movement militancy failed to impose its programme anywhere in Latin America, a far cry from his earlier optimism (Petras 2007b, 1997). This suggested failure is perhaps most stark in Brazil (see Branford below; Stédile 2007).

Citizenship under 'pink tide' governments

An obvious problem here is that popular expectations, because they are so insistent, so immediate, can quickly turn into disenchantment (see Motta below). So, while their demands for empowerment, and for the establishment of participatory and transparent governance, have not been ignored, they often seem to be put on the back burner. This has varied between 'pink tide' governments, but the latter need to sustain a healthy relationship with civil society by responding quickly and substantially to its needs (see Guarneros-Meza below). If governments appease domestic and international powerbrokers, they risk losing the support of their constituencies. We also need to ask how committed 'pink tide' governments have been 'to push[ing] the state form to the limit, to open[ing] it out into real forms of popular control' (Holloway and Sitrin 2007). Of course, social movements also try to maintain their autonomy vis-à-vis the state. At the farthest point of the spectrum, the Mexican Zapatistas reject all participation in conventional politics. But significant organizations such as the Brazilian Movimento dos Trabalhadores Rurais Sem Terra (MST, the Landless Workers' Movement), and the Bolivian Coordinadora del Agua y por la Vida, which coordinates struggles against privatization of resources such as water, as well as many indigenous, squatters', rural peasants' and women's groups, do look to 'pink tide' governments to represent their interests. If disaffection sets in, governments risk undermining their own legitimacy. To take some random examples: Kirchner was widely criticized for trying to divide and manipulate Argentinian *piquetero* (street blockade) groups. One reading of the defeat of Chávez's constitutional reform referendum in 2007 was that many *chavistas* abstained, feeling that the government had become isolated from their concerns (see Lievesley below). Within the Bolivian indigenous movement, many linked to Felipe Quispe and the *Nación Aymara* were suspicious of what they saw as Evo Morales's opportunism, fearing that he might sacrifice what he terms 'indigenous nationalism'.

If we focus on one social movement – women – we need to ask a number of questions about how 'pink tide' governments have responded to their political agendas. One question would be how women have fared in terms of their election to political bodies, whether efforts have been made to improve their representation, and whether this has had any perceptible impact (Miguel 2008). Another would be to consider how female political leaders are judged. Although it is too early to evaluate Cristina Fernández's performance in Argentina, Michelle Bachelet in Chile has been heavily criticized for not demonstrating strong leadership: a habitual masculine critique of women in politics. There is also the undeniable fact that there are often very difficult relationships between, on the one hand, women in positions of power in government, in bureaucracies and in NGOs, who will themselves have to frequently contend with male-dominated institutional cultures and, on the other hand, women activists and those in grassroots movements. Women elected to public office are generally there because of advantages of class, education and wealth, and there is no reason to expect them to share the same attitudes and priorities as poor women. To progress through the hierarchies of government, they will also tend to seek compromise policies which will, in turn, distance them from women activists. It also needs to be remembered that, historically, the Latin American left has responded inadequately to women's demands, and that disparagement and marginalization of women led to the creation of autonomous feminist groups (Vargas 1982; Guzmán and Portocarrero 1985).

Have 'pink tide' governments introduced women-friendly policies? The left in power has made an undeniable difference to the living conditions of poor people, which must necessarily help women, who are still mainly responsible for family survival strategies and who cluster at the bottom of the labour market, with initiatives such as Venezuela's *misiones*, Brazil's *Bolsa Familia* ('family bag' of essentials covered by the payments), similar strategies in other countries, as well as progress in areas such as land reform (contentious in Brazil), health, education and employment. It has been suggested, however, that women may jettison their gender-specific demands in order to defend collective family or community interests, or to press for other progressive developments. Thus, Venezuelan *campesinas* and *pobladoras*, peasants and township dwellers, may vote for Chávez and defend his government against its opponents, because they believe that it will improve the lives of the poor generally, rather than demanding priority for women's issues (Espina 2007). The gender rights in Venezuela's Bolivarian constitution, including the definition of homemakers as productive and entitled to social security, the Banmujer (Women's Bank), Misión Madres del Barrio (Mothers of the Slums Mission), and other microdevelopment projects for and by women, and recently the creation of a Ministry for Women's Issues, are very significant initiatives. But it will take time to discover how fundamentally they disturb existing structures of discrimination and disadvantage.

Bachelet has championed sexual and reproductive freedom. Introducing a scheme to distribute free emergency contraception at public hospitals to girls as young as fourteen, she presented it as a matter of public health rather than a controversial issue. Chile remains a highly conservative society, however, and her critics used the plan as proof of her dangerous feminist convictions, undermining the family and so on. When the Argentinian health minister, Ginés González, announced in summer 2007 that legalizing abortion would reduce maternal mortality, it appeared that a seismic shift in public discourse might have opened. The new governments have not generally challenged prevailing gender relations and the cultural and legal construction of sexuality, however, and there has been a right-wing and Catholic backlash. It should be to his everlasting shame that one of the 'pink tide' leaders, Daniel Ortega of Nicaragua, supported the penalization of therapeutic abortion in order to get elected in November 2006, in the sure knowledge that increased deaths in backstreet abortions would follow. Equally disappointing was Tabaré Vázquez's March 2006 statement that he would veto a bill in Uruguay on sexual and reproductive health, including decriminalizing abortion. Women still face many political, economic, legal and cultural obstacles that they need to fight against in order to achieve empowerment (Lievesley 2006). For many, the 'pink tide' is resolutely male.

Norms and types

The second general caution we wish to issue in this introduction is about the particular typologies and terminologies used to describe the left in Latin America (general definitions of social democracy and socialism are discussed in our concluding chapter below). A number of questions need to be asked in assessing the utility of typologies. What aspect of political behaviour or ideas is the subject matter? If it is original, what research method has been used to create it, or is it rather simply asserted? And, crucially, what is its purpose? Is it academic or historical, or designed to help political actors make decisions? Or is it simply a device to damn by association, and influence domestic or international opinion? Some recent typologies illustrate the need for critical caution. In 1993, in his extremely influential study, Castañeda offered four 'shades' of the Latin American left: communist, social democratic, Castroist and political-military (Castañeda 1994: 4). He was welcoming the decline of the revolutionary left and pressing for a new, modified and moderate social democracy. His view that the defeat of the revolutionaries meant the end of the need for revolution was, of course, immediately challenged (Fernandes 1996). By 2006, though, in the face of the 'pink tide', Castañeda had boiled his types down to the 'right left' and the 'wrong left', with Chávez condemned as epitomizing the 'wrong' left.

This shift illustrates very well the need to understand the contexts and frequently normative purposes of typologies. In his 1993 study, Castañeda had developed an extended critique of Latin American societies, and suggested policies that serious egalitarians should pursue. Among these were: the commitment to multi-party democracy; the centrality of deepening democratization; the unavoidability of redistributive social policy given the extremes of poverty; the acceptance, once the teleological view of socialism as a specific stage on the road to communism had been abandoned, that a wide variety of minimalist and maximalist policies was valid; the need to 'take up the banner of regional integration in general' and adopt a regional 'social charter', EU-style, to regionalize minimum social standards; to bring in the millions excluded from electoral processes; to build relationships between the state and social movements; to deepen democracy beyond electoral politics, reinforce civil society and decentralize in the context of a strong central state, giving local powers to urban social movements, creating councils of providers and recipients of services; to bring social and economic matters into the domain of political democracy; and to institutionalize movements such as squatters, women, indigenous, gay, consumer networks in transport, housing, health, schools, etc. (Castañeda 1994: 138–40, 153–4, 313, 317, 330, 363–4, 389–90). Given that Venezuela's Bolivarian programme is probably the continent's most advanced manifestation of everything on this list (Wilpert 2007, for details), it is tempting to ask how on earth Chávez ends up on Castañeda's 'wrong left'? The plainest difference between Castañeda's two typologies is that the early version was based on a historical overview of the past, the second on a polemical view of

15

the future. Both have a legitimate normative political purpose. The first asserted that only one, social democratic, road remained open to the left. The second typology advised US policy-makers how to best combat the 'wrong left'. Consistent in both are Castañeda's commitment to free market economics and his dismissal of Latin American 'populism', with which he identifies Chávez.

By contrast, an alternative typology has been offered by another prominent academic-activist, one far to the left of Castañeda. James Petras divides Latin American politics today into four blocs. The 'radical left' includes the FARC guerrillas in Colombia, various sectors of social and labour movements, and some small Marxist groups. A 'pragmatic left' encompasses Chávez, Morales and Fidel Castro, plus a considerable list of electoral parties, social and labour movements, and the majority of left-wing intellectuals. A third bloc, of 'pragmatic neoliberals', groups Lula and Kirchner, the Sandinistas in Nicaragua, and various political and business organizations. Fourth, 'doctrinaire neoliberal regimes' include Calderón in Mexico, Bachelet in Chile, most Central American governments, and of course Uribe's Colombia (Petras 1997). On this account, then, Castañeda's 'right left' are in the 'wrong', neoliberal blocs, while his 'wrong left' are to be found in Petras's 'right' radical and pragmatic leftists. It is important to be aware of the origin and purposes of typologies!

It should also be noted that Castañeda's assertion, that in Latin America the 'third way' developmental state is the only viable social democratic path, an approach recently advocated at length by Michael Reid, has been challenged (Reid 2007). Richard Sandbrook et al. identify three types of social democratic programme in the 'global periphery': radical, classical and 'third way'. All, they argue, are achievable in developing states, although in conditions of more complex class compromises than in Europe. They suggest that the absence of hegemonic labour movements, and the labour movement conservatism noted in many Latin American contexts, has produced a greater emphasis on welfare policy to combat poverty, as opposed to tripartite wage bargaining (Sandbrook et al. 2007). This emphasis is certainly visible in Latin America today (see Silva, Crabtree, Buxton, Branford below).

The spectre of populism haunting colonial supremacism

Castañeda's negative use of the term populist to attack Chávez raises a terminological and conceptual problem for students of Latin American politics, although, as one reviewer noted, he himself 'does not go far down the treacherous road of defining populism' (Dunkerley 1994: 30). Its use in this volume, for example, ranges from a rejection of the term as a dismissive cold war concept, to, on the other hand, a term used on the left to warn against the risk of an authoritarian backlash against populist politics (see Vivares et al., and Silva, below). In our concluding chapter we return to this problem and suggest that left-wing populism can be seen as part of a continuum of social democratic and socialist politics. There is also a particular problem with the concept of populism in Europe, where it has become used to describe an enemy of social democracy on the far right, characterized by the rise of racist anti-immigrant parties (Cuperes 2003: 30; Fabius 2003: 251). For right-wing American commentators 'populist!' is an insult thrown at leaders like Chávez and Morales, intended to conjure up images of an alliance of charismatic leaders and unstable masses, threatening traditional oligarchies, circumventing established political mechanisms, and challenging a democratization based on the 'polyarchic' alternation of governing elites. At times the concept seems to be used in a racist manner to portray the non-white masses as too infantile to participate responsibly in politics, hence their need for no-nonsense, dangerously charismatic leadership. Part of the explanation for the 2002 coup in Venezuela, and for the demonizing of Chávez and Morales, certainly lies in the racially divided societies they now preside over. Their challenge to economic exploitation and racial discrimination has prompted a violent and hysterical supremacism that led one veteran analyst to invite us to view these as settler societies (Gott 2007). In other words we in Europe should have in mind the brutal supremacism of white settlers in Africa and Asia when they were threatened by democracy and reform. It is no accident, given this history of racial exclusion, that the most controversial attempts to widen and deepen democratic institutions and culture, to empower previously excluded racial and social groups, and to introduce structures for participatory democracy, have been in some of the Andean states where large indigenous populations survived the Spanish conquest.

A continent that threw off imperial rule in the early nineteenth century, building most of the world's first modern republics, is now, often recalling that history, witnessing a far more complex political struggle to assert the sovereignty of the people, to renegotiate the terms of their relations with the global economy, and to resolve the poverty and discrimination that have been the legacies of centuries of formal and informal empire. In attempting to capture some of the complexity of this process, we have included chapters (Dominguez, Lievesley) that offer general analyses of the ideological and political processes at work, and chapters dealing with what, at the time of writing, have been vital national sites of these processes. On Brazil and Venezuela, we have included two chapters each. In terms of economic weight (Brazil) and of political radicalism (Venezuela), these are arguably the most important 'pink tide' states. They also represent exactly the kind of differences in economic and political strategy that demonstrate the limitations of the 'pink tide' analogy. Further, these chapters offer an opportunity to discuss both national and local factors involved in the progressive changes taking place. The importance of local initiatives underpinning the emergence of some of the left-wing challenges is also represented in a chapter on Mexico, though in this case the argument is that the left's narrow and disputed loss in 2006 at the national level was related to its local record. In terms of the apparent degrees of radicalism within the 'pink tide', the book covers the main ALBA member states, Venezuela, Cuba, Bolivia, and Nicaragua. It also covers presidencies whose radicalism is less associated with public denunciation of the USA or of capitalism: Brazil, Argentina and Chile. We have discussed other key states, notably Uruguay, in one of the overview chapters (Lievesley). The book includes the work both of experienced and of younger specialists. It is based on recent research, some carried out at very local levels, some at the national and regional levels. It is all the work of students of politics, and from a variety of perspectives. We hope that this variety of perspective and focus makes the book more useful and interesting. The coverage cannot hope to be comprehensive, but we hope the reader will agree that the range of national and sub-national politics discussed in the book offers substantial insights into the character and content of the left's political revival. We hope it will stimulate further reading, and further writing. Above all, we hope that this latest reinvigoration of the struggle for social justice in Latin America will be sustained and extended. In his 2007 lecture, Hugh O'Shaughnessy also called on academics to 'pitch in much more actively than we have hitherto on the side of those who want to put the region's often murky past behind' (O'Shaughnessy 2007). For our part, this is one modest pitch on that side.

ONE | **The left in Latin America**

1 | Is Latin America moving leftwards? Problems and prospects

GERALDINE LIEVESLEY

Suppose we rave a bit? Let's set our sights beyond the abominations of today to divine another possible world. (Galeano, E. 2000: 334)

When Tabaré Vázquez and the Frente Amplio (Broad Front) won the October 2004 general election in Uruguay, their success was hailed by Hugo Chávez, the president of Venezuela, as 'another step on the road to building ... a new Latin America, a new world' (Navarrate 2005: 1). A sense of momentous events taking place was underscored with victories for left-of-centre governments in 2006, 2007 and 2008 in Bolivia, Chile, Nicaragua, Ecuador, Argentina, Guatemala and Paraguay, in addition to the re-election of both Chávez and Luiz Inácio Lula da Silva as president of Brazil in 2006. The seemingly inexorable progress of radical social democracy had, however, appeared less sure in the year before the Brazilian poll when the legitimacy of the ruling Partido dos Trabalhadores (PT, the Workers' Party) was put into doubt by a major corruption scandal which convulsed its upper echelons, while Chávez's inaugural commitment to introduce 'Twenty-First Century Socialism' was dealt a serious blow by the December 2007 referendum defeat of his proposed constitutional amendments, and Evo Morales faced threats of secession from four dissident provinces throughout 2008. Additionally, there was a resurgence of right-wing political parties and think tanks – backed by the US government – across Latin America as elites organized to resist popular empowerment and to defend their control over natural resources (Zibechi 2008; Dangl 2008).

Of fundamental concern is that some politicians labelled as 'pink tide' offer very indistinct and ambiguous political identities. Known as the 'red bishop' (he abandoned the priesthood in 2007 to run for office), Fernando Lugo was elected president of Paraguay in April 2008. His electoral victory brought to an end the rule of the Colorado party and its six decades of corruption and repression. During the campaign, Lugo's Patriotic Alliance for Change stressed the need to attend to the grievances of the rural poor and indigenous communities and resolved to secure a fair price for the country's natural resources (particularly hydroelectricity and soya beans), but also promised to attract foreign investment and privatize public companies. The new Congress had a Colorado majority, which would likely block progressive legislation, and the Patriotic Alliance is a loose and possibly fractious bloc of Liberals, dissident Colorados, socialists and social movements. Lugo, who described himself as a 'man of the Centre who has a certain distance from Left and Right but with the capacity to unite both', may find his optimism to be unfounded (Hennigan 2008: 41). Sending out similarly mixed signals was the front-runner for the 2009 elections in El Salvador. Representing the Frente Farabundo Martí de Liberación Nacional (FMLN, Farabundo Martí Liberation Front) which waged a guerrilla struggle against the authoritarian Salvadorean state over many years, Mauricio Funes, an ex-journalist, was neither a fighter nor indeed a member of the front-turned-political-party. He described himself as embodying 'the left of hope, we are a sensible left, a reasonable left, a left that is betting on change, a stable change ... We do not aspire to build socialism in El Salvador' (Shank 2008: 2–3). His government would not stand close to either Venezuela or the United States. It would withdraw the country's troops from Iraq but would not withdraw from the Free Trade Agreement with Washington. In reading remarks by both Lugo and Funes, one is left with the impression that these politicians are trying to appeal to everyone while not offending anyone.

The trend leftwards has also been blocked by the defeat of centre-left candidates in Mexico, Peru and Colombia. The ex-mayor of Mexico City, Andrés Manuel López Obrador, lost a highly contested (and many would argue fraudulent) election in July 2006. He had identified himself as a centrist but had promised to renegotiate the neoliberal North American Free Trade Agreement (NAFTA) and reduce US influence, and his election would have been a strategic blow to Washington. The candidate of the incumbent Partido de Acción Nacional (PAN, the National Action Party) government, Felipe Calderón, was finally declared the victor by the National Electoral Commission in late 2006 after López Obrador supporters had occupied the main squares and avenues of the capital city. The political situation was further complicated by the fact that the Zapatistas (Ejército Zapatista de Liberación Nacional, the Zapatista National Liberation Army) refused to support López Obrador and the Partido de la Revolución Democrática (PRD, the Party of the Democratic Revolution), and refused to engage in electoral politics and conducted their own 'other campaign', concentrating upon popular empowerment.

In June 2006, Alan García's narrow defeat of Ollanta Huamala in the Peruvian presidential elections led some commentators to suggest that the 'Chávez effect' could be counterproductive as García (previously president between 1985 and 1990 and an avid neoliberal acolyte) made political capital in describing Chávez's strident support for Huamala as interference in another state's domestic politics. Huamala's politics were indistinct: broadly populist, anti-imperialist (he had promised to nationalize multinational companies operating in Peru) and indigenous. His heartland was the impoverished south and the shanty towns surrounding Lima and other cities where demands for social justice have become increasingly vocal. Although he was defeated this time, the intense polarization of Peruvian society may cause more radical candidates to emerge. Indeed, at the People's Summit held in Lima in May 2008, Peru's indigenous associations announced that they would field their own presidential candidate in 2011. Their goal, according to one leader, was to 'elect a Peruvian Evo Morales' (Salazar 2008).

The most decisive setback for radical social democracy came in May 2006 when, having rewritten the Colombian constitution in order to stand for a second presidential term, Alvaro Uribe obtained a comfortable victory with 62 per cent of the vote. Left-wing senator Carlos Gavria came a dismal second with 22 per cent. Colombia is the USA's closest ally in the Americas and Washington has invested huge amounts in Bogotá's counter-insurgency and drug eradication programmes. The guerrilla war waged by the Fuerzas Armadas Revolucionarias Colombianas (FARC, the Revolutionary Armed Forces of Colombia) since the 1960s may be winding down following the death of its veteran leader Manuel Marulanda in May 2008, an event shortly followed by Hugo Chávez calling upon the fighters to lay down their arms. The consolidation of an organized radical social democratic organization with social movement support has been impeded by the widespread state and paramilitary repression that has characterized Colombia for many decades. Colombia will be the hardest nut for the 'pink tide' to crack.

The origins of the contemporary trend towards radical social democratic governments can be found in municipal victories in Peru and Brazil, among other countries, in the 1980s and 1990s, and national elections in Venezuela (1998, Chávez), Chile (1999, Ricardo Lagos), Brazil (2002, Lula) and Argentina (2003, Kirchner). As the introduction to this book suggests, however, the use of descriptors such as 'radical social democratic', 'left-leaning', 'left of centre' and 'pink tide' suggests a problem of identity and definition. Can these governments and the parties and alliances that support them be grouped together under a common political profile; do they share similar objectives and pursue them through similar strategies? The answer is no. Although all offer commitments to alleviate poverty and to seek regional consensus, they possess a hybrid profile, mixing and matching elements of personalism, populism, nationalism and socialism, and some go about the process of governing in elitist and exclusive ways. Some reject neoliberalism while others regard it as a necessary evil, and Chile embraces it. We need to question how transformative their social programmes have been in terms of improving the quality of life of the poor and whether they have empowered women and indigenous communities. We also need to ask how embedded in their political cultures these governments are. Here questions of legitimacy and policy transparency and the absence of corruption will come into play.

Different strategies, the same objectives?

Lula's domestic programme has been predicated upon reform through market-led growth, while both the Lagos and Bachelet governments in Chile continued the neoliberal model embraced by the Pinochet regime in the 1970s, albeit while inserting a modicum of social justice. Both experiences contrast sharply with Chávez's mobilization of the traditional left's social base, state interventionism and defiance of international capital, and Morales's commitment to land reform and his championing of indigenous rights. Even Chávez and Morales, however, have not yet sought to abolish the essential elements of capitalist production, namely private profits, foreign ownership and profit repatriation, nor have they outlawed future foreign investment. In a sense, what they are doing is normalizing regulatory relations in the face of exceptional profits. Thus, their governments have renegotiated contracts and prices with foreign companies, converted some business relationships into joint ventures and allowed for some form of profit sharing. Given their natural resource richness, astute multinational corporations are likely to agree to such refashioning if they wish to continue doing business with Venezuela and Bolivia. Although Chávez has introduced many radical changes in Venezuelan society – particularly his embrace of participatory democracy – there are limits to what his government can do economically, which may prove problematic in the future. The crux of the matter is whether his – and other governments – are able to balance popular expectations with the delivery of speedy and qualitative reforms.

My analysis of the prospects of these present and possibly future governments has recourse to some thoughts about the classical revolutionary/reformist socialist debates of the late nineteenth and early twentieth centuries. I refer particularly to Lenin and Luxemburg's critiques of Karl Kautsky and of Bernstein's model of evolutionary socialism. The question of whether radical social reform could be implemented through taking state power, inheriting old institutions and practices and then, over time, transforming them in order to maximize social justice and participatory democracy was clearly relevant to earlier experiments in radical social democracy, such as Guatemala under presidents Arévalo and Arbenz (1944–54) and Chile under the Unidad Popular (Popular Unity) (1970–73). In both countries elected governments attempted to introduce wide-ranging social reform but were overthrown by the military with the endorsement of the United States. It was also evident in the debates in which the left has been engaged and the changes it has gone through since the 1960s (here it might be more useful to talk about 'the lefts' given the ideological heterogeneity of parties). What are the differences between those times and these? One element that contrasts sharply with earlier times (and, indeed, with the situation in 1914 as the bulk of the Second International surrendered to nationalism and repudiated international solidarity on the eve of the First World War) is that many Latin and Central American states are attempting to create a regional consensus with respect to trade, development and diplomacy. This is an important initiative given a history where such unity has been under-mined by, for example, the IMF's refusal to hold collective talks on debt restructuring, preferring to impose conditionality on individual states. The creation of the Bolivarian network, the possibility of an Organization of American States (OAS) in which the USA is no longer hegemonic, the May 2008 establishment of Unasur, a project for the integration of Latin American countries, and the proposed Latin American Defence Council (with the USA being excluded from the last two) are all aspects of this new and dynamic approach.

Since the 1980s, the election of municipal and national social demo-cratic governments has been accompanied by – and many, this author included, would argue facilitated by – intense and widespread popular mobilization against global capitalism and its application of neoliberal privatization policies. If Latin and Central America are moving leftwards in a substantial and sustainable fashion, then these popular struggles must be seen as vital to the process. Their political influence has been highly significant (to take just one example, the intensity of popular mobilization forced three governments from office – in Ecuador, Bolivia and Argentina – between 2001 and 2004) and the momentum of earlier mobilizations was also greatly responsible for the transitions from mili-tary and authoritarian regimes to civilian, elected governments which began to take place after 1980. We need to explore the relationship be-tween elected 'left' governments and radical popular movements and to consider whether the policies and development models adopted by social democrats in power can satisfy the needs and aspirations of their poor constituents. Of particular concern is whether such governments can provide a viable alternative to neoliberal orthodoxy; whether they endorse participatory democracy and transparent, responsible government rather than the traditional top-down approach to political rule; and whether they contribute to a redefinition of the political contours and socio-economic structures of Latin and Central America. The global political economy with which these governments interact is inimical to the agendas popular movements endorse. This creates tensions between governments, parties and movements and may also provoke tensions within the latter as they find themselves caught up in the institutional agenda of the state. Such was the case, for example, for the *piquetero* network (groups of unemployed people who set up roadblocks during and after the 2001–02 economic crisis in Argentina), which suffered severe fragmentation when one of its largest elements – the Federation of Land and Housing – latterly chose to join the Kirchner government. This assured it of access to resources and satisfaction of its demands (although getting into bed with the state does not always bring the outcomes co-opted social movements expect) but at the cost of undermining its credibility within the wider popular movement. Conversely, groups that try to maintain their autonomy have no hope of official legitimization, and this may, over time, cause them to lose cohesion and resolve. People, of course, mobilize out of necessity and often for their very survival, and popular organizations can fragment if they cannot deliver speedily and effectively. The manner in which radical social democratic governments address popular concerns and enhance policy transparency must be seen as central to the way in which their performance is judged and their legitimacy ensured.

Historical antecedents: another form of revisionism?

The theoretical debates of nineteenth- and early-twentieth-century Marxism were of immense importance in the shaping of the Latin American left's ideological discourse.In his book *Evolutionary Socialism* (1961 [1899]), Eduard Bernstein argued for the possibility of the working class achieving practical legislative gains within the bourgeois-democratic structures of capitalism without recourse to revolutionary struggle. His views were forcibly rebuffed by Rosa Luxemburg (in *Social Reform or Revolution?*, published in 1900). She maintained that such a strategy would result only in the proletariat's incorporation into the capitalist system and its acceptance of its ideology and values. A similar debate occurred between Karl Kautsky and Lenin. In *The Dictatorship of the*

Proletariat (1981 [1918]), Kautsky talked about the potential for a radical extension of socialist democracy into the executive arm of the state. Lenin rebutted this perspective; citing the Paris Commune as inspiration, he argued, in *The Proletarian Revolution and the Renegade Kautsky* (1970 [1918]), that a proletarian state must sweep away all vestiges of both liberal democracy and capitalism. Luxemburg further contended that any revolution which attempted to replace popular empowerment with the surrogacy of party or state (which she accused the Bolsheviks of doing) was doomed to failure. The question of who controlled the state was central to one of the most contentious political episodes of the century, which was the Chilean Unidad Popular government. After its fall, many on the left criticized it for failing to defend the working and popular sectors against right-wing subversion and for believing that it could recalibrate the structures and purpose of a capitalist state. As Sader has recently commented, the UP 'underestimated the class nature of the state. It neglected ... to institute an alternative power outside the traditional apparatus which ultimately cornered and smothered the executive' (Sader 2008: 4). Many others, of course, including many Chilean socialists, argued that the UP should have accommodated itself even more to the imperatives of liberal democracy.

While the Latin American left was shaping its ideological profile, it was doing so in a very difficult and often deadly political environment. In the early twentieth century, Latin American governing elites sought to avoid the potential revolutionary challenge of the new urban social classes produced by processes of industrialization and modernization. The old oligarchies were compelled to accommodate demands for political inclusion which came from the middle classes and organized labour, although they were unwilling to do so and fought hard not to. The enlargement of political elites was accompanied by the attempted incorporation of 'the masses' through populist and corporatist strategies. At the same time, diverse organizations competed for the loyalty of the working class (peasants and the urban poor were generally not seen as possessing revolutionary potential). Communist parties followed the zigzags of Comintern policy changes; thus, in 1935, the launching of the Popular Front led them to some strange bedfellows. The Partido Comunista Peruano (PCP, the Peruvian Communist Party) dallied first with the military dictatorship of General Benavides (1933–39) and then the strongly pro-US President Manuel Prado (1939–45), while the Partido Comunista Chileno (PCC, the Chilean Communist Party) engaged with the right-wing Radical Pedro Aguirre Cerda in the late 1930s and Cuban communists moved close to Fulgencio Batista in the early 1940s.

Invariably these ill-conceived alliances produced no positive results but certainly undermined labour support and compromised communist legitimacy. Over time, communist parties adopted the revisionist line and, turning against armed struggle and the revolutionary seizure of the state, sought respectability within political systems. Of course, the latter tried their hardest to co-opt or destroy the communists, who in their desire to please went to great lengths to demobilize and sanitize trade unions and other popular sectors.

Trotskyist and Maoist parties took up the banner of revolution but their political influence was limited by their sectarianism and predilection for ideological schism. Thus the Latin American Trotskyist movement was divided between the proletarian tendency (which viewed the fight against capitalism and imperialism as indivisible) and the national liberation tendency (which saw imperialism as the biggest enemy and argued for an alliance of all anti-imperialist forces, including progressive capitalists). Stalinists, Trotskyists and Maoists were challenged by the New Left, which was fascinated with the Cuban revolution and which advocated the launching of the armed struggle without waiting for the objective conditions which the 'Old' Left maintained were essential for success. The 1960s saw ideological splits within parties and the launching of generally ill-fated guerrilla wars which provoked the military to intervene, beginning with the Brazilian coup of 1964.

Apart from arguing among themselves on matters of tactics and strategies, left-wing parties also competed for popular support with national-populist movements such as Peronism in Argentina, APRA in Peru, Vargas in Brazil and Cárdenas in Mexico, and also with reformist parties. Thus, Acción Democrática (AD, Democratic Action) in Venezuela occupied a significant position within the political landscape after the *Punto Fijo* of 1958 (an electoral pact between the AD and the Partido Social Cristiano de Venezuela – COPEI, the Venezuelan Social Christian Party) and sought working-class support through oil-financed welfare provision and labour legislation. There were also a number of instances of the left falling in love with radical military leaders – *caudillos* – such as the PCP and General Juan Velasco Alvarado, leader of the Peruvian Revolution of the Armed Forces (1968–75), and succumbing to the fascination that General Omar Torrijos exerted over the Panamanian left in the 1970s. Some would place Chávez in this category (Castañeda 1994; Gott 2000).

By the 1960s, mobilization in support of citizenship rights, land reform and greater equity of income distribution and social provision was 'channelled by various left-wing armed and non-armed movements into assaults on the *status quo* and to capture the state for a distinct political project' (Pearce 2004: 494). In the main, these movements viewed the popular sectors as subjects to be led and directed by left-wing intellectuals who best understood the revolutionary road (what came to be known as *vanguardismo*). Rural land invasions and urban squatter movements were too often treated by left parties as 'mobilisation platforms for their own political initiatives' (Castells 1983: 25). Their emphasis upon securing state power led many left-wing parties to regard popular empowerment as instrumental to this end rather than intrinsically important as a means of securing fundamental societal change. Tensions between ideologically hidebound parties and popular activists undermined collective actions and fostered relations that were often tainted by the dogmatism of the former and the latter's suspicion. Such problems were compounded by the authoritarian and repressive political environments in which both operated, particularly during the military dictatorships which so many countries experienced after 1964.

Military rule and repression produced an ideological crisis on the left. To take one example, following the military coup in Chile in 1973, a wide-ranging debate took pace between socialists and communists. The socialist Renovación (Renewal) group maintained that the Unidad Popular had failed to achieve broad social support and had not explored the possibility of an alliance with the Christian Democrats, their rivals on the centre-right, which would have produced this. It accepted the necessity of such an alliance and a role in a transition structured by the military, which would eventually lead to the creation of the first Concertación government. The communists and dissident socialists led by Clodomiro Almeyda opted for a strategy of armed struggle and, as a consequence, became politically marginalized (Loveman 1993). As civilian transitions emerged and militants began to return from exile and imprisonment, left-wing parties reconstituted themselves and embarked upon a re-evaluation of democracy and the prerogatives of citizenship. The left's priorities shifted with constitutional principles and democratic conventions replacing social and economic rights. Many now saw fiscal stability as more important than social expenditure and inclusive social policies and accepted a reduction in the role of the state and an increase in that of the private sector in economic management. For a large majority, 'the antagonism between authoritarianism ... and democracy [had] largely superseded that posited between capitalism and socialism' (Munck 1990: 113). This was a very different left, which repudiated armed struggle and sought to maximize its electoral attractiveness by wooing new constituencies – rural communities, squatters, women – and by embracing the politics of diversity and identity. Old habits die hard, however, and there continued to be difficult relationships between lefts in government – at local and national levels – and popular movements.

The contemporary period: avoiding the mistakes of the past

I began this chapter with the Frente Amplio's 2004 election victory in Uruguay. The Frente was formed in 1971 as a coalition of communists, socialists and Christian Democrats with the aim of breaking the stranglehold that two parties – the Blancos and the Colorados – had exercised over the country since independence from Spain in 1830. The Frente's founders formed *comités de base*, grassroots committees which they hoped would promote participatory democracy and contribute to the transformation of what was a hidebound political system. The new coalition dedicated itself to a programme (known as the 'First Thirty Measures') that included agrarian reform, the nationalization of private banks and the reinvigoration of the public sector. The Frente found itself caught up in intensifying repression as the government battled with the urban guerrilla movement, the Tupamaros. Following the military coup of 1973, the Frente was outlawed; it re-emerged in 1984, obtaining 21 per cent of the vote in the first democratic elections in the best part of a decade. Despite experiencing a split in mid-1989, its candidate, Tabaré Vázquez, was elected mayor of Montevideo later that year.

With its electoral momentum growing, the Frente gained nearly 40 per cent of the vote in the first round of the 1999 presidential elections but lost in the second round to the National Party. There was tremendous optimism as the 2004 elections approached that it would finally win power and be in a position to implement its political programme. Victory was secured but many expectations were subsequently dashed. Although there has undoubtedly been much progress in many areas, the 'First Thirty Measures' have not been adopted and, although Vázquez has been involved in various regional initiatives, Uruguay has also signed a trade and investment agreement with the United States, the precursor to a free trade treaty. It also broke its promise not to pay its foreign debt and, indeed, made advance payments to the IMF, channelling funds that could have been used for social development programmes.

In attempting to explain the Frente's political journey, there has been much criticism of Vázquez himself: he was not a militant under the dictatorship and he has always argued for the need to occupy the centre ground and not antagonize conservative sectors. Thus radicals have been outmanoeuvred and excluded from his cabinets, his economic policy has not moved far from a neoliberal position and he has pragmatically used his good relations with Washington to enable Uruguay to defend its corner against its much larger neighbours, Argentina and Brazil. Since 2004, a growing distance has developed between the Frente's ambitious hierarchy and its grassroots (a situation very similar to that pertaining in Brazil). Veteran activists do not share the same values as younger Frente members, who have no memories of the years of clandestinity and struggle, and view the organization as a means to further their careers (Fox 2007). Of course, the fact that the Frente was a coalition from its inception has always meant that it would be susceptible – again, as with the Brazilian PT – to factionalism because a common political consensus has never existed. Both the Frente and the Workers' Party have experienced critiques from the left, from within their own ranks and from social movements. Asambleas Populares (Popular Assemblies) emerged in 2006 in Uruguay with the express aim of re-radicalizing the Frente while the PT has been severely criticized by the Movimento dos Trabalahadores Sem Terra (MST, the Landless Workers' organization). While the MST initially supported the PT, their relationship has deteriorated, with the MST being particularly incensed by the government's slow progress on land reform. At the MST's Fifth Congress in June 2007 – to which Lula was not invited – it lambasted him for his abject surrender to neoliberalism (in its most recent guise, his embrace of biofuel technology) and adopted what it termed a 'democratic agricultural model'. This advocated taking land from multinational companies and returning it to family agriculture, turning from the external to the internal market, and pursuing an environmentally friendly 'agroeconomy' (Zibechi 2007). For the MST, Lula was no longer a friendly president; he had joined the enemy's camp. Many commentators point to the negative consequences that power brings, and particularly corruption, both personal and institutional. Thus someone like Lula, a radical trade unionist in the 1970s, could now be seen as a man who felt more at home attending the World Economic Forum in Davos than the World Social Forum in Porte Alegre.

Lula's 2002 victory was hailed by many in Brazil and the rest of Latin America as on a par with Salvador Allende's election in 1970. His government was soon being criticized, however, for its capitulation to global capitalism. Its pursuit of the World Bank's mantra of 'growth with equity' led former Bank president James Wolfensohn to laud it as the 'most important experiment in Latin America today' (Grandin 2006: 2). It is well known that the PT's political agenda was predetermined before the 2002 election when Lula held talks with the international financial institutions (IFIs) and domestic capital and agreed not to interfere with the neoliberal model. João Pedro Stédile, an MST spokesperson, contended that Lula and other leaders betrayed the PT's founding principles of participatory

31

democracy and social justice in the pursuit of short-term political ambition, and that this sell-out was demonstrated by the slow implementation and superficial nature of reform (Stédile 2003). Even the government's most praised policies were handicapped. Thus, the impact of its food programme, Zero Hunger, was stymied by strict monetarist budgetary constraints and was also responsible for creating a dependency culture, while the *Bolsa Familia* (literally 'the family bag' – the distribution of funds to the poorest families) created political support for the PT, but it was support based upon the state's largesse rather than approval of its actions, and one that could prove to be extremely fickle. Such token reforms – although undeniably helpful to many households – did not seriously challenge the roots of poverty, racism and social exclusion.

Other governments have been similarly castigated. Daniel Ortega has been criticized for trying to stifle dissent and for using unconstitutional means to ensure he stays in power. A consummate politician, he faces an opposition that can potentially frustrate his plans, and so he resorts to intra-elite deals which many Nicaraguans disapprove of. In November 2007, he barred two parties from taking part in municipal elections. A leader of one of these, the Movimiento Renovación Sandinista (MRS, Sandinista Renovation Movement), Dora María Teller (once a guerrilla fighter and a revered political figure), went on hunger strike in June 2008 to condemn what she described as Ortega's dictatorship. Citing his government's failure to tackle high inflation and structural poverty, she also attacked him for shutting down the political spaces for representation and criticism (Carroll 2008). In Argentina, the Kirchners have both been accused of presiding over governments that are overly centralized and which have decision-making processes that have little regard for grassroots concerns. Farmers' strikes plagued the first months of Cristina Fernández's presidency; the protests centred on opposition to an increase in taxes on soya and other agricultural exports and to rising food prices. Towns and cities experienced roadblocks and middle-class neighbourhoods saw angry 'pots and pans' demonstrations while supermarkets were looted. The government argued that the tax measures were aimed at redistributing income, but critics maintained that there had been no dialogue between state and country to explain the policy's rationale, and this reflected the Kirchners' increasingly imperial governing style (Valente 2008).

Michelle Bachelet's government in Chile has had to contend with recurring strikes by teachers and students provoked by the impact privatization has had on the quality of education; by copper miners demanding better wages and conditions and calling for renationalization of the industry; and by the Mapuche indigenous community (many of whose leaders languish in jail) arguing for constitutional recognition of its rights and a return of the land stolen from it by logging companies. President Rafael Correa has been criticized for continuing neoliberal economic policies and also for failing to address structural racism. In May 2008, the Confederation of Indigenous Nationalities of Ecuador (CONAIE) published a blistering critique of his opposition to the creation of a plurinational state that would recognize the country's ethnic and cultural diversity in the form of a new constitution (similar demands have been made in Peru and Mexico and are at the core of Evo Morales's plans for Bolivia). CONAIE also condemned the government's tolerance of the activities of large-scale mining companies which are responsible for environmental devastation and threaten the survival of rural and indigenous communities. CONAIE has talked of launching a national indigenous rising (Denvir and Riofrancos 2008).

Michelle Bachelet – a divorced mother of three, an agnostic and a socialist – has been criticized for the lack of progress in women's empowerment. While her election reinvigorated the gender debate, no party is willing to offer overt support for more rapid legislative progress. The nature of coalition government in Chile means that the socialists must maintain their relationship with their partners, the Christian Democrats, and the latter hold conservative views on issues such as reproductive freedom and abortion (Ríos Tobar 2007). Although the government of Patricio Aylwin created the Servicio Nacional de Mujeres (SERNAM, the National Women's Service, essentially a ministry for women) in 1990, it encountered institutional and financial obstacles that hampered its remit. It has been condemned as being an arm of the state by popular women's organizations and feminists have also criticized it, but paradoxically many have been employed by SERNAM and gone through a process of institutionalization themselves (Waylen 1996). The incorporation of women's demands into official policy-making structures may be a positive move but it is not sufficient in itself; there remains the need to change what are still resolutely male cultures and to bring substantive changes to women's lives, especially those of poor and indigenous women.

Even Venezuela has not been immune from criticism. James Petras has argued that Chávez has not yet attacked capitalism; that the richest reserves of oil are still owned by foreign capital; that his 'radical' measures are merely 'modernising and updating petrol–nation state relations' (that is, tax and royalty increases from 15 to 33 per cent). He talks about 'grandiose gestures' which fail to affect structural change (Petras 2006: 4). This assessment was challenged by Diane Raby, who believes that

Chávez's role is pivotal as a unifying point for the Venezuelan left and for much of the population. She contrasts this situation to the lack of leadership shown by Lula and the PT. Furthermore, the various *misiones* and *consejos comunales* (the first, community initiatives in health, literacy and education and housing; the second, the organs of popular democracy) have captured the popular imagination and stimulated community self-organization. Their ongoing achievements are important, but so are the processes of empowerment and consciousness-raising that they engender (Raby 2006b). They can also be seen to be bypassing old bureaucratic structures, in effect redesigning the nature of the state and aiming to consolidate popular control over it. To a point this appears true, but it does not detract from the nature of Chávez's political style, the suspicion that he believes that he is the only person capable of leading Venezuela into this bright future, and the fact that commentators point to the growing gap between the *chavista* governing elite and the popular movement, which may account for the fact that many *chavista* rank and file abstained from the government's constitutional referendum in December 2007, leading to a close but significant defeat for Chávez (Rosen 2007). Raby's central contention is that radical processes need populist, charismatic leaders who are 'rooted in popular culture', who are 'ideologically pluralist' and whose governments are 'democratic in both political practice and institutional structure' (Raby 2006a: 257). The question is: how do you ensure these conditions?

Radical social democracy and popular empowerment

It is evident that 'the importance of the rise of the "left" governments is that they are a reflection of the strength of struggle in the continent as a whole ...' Governments have sought to give this struggle a 'state form' with the aim of defusing it. Despite ongoing problems and contradictions, it may be that only in Venezuela (and possibly Bolivia) has there been 'a genuine attempt to push the state form to the limit, to open it out into real forms of popular control' (Holloway and Sitrin 2007: 1) The most significant developments are taking place within social movements such as the Zapatistas, the *piqueteros*, workers' cooperatives, communities mobilized against water and other natural resource privatizations and in many other sites of activity. It is in the nature of governments to try to control and fragment such expressions of resistance. They create institutional spaces and linkages for the movements in order to dictate their boundaries and behaviour. It is very difficult for social movements – which aspire to be non-hierarchical – to deal with the power of the state. Co-optation is always a danger. In Bolivia, the

Federación de Juntas Vecinales (FEJUVE, the Federation of Neighbourhood Councils) of El Alto (an enormous township close to La Paz) was prominent in struggles against the privatization of national gas reserves in 2003 but then suffered internal strife and grew far less radical. One of its leaders, Abel Mamari, was appointed head of the new water ministry in January 2006 but was subsequently dismissed in 2007 after a series of scandals (Spronk 2008). Social movements operating in hostile political environments continue to endure repression. The Asamblea Popular de los Pueblos de Oaxaca (APPO, the Popular Assembly of the Peoples of Oaxaca) in southern Mexico grew out of the repression of a teachers' strike by state governor Ulises Ruiz in spring 2006. Since then it has gained momentum, representing hundreds of grassroots organizations in what is essentially a de facto alternative government based upon participation and transparency (Esteva 2007). It has had to withstand internal divisions between those who wish to use it as a means of institutionalizing popular organizations in a more traditional hierarchical manner and those who reject electoral politics and want it to 'remain a broad space of decision making and organizing that respects the political autonomy of its members' (Rénique and Poole 2008: 30). Notwithstanding these pressures, government repression and the efforts of political parties to co-opt it, the APPO template has been imitated in other municipalities throughout Mexico and elsewhere. The aim of these movements and of the more famous Zapatistas is 'to articulate local autonomy practices to other struggles ... in an effort to strengthen ... autonomy initiatives and ensure that they continue to tackle broader structural inequalities' (Mora 2007: 65).

Radical social democratic governments can support social transformation but they cannot develop, consolidate and sustain it. This can only really be done by people themselves, working in communities and forging links with other, like-minded communities within and across national borders. This does not mean that such groups should not deal with the state – this is inevitable – but that they should structure and take control of that relationship. Evaluating the PT's experience, Hilary Wainwright has argued that it should act as a warning to other left-leaning governments that the most important lesson to be learnt is that 'electoral success does not on its own bring sufficient power even to initiate a process of social transformation but ... an electoral victory can be used to activate a deeper popular power' (Wainwright 2005: 4). Radical social democratic governments cannot take popular support for granted; a widening gap between promises and satisfaction will produce anger while making concessions to global capital at the cost of postponing or watering down

2 | The Latin Americanization of the politics of emancipation

FRANCISCO DOMINGUEZ

In 1993, Jorge Castañeda wrote in the opening sentences of his *Utopia Unarmed* that 'The Cold War is over and Communism and the socialist bloc have collapsed. The United States and capitalism have won, and in few areas of the globe is that victory so clear-cut, sweet, and spectacular as in Latin America' (Castañeda 1994: 3). Events, my dear boy: events before the ink in Castañeda's book had even dried began to disprove the excessive triumphalism of his assessment. *Utopia* was published in 1993; the Zapatista uprising in Chiapas began on 1 January 1994, against the US-inspired North American Free Trade Agreement (NAFTA) treaty. What was special about the Zapatistas was their insistence on defeating NAFTA and its neoliberal agenda as a precondition for indigenous peoples recovering their ancestral rights in Chiapas, and in Mexico as a whole. Notwithstanding Fukuyama's post-Soviet contention that history had ended in the global triumph of liberal capitalism, history was being made along lines that defied conventional theoretical analysis (Fukuyama 1992). Furthermore, within five years a political earthquake in Venezuela, with continental reverberations, was to smash to smithereens any notion of the final victory of capitalism, in Latin America at any rate. An intriguing and vocal military officer, Hugo Chávez Frías, had sparked the nation's imagination, and in 1998, following a failed uprising in 1992, he was elected president of Venezuela, one of the largest oil producers in the world. Once elected, he embarked upon a process of reforming the nation, on a path towards what he has labelled Socialism of the Twenty-first Century.

What was common to these two momentous developments was the role of national leaders deeply ingrained in their countries' histories, with Emiliano Zapata and Simón Bolívar representing the aspirations and objectives of the respective socio-political movements in Mexico and Venezuela. The Latin Americanization of politics in the continent had begun to crystallize in political movements that sought legitimacy in a radical reinterpretation of history. To contend that Zapata's views are perfectly consistent with the objectives of the EZLN (Ejército Zapatista de Liberación Nacional, Zapatista Army of National Liberation) in Chiapas, including armed struggle, is pretty accurate historically. But to suggest that Simón Bolívar somehow pre-announced Venezuela's Socialism of the Twenty-first Century may be overstretching the reinterpretation of history.

In recent decades powerful social and political movements have emerged in many a Latin American country, commonly displaying ideological dimensions that link iconic historic figures with contemporary struggles, and drawing inspiration, and key principles of their political identity, from the thought and legacy of such figures. As in the cases of Zapata and Bolívar, the prominence of José Martí has greatly increased in Cuba's struggle for survival and national sovereignty since the collapse of the Soviet Union. The quest for such historic figures can similarly be found in Ecuador, Bolivia and Peru, where mass indigenous movements portray their contemporary mobilizations and objectives as a continuation of the struggles waged by their ancestors back in colonial times. Furthermore, similar developments have been apparent in Nicaragua, with Augusto Cesar Sandino; El Salvador, with Farabundo Marti; in Peru, with Andrés Avelino Caceres; and to a lesser degree with José Artigas in Uruguay and Manuel Rodríguez in Chile. These examples are by no means exhaustive. These individuals are re-created in the contemporary setting as the embodiment or crucial source of inspiration for current objectives. This new type of politics in the region is producing formidable results for the emancipation of the nation and the 'people', the lower classes. Its symbols, its historic and cultural references, its ideologies, its discourses have a domestic origin. This chapter explores this relationship between contemporary movements for the emancipation of peoples and nations, and historic legacies. Such legacies stem notably from periods of political crisis and tension: during the colonial period; in the era of anti-colonial liberation; during the waves of radicalism and repression inspired by the Russian revolution; and in reaction to the cold war and the Cuban revolution. The chapter also draws attention to the commonalities in the political outlook of today's emancipatory movements and governments, commonalities that help account for the unprecedented levels of political collaboration emerging across the continent.

Cultural resistance

There has been a long intellectual and literary tradition in Latin America that seeks to link past resistance against, firstly, colonialism and, later, oligarchic injustice, in works such as Pablo Neruda's *Canto general* (General Song), published in 1950 in Mexico but started by the Chilean poet in 1938; and more recently, Eduardo Galeano's trilogy *Memoria del fuego* (Memory of Fire). *Canto general*'s narrative poetry, like *Memory of Fire*'s poetic prose, covers the centuries from the pre-conquest up to contemporary developments as a continuum of resistance, whose ultimate emancipatory conclusion is a classless society. Overcoming the specificities of national capitalism will make equality and social justice prevail (Neruda's penultimate poem in the work is a homage to the Communist Party). Neruda's epic poem is a song of rebellion as the history of Latin America. His immortal 'Macchu Picchu' ends with a call to battle: 'Give the silence, the water, the hope / Give me the struggle, the iron, the volcanoes [...] / Come into my veins and into my mouth / Speak through my words and my blood' (Neruda 1984: 37). Galeano also announces that unless there is justice there will be no social peace: 'Those who have been vanquished dream with Zumbí; and the dream knows that while a man owns another in these lands, Zumbí's ghost will continue to roam the roads [...] and will continue to struggle throughout Brazil. Zumbí will be called the leaders of the incessant black rebellions' (Galeano 2004: 312). The symbolic Zumbí threat could easily be across the continent. Zumbí was not only a slave rebel, he was also one of the ablest leaders of Palmares, a *quilombo*, a settlement of Maroons (escaped slaves) in the interior of Recife that, at its height, had about thirty thousand members, lasted about a century, and resisted more than forty military expeditions against it (Anderson 1996: 545–66). In these few samples we can identify struggles for the nation, class, freedom, identity, and justice. Over five centuries Latin Americans seem to have had the knack of turning particularistic struggles into legitimate battles for universal principles. Even a right-wing neoliberal politician/writer, Mario Vargas Llosa, a Peruvian and naturalized Spaniard, said this about the performance of the Chilean musical group Los Jaivas of the poem 'Macchu Picchu', which took place in the eponymous Inca ruins:

> The poem ends up with an awesome argument against the historic injustice which suggests that the price for the beauty and sublime [ruins] is the suffering of large numbers of human beings [...] thus for 'Alturas de Macchu Picchu' these rocks besides being a set of art and human sacrifice, majestic landscape, and strength and bewitchment of nature [...] are a symbol of the common Latin American patria. (Vargas Llosa n.d.)

Such an interpretation is not just an imaginative historical account by radicalized intellectuals, but is pretty much borne out by actual developments. The leaders of many rebellions have couched their programmes in universal terms, giving their pronouncements validity well beyond their period. Furthermore, the need to define an identity, a pretty intractable issue in the region, has led governments since independence from Spain to glorify, in the abstract, the struggles of their indigenous ancestors, even though the contemporary descendants of those lionized warriors are despised in reality. Many official textbooks praise indigenous leaders such as Cuauhtemoc, Caupolican, Manco Capac, Pachakuti, even though the glorification of the indigenous is sometimes driven by racism. For example, the officially sponsored Indianista movement in nineteenth-century Brazil, at a point when the indigenous population had almost been wiped out, proclaimed the country's national identity as *mestizo* (mixed race). But this *mestizaje* was of Portuguese and indigenous blood: it was explicitly excluding black Africans. In other countries, such as the Dominican Republic, similar racial constructs can be found.

Furthermore, the independence of Latin America from Spain, at the beginning of the nineteenth century, was preceded by events in Europe that shook the contemporary world to its foundations by dealing a severe blow to English colonialism, and abolishing the French feudal order. American independence and the French Revolution, despite their political limitations, supplied a democratic ideological foundation to the new Latin American republics. Local oligarchies possessed no independent thinking beyond this uncomfortable European radicalism, embraced as a bulwark against monarchic restoration. Their ideological caution was based on concrete social fears. Their timidity in pursuing independence reflected not only an aristocratic class outlook, but also the terrifying spectacles of the social revolutions of 1780 and 1781, in Peru and Colombia, which challenged not only Spanish despotism but also their own oligarchic privileges (see Williamson 1993). And one such rebellion succeeded: Toussaint L'Ouverture, Henry Christophe and Jean Jacques Dessalines led the astonishing slave rebellion that established in Haiti history's first independent black republic, preceding the independence of Latin America by more than a decade (see James 1980). In Peru and Colombia, the oligarchies knew that any democratic impulse might destroy their control over land and labour. In Haiti, the underdog had overthrown not just colonialism but the class system that underpinned it. The revolutionary implications of republicanism were spelled out by Simón Bolívar:

> A republican government, that is what Venezuela had, has, and it should have. Its principles should be the sovereignty of the people, division of powers, civil liberty, prohibition of slavery, and the abolition of monarchy and privileges. We need equality to recast, so to speak, into a single whole, the classes of men, political opinion and public custom. (Lynch 2006: 29)

Genuine radical democrats like Bolívar and José Antonio de Sucre, however, were exceptions in this deeply conservative creole oligarchy, as Lynch has recently detailed (Lynch 2006). And ever since, Latin American elites have rested uneasily in their states. And since the rise of the hegemonic United States and its military occupation of Cuba in 1898, these elites have been acutely aware of their own weaknesses and have relied on the US empire to put down many a democratic challenge. Thus, the formal democratic foundations of the state in Latin America have regularly been trampled upon, externally by the United States and its allies, and internally by authoritarian and dictatorial regimes, usually with deadly consequences. Latin American history in the twentieth century is littered with 'interruptions' of a formal democracy that, given their liberal democratic constitutions, ought to have thrived in the region's states. Yet, with very few exceptions, it could be said that brief democratic interludes actually interrupted a normality of violent and authoritarian regimes imposed and/or propped up from outside. The continent's intellectual, literary and cinematographic production has been dominated by violent historic events.[1] The 'exceptions', Mexico and Colombia, confirm the elite's attitude towards democracy. Force, however, could never be the only expedient utilized by the USA–oligarchy alliance. The democratic foundations of the state made it highly problematic to legitimize elite rule. Social, political, racial, gender and any other form of exclusion have been paramount for the elite to sustain consensus and its class dominance. Thus, since the origins of the republics, large groups have been denied participation in politics, through a combination of terror and socio-economic marginalization. It could not be otherwise, since all the countries of the region have always had the potential of becoming explosive social and political cocktails. The question is why rebellion from below seems to be succeeding in the twenty-first century where it mostly failed rather miserably in the twentieth?

Particularities of Latin American society

Latin America's social formation is indeed peculiar. Conventional concepts such as proletariat, bourgeoisie, peasantry, although useful as conceptual guides, can become doctrinaire obstacles to grasping the reality of the region's social and political dynamics, if rigidly applied. Key thinkers recognized this and produced imaginative frameworks and analyses to attempt to define the central historic task of their epoch. Intellectuals of the calibre of Simón Bolívar, José Martí, Julio Antonio Mella, José Carlos Mariátegui, José Enrique Rodó, and so many others, grappled with the intractability and complexity of their countries' social formation, seeking an always elusive strategy to fulfil the promise of the republics.[2] Far beyond the drafting of manifestos or political programmes for others, they fought, and often died, leading revolutionary social and political movements.

Mella and Mariátegui produced impressive analyses of the social realities of their respective countries, Cuba and Peru. They had embraced Marxism, which they indigenized by looking at the interplay and dialectics of the actually existing forces for social change. Following in the footsteps of Martí and Rodó, they began to posit inclusive theories of nationalism against the predominant Social Darwinist views of the nineteenth century, which excluded Indians and blacks from nationhood (see Miller 1999). Furthermore, they developed strategies of emancipation in which excluded groups played a central role. Mella was of course aware of the central role black slaves played in the Cuban wars of liberation in 1868 and 1895. He and Mariátegui observed the role the indigenous peasantry had played in the 1910–20 Mexican revolution. Mariátegui's approach to the Indian 'question' contradicted the ideologies of assimilation and 'whitening' that underpinned the de facto exclusion of the non-white masses:

> It has invariably tended to serve the interest of the ruling class – first Spanish then Creole – to explain the condition of the indigenous races with arguments about their inferiority or their primitivism. In this, that class has done nothing but reproduced, with respect to this internal national question, the white man's rationale for his treatment … of colonial peoples. (Cited in Miller 1999: 157–8)

For Mariátegui, the Indian 'question' could be resolved only by tackling the material bases that perpetuated it over the centuries, *latifundia* (great estates) and the associated power of the *gamonales*, the Peruvian landowners. Furthermore, the maintenance of communally held land in the form of the Inca *ayllu* offered a socialist solution to the Indian question. He assumed that four-fifths of the Peruvian population were peasant and indigenous and therefore, he concluded, 'Our socialism would not be … Peruvian – it would not even be socialism – if it did not declare solidarity first of all with the claims of the indigenous peoples' (cited in Miller 1999: 160). Given that the Peruvian bourgeoisie is subordinated to the landed aristocracy and foreign capital, Mariátegui concludes that it has proved incapable of developing capitalism and, therefore, incapable of making progress towards modernity and economic development, thus condemning Peru to perpetual underdevelopment. In *Siete ensayos* (Seven Essays), Mariátegui portrays the political relationship between nation, class and race as part of an emancipatory political project that necessitated not only drastic socio-economic transformations, but also the refoundation of the cultural bases of the state (Mariátegui 1974).

In opposition to Mariátegui stood Víctor Raúl Haya de la Torre, also Peruvian, who similarly drew his intellectual inspiration from Marxism but who reached diametrically opposite conclusions. Haya de la Torre examined Peruvian reality through the prism of modernizing theory, since for him

> Imperialism [had] initiated a process of capitalist development which coexists with feudal relations from the colonial period [...] the revolution has to be anti-feudal and anti-imperialist so as to liberate the nation from feudal and foreign domination. It cannot be a socialist revolution as [...] it is not possible to skip the historical stages of development, and thus, it is necessary first to develop capitalism fully. (Kay, C. 1989: 16)

There is, of course, a culturalist reading of Mariátegui's views, and the issues of indigenous and non-indigenous identities in Peru are indeed complex, and simply implementing Mariátegui's programme would not be likely to resolve them. But we are here interested in his political methodology. Mariátegui's perspective had to contend with the most doctrinaire period of the Communist International, to which his party affiliated after his death. Stalin's Comintern had 'bolshevized' world communist parties after 1928, imposing incredibly rigid formulations, which in Latin America were driven by its Buro Sudamericano (South American Bureau) and a doctrinaire zealot, Vittorio Codovilla, an Argentine communist. The Comintern clashed on almost every point with Mariátegui's views. The Comintern's reductionist 'class-against-class' Third Period had negative consequences, and was followed by the equally rigid schema of the 'popular front'. The latter required an alliance with the 'progressive bourgeoisie', in order to fully develop capitalism: a revolution in stages, to create the objective conditions for an eventual socialist outcome (see Löwy 1981: 70–79).

It would be mistaken to attribute the terrible setbacks that the efforts for emancipation suffered in the 1930s up to the Cuban revolution in 1959 to the wrong policies of communist parties in the region. Nevertheless, their schematic and dogmatic approach, under the direction of the powerful Soviet machine, impoverished left-wing politics. Cuba's communists, for example, joined the 1940 Batista government and had grave reservations about the 26 July Movement, and about its leader, Fidel Castro (Thomas 1971: 733, 1219). The official paper of the Cuban revolution, *Revolución*, harshly attacked Blas Roca, Cuba's leading communist. The

Cuban revolution changed the communist perspective. Fidel and the 26 July Movement succeeded because they were capable of bringing together all the strands of *cubanía revolucionaria* (revolutionary Cubanness), with its roots in Martí and the *mambises* of the second independence war (after a Dominican freedom fighter, John Mamby), in Mella in the 1933 revolution and in Guiteras. In this regard, Raby has aptly pointed out that

> Figures like Mella and Guiteras formed part of what could be called the Latin American independent Marxist tradition, a school of thought derived from Marx and Lenin but adapted to the realities of the colonized Afro-Indian-Latin-American world and formulated by such thinkers as the Peruvian José Carlos Mariátegui. (Raby 2006a: 97)

Arguably, the Cuban revolution readopted the politics of Mella and Mariátegui, but this unfortunately did not spread to the rest of the continent. Instead, partly due to Cuban pressure, what was promoted was one form of struggle, the guerrilla *foco*, which was elevated to the status of strategy, when it is, at best, a tactic, and a bad tactic at that (for the classic defence see Debray 1967).

Thus the adaptation of the emancipatory project to the Afro-Indian-Latin-American world was partial. The precursors of today's movements did not seek to establish a political, spiritual, intellectual link with struggles and leaders of the past. As Roberto Fernández Retamar lamented in 1971, '... it is now, after the victory of the Cuban Revolution, and thanks to it, that Martí is being "rediscovered and reassessed"' (Retamar 2000: 40). Retamar also bemoans the lack of knowledge in the region about not only Martí, but also Artigas, Recabarren, Mella, Mariátegui and Ponce, and attributes it to the strength of a colonialist ideology that leads people to read not local but metropolitan anti-colonialist writers (Retamar 2000: 40). Perversely, it was neoliberalism which was to create the material conditions for a hegemonic struggle for emancipation.

Dictatorship, neoliberalism and the rise of social movements

In the mid-nineteenth century, as Latin America's rulers were stabilizing their post-colonial supremacy, the revolutionary potential of a new force, capitalism, was being identified in Europe, and a radical vision of it stated: 'constant revolutionizing of production, uninterrupted disturbance of all social conditions, everlasting uncertainty and agitation distinguish the bourgeois epoch from all earlier ones. All fixed, fast frozen relations, with their train of ancient and venerable prejudices and opinions, are swept away ...' (Marx 1971: 35). Never was the dire dictum of the 1848 Communist Manifesto more true in Latin America than in the three decades that began in the 1970s. Indeed, 'fixed' realities of Latin America's social formation, like the Bolivian mining unions, once as certain as the rising sun or the eternally snow-capped peaks of the Andes, evaporated under neoliberalism. This was not just the result of unbridled market forces, but of deliberate political action. In the 1970s, an iron fist descended upon the whole region, demolishing whatever modicum of social contract had existed. Military dictatorships and intensely authoritarian regimes were established, terrorizing and eradicating many of the social organizations built in long decades of organizational efforts, political endeavour and social struggles. US-inspired and US-supported military dictatorships were established in Brazil in 1964, Bolivia in 1971, Chile in 1973, Uruguay in 1973, Argentina in 1976. CIA destabilization plans created the conditions for the electoral defeat in 1980 of Michael Manley's progressive government in Jamaica. Furthermore, there were already dictatorships in Paraguay, which lasted from 1954 to 1989; in Nicaragua under the Somoza dictatorship installed by the USA in 1933; in Honduras and neighbours El Salvador and Guatemala. By 1980, nondictatorial states such as Venezuela, enjoying super oil revenues, Colombia, enduring the mixed blessing of the cocaine cartels, and Mexico, taking big strides towards neoliberalism, were all solidly pro-USA and anything but democratic.

The US ruled its backyard through the terror of its National Security Doctrine, implemented by ruthless local proxies, whether legal or illegal. The challenges posed by revolution and guerrilla warfare in Central America in the 1980s would only intensify the terror. 'Low-intensity' warfare under Ronald Reagan increased political violence to unprecedented levels, with appalling consequences for the human rights of hundreds of thousands of ordinary Latin Americans. The human 'collateral' damage of the brutality of imperialist reassertion in its backyard was indeed horrific. In rounded figures there were 5,000 assassinations in Chile, 30,000 in Argentina, 50,000 in Nicaragua, 80,000 in El Salvador and 120,000 in Guatemala. According to Amnesty International,

> It is estimated that between 1966 and 1986 some 90,000 people 'disappeared' in countries including Guatemala, El Salvador, Honduras, Mexico, Colombia, Peru, Bolivia, Brazil, Chile, Argentina, Uruguay and Haiti. This figure includes young children and babies born during their mothers' detention in countries such as Argentina, El Salvador, Guatemala and Uruguay, some of whom are believed to have been subsequently given up for adoption. (Amnesty International 2001)

The activities of trade union organizers, in both rural and urban areas, became extremely hazardous. In fact, almost no lower-class organization of civil society could operate under such dangerous conditions. Repressive policies were designed precisely to prevent any obstacle to the implementation of full-blooded neoliberal economic policies. Trade union and similar activities were banned, in most cases *de facto*, in others, such as in Chile, *de jure* through Pinochet's highly restrictive Labour Plan. Civil society was terrorized by the killing, imprisonment or exile of traditional political, social and cultural representatives (the interest in civil society this sparked has led some to conflate civil society with popular movements, a serious error given that death squads are also part of civil society). Thus, whereas neoliberalism was officially proclaimed in 1979/80 with the elections to office of Margaret Thatcher and Reagan, the restructuring of the Latin American economies had begun in earnest several years previously, when Pinochet invited the 'Chicago Boys', neoliberal academics from the USA, to run the dictatorship's economic policy. The socio-economic consequence for the majority in Latin America was catastrophic devastation.

There were 76 million fewer poor people in the region in 1970 than in 1990 (O'Donnell 1996). Neoliberal policies increased the proportion of people in poverty to 40.5 per cent in 1980; it reached a staggering 48.3 per cent in 1990 and 44 per cent in 2002. The total poor population of the region in 1980 was 135.9 million, rising to 200.2 million in 1990 and to 221.4 million in 2002. By 2003 the equivalent figures were 44.3 per cent and 226 million respectively (ECLAC 2004: 56). Economic growth fell from an average of 3.11 per cent in the period 1970–79 to –0.28 per cent in 1980–89, recovering weakly in 1990–99 to 1.32 per cent (Bustillo 2007). This was not the result of the 'invisible hand' but of the deliberate hand of the state, which supplemented the invisibility of the market with policies such as: elimination of protection for national industry; favouring exporting sections of the economy; elimination of restrictions on the influx and operation of foreign capital; privatization of all state assets; and the elimination of most, if not all, welfare provision. Inevitably social exclusion grew massively.

> From 1990 onwards, employment grew faster in low-productivity sectors. In the ECLAC region as a whole, the share of the informal sector in urban employment rose from 42.8 per cent in 1990 to 47.4 per cent in 2003 ...
> In a sample of 18 Latin American countries in 2003, the urban unemployment rate was 11.4 per cent, while the rate for young people (15–24 years) was 21.3 per cent. (United Nations 2006: 10)

Most importantly (an insufficiently examined dimension), large segments of the middle classes were pauperized in the long neoliberal wave. Chile, the region's neoliberal showcase, saw wealth concentration sky-rocket to the detriment not only of proletarian and peasant groups, but also of the petty bourgeoisie. Twenty years after the systematic application of neoliberal policies, income distribution in Chile was as follows: the wealthiest 15 per cent (2 million people) received equivalent to 54 per cent of GDP; the 27 per cent of the population (4 million) classed as middle income earners received the equivalent of around 25 per cent of GDP; and the 58 per cent of Chileans (8 million) classed as low income earners shared a paltry 21 per cent of GDP (Cademartori 1998: 47; and see Dahse 1979).

Traditional popular organizations mostly either ceased to function or carried on an extremely precarious existence, dramatically changing the continent's political complexion. One such change was the rise of social movements with political agendas far broader than the radical cor-poratism of class-driven organizations. The new movements concerned themselves with issues such as poverty, the environment, privatization, land reform, social services, rights of indigenous people, unemploy-ment, youth, women, ethnicity, democracy and democratization, justice, multinational capital, human rights, imperialism, colonialism, racism, free trade agreements, and exploitation. The second such change was the decline, in some cases total, of traditional political parties such as AD (Acción Democrática, Democratic Action), and COPEI (Partido Social Cristiano de Venezuela, the Venezuelan Social Christian Party) in Venezuela. Such parties had managed to channel and/or give expres-sion to lower-class groups within the dominant class hegemony in the region. At same time new mass counter-hegemonic parties arose, such as the Brazilian Workers' Party (PT, Partido dos Trabalhadores) and the Bolivian MAS (Movimiento al Socialismo, Movement towards Socialism). Paradoxically, the rise of the social movements was significantly aided by the disappearance of some of the left's rigidity following the collapse of the Soviet bloc (see Petras 1990). Even more paradoxically, the process of capitalist globalization brought movements together across national borders, in events such as the World Social Forum in the iconic city of Porto Alegre, which, with its participatory budget, had showed that neoliberalism could be challenged. Declaring another world possible, these movements set out to build it from the bottom up.

The nationalization of the politics of emancipation

It would obviously be mistaken to portray the new counter-hegemonic social and political movements as sharing identical roots. They originate

47

in the unique domestic realities of a mosaic of continental diversity. Their commonalities, however, constitute a key factor in shaping their outlook, as I have written elsewhere:

> These movements seek to 'complete' what their historic national political ancestors began, and are Bolivarian in a *Latinoamericanista* sense: they share a common history, a common 'enemy', face similar obstacles to their progress, are mortgaged to the same international financial institutions, suffer similar kinds of discrimination, similar kinds of social, cultural, economic and political exclusion, and are in the grip of the same straitjacket, namely, neoliberalism. (Dominguez 2006)

Where movements focused on direct action moved into the electoral arena to pursue their objectives, and constituted political parties, many retained the dimensions of mass movements and, conversely, many mass movements behave like political parties in their focus on forcing national political change. The Brazilian PT originates in the militant trade unionism of the 1970s, and the Bolivian MAS originates in the *cocalero* union of coca growers. The Federación de Juntas Vecinales of El Alto (FEJUVE,

---

Box 2.1 Invoking history and identity

With Guaicaipuro, with Paramconi, with Anacaona, with Hatuey we have to side, and not with the flames that burned them, nor with the ropes they tied them up with, nor the steel with which they slit their throats, nor with the dogs that bit them. (José Martí)

Still, with absolute precision, we have not even a name, we are practically un-christened: maybe Ibero-Americans, maybe Indo-Americans. For the imperialists we are no more than despicable and despised peoples. At least we were. Since Girón they began to think a little differently. Racial scorn. To be Creole, to be Mestizo, to be Negro, to be simply Latin American is for them a motive of scorn. (Fidel Castro)

They will not be able to defeat us! In Venezuela are the ashes of Simón Bolívar, the ashes of our grandparents, the ashes of Guaicaipuro! They will have to annihilate all of us to be able to take possession over this land! (Hugo Chávez)

Sources: Retamar 2000: 36–7, 42–3; Bolivarian Republic of Venezuela 2006

Federation of Neighbourhood Councils), though not a political party, has been responsible for the ousting of three Bolivian governments. The Confederación de Nacionalidades Indígenas de Ecuador (CONAIE, Confederation of Indigenous Nationalities of Ecuador) joined the short-lived government led by radical military officers, headed by Colonel Lucio Gutiérrez, following a semi-insurrection against the ousted government's decision to dollarize the economy. CONAIE has a politico-electoral arm, Pachakutik, that fields candidates. In Argentina it was mainly the four-thousand-odd actions of the *piqueteros* (roadblockers) which led to President Fernando de la Rua's ousting in December 2001 (*El Clarín* 2002). The Zapatistas in Chiapas claim not to have a strategy of state power, yet are an armed movement that has defied the dominant politics, even of those of the left such as the PRD (Partido de la Revolución Democrática, Party of the Democratic Revolution) in Mexico. In Central America, former guerrilla groups such as the FMLN (Frente Farabundo Martí de Liberación Nacional, Farabundo Martí National Liberation Front in El Salvador), FSLN (Frente Sandinista de Liberación Nacional, Sandinista National Liberation Front in Nicaragua) and URNG (Unidad Revolucionaria Nacional Guatemalteca, Guatemalan National Revolutionary Unity) are now parties with strong links to social movements of workers, peasants, urban poor, women, indigenous groups, squatters, street vendors and suchlike. FSLN commander Daniel Ortega's return to office in Nicaragua in 2006 shows their continuing potential. In Venezuela, the MVR (Movimiento V [Quinta] República, Fifth Republic Movement) never quite acquired the nature of a political party, being rather a group of personalities led by Chávez, on the back of a gigantic and varied social movement based in the *barrios*. In Uruguay, the Frente Amplio (Broad Front) is a coalition that includes former Tupamaro guerrillas, trade unionists and left-wing social democrats. Other examples could be added: there are varieties of social-movements-cum-political-movements also in Colombia, Paraguay, Chile, Costa Rica, Peru, the Dominican Republic and Puerto Rico. What is clear is that the political landscape has been significantly modified: Latin America is adopting a different kind of politics.

The new politics had to shake off old intellectual paradigms that had become obstacles to an emancipatory project. This was a project that now incorporated a broader social alliance than conventional socialists had envisaged, and it took into account the specific socio-economic and class configurations of the region's nations. More conventional emancipatory paradigms, revolutionary nationalism and Marxism, were not abandoned. They had endowed Latin American politics with a heroic and honourable tradition of struggle, and with formidable intellectual tools. They had neglected key socio-economic realities, however, such as racial and gender discrimination, and the environment. Their politics rested on a mechanical and deterministic view of modernization, in which some key social concerns were seen as backward-looking, notably the Indian and the peasant questions. In Latin American terms, they were more Haya de la Torre than Mariátegui (for opposite sides of the more general 'civilization–barbarism' binary, see respectively Sarmiento 1998 and Martí 2007). Alvaro García Linera, former guerrilla fighter and current vice-president of Bolivia, has shed light on how to understand the influence and limitations of this perspective, thus it is worth quoting him at length:

> Marxism came to be part of a political culture ... based on the primacy of proletarian identity above all other identities, on the conviction of the progressive role of industrial technology ... the central role of the state with regards to property relations and distribution of wealth, the cultural nationalization of society around these moulds of the historic and class 'inferiority' of the majority peasant societies in the country. This modernizing and teleological narrative of history ... would create a cognitive bloc and an epistemological inability about two realities which will be the point of departure of another emancipatory project which with time will superimpose itself over Marxist ideology: the peasant and ethnic issues in the country. (García Linera 2007: 2)

In short, unless Marxism, or any other ideological framework, however socialistic its proclaimed objectives, moves away from a narrow class-corporatist frame of analysis and incorporates in its emancipatory project the fundamental questions of oppression and exclusion that characterize most Latin American societies, no progress towards socialism or modernization can be achieved. As García Linera goes on to argue, since the founding of the contemporary Latin American republican state, there has been a power structure based on the exclusion and extermination of the Indian. For the Indian question to be resolved, the Indians must be at the head of the state, or be part of a national-popular coalition, which is exactly what the Evo Morales government has achieved.

Evidently, the Indian issue does not apply everywhere in the region, but it is central in Ecuador and Guatemala, in Peru and Paraguay, while the defence of Mapuche ancestral lands against capitalist encroachment has become a political battleground in Chile. The history of ancestral resistance is a key feature of such politics, together with the necessity of transforming the state to promote their interests. In this regard, a public letter sent by CONAIE to President Rafael Correa of Ecuador is revealing, in that it makes their support conditional on the transformation of the state into a pluri-national state, to strengthen the autonomous self-government of the indigenous communities (CONAIE 2008). They have made progress, since Correa is pushing for a new constitution recognizing the right of indigenous communities to exert jurisdictional authority on the basis of their ancestral traditions (Constituent Assembly of Ecuador 2007).

The Brazilian MST (Movimento dos Trabalhadores Rurais Sem Terra, Landless Workers' Movement) is the epitome of the social movements in Latin America with an impressive record of success, as they themselves state:

[The] Movimento dos Trabalhadores Rurais Sem Terra (MST) is the largest social movement in Latin America with an estimated 1.5 million landless members organized in 23 out of 27 states. The MST carries out long-overdue land reform in a country mired by unjust land distribution. In Brazil, 1.6 per cent of the landowners control roughly half (46.8 per cent) of the land on which crops could be grown. Just 3 per cent of the population owns two-thirds of all arable lands. Since 1985, the MST has peacefully occupied unused land where they have established cooperative farms, constructed houses, schools for children and adults and clinics, promoted indigenous cultures and a healthy and sustainable environment and gender equality. The MST has won land titles for more than 350,000 families in 2,000 settlements as a result of MST actions, and 180,000 encamped families currently await government recognition. Land occupations are rooted in the Brazilian Constitution, which says land that remains unproductive should be used for a 'larger social function'. (MST 2008)

The MST is much more than a social movement; it is a university of radicalism that runs seminars, conferences and schools; owns a publishing house, Expressão Popular; establishes libraries for its own centres of formation throughout the nation; and does much, much more. Its virtual library has a rich collection of articles vindicating the struggles of Zumbí, Luiz Carlos Prestes, Chico Mendes, and a gallery of 'heroes of the people', among which we find Gramsci, Sandino, Camilo Torres, Che Guevara, João Pedro Texeira (leader of the Peasant Leagues of the 1950s), Pablo Neruda, Salvador Allende, Tupac Amaru and Toussaint L'Ouverture (the library is at www.mst.org.br). The MST programme requires a complete overhaul of the Brazilian state apparatus.

The list could be longer, but the sample examined here will suffice to demonstrate the depth of the Latin Americanization of the politics of emancipation. Through a different type of politics, it aims at taking power, and is positioning the mass of the people to successfully challenge the hegemony of their comprador elite and its imperialist mentors. This type of politics is indeed generalized and actively promoted in the region. The website of the Alternativa Bolivarian Para los Pueblos de Nuestra América (ALBA, Bolivarian Alternative for the Peoples of the Americas) contains works in its *Memoria histórica* (Historical Memory) section on many key events and personalities of Latin American radicalism.[3] Furthermore, ALBA sees its own ancestry in 'the dream of Martí and Bolívar of a solidarious Latin America united in social justice, the realization of the human potential of its inhabitants, the defence of their culture and the conquest of a dignified position in the century that begins' (Correa Flores 2005: 16).

In the '*Antedentes históricos del ALBA*' (historical antecedents) section of ALBA's official site we find a selection of classical statements of Latin American revolt and radical politics.[4] Latin American history is an inexhaustible reservoir of inspiration to contemporary battles. Nowhere is this process more advanced than in Venezuela. In the Bolivarian revolution in Venezuela, Hugo Chávez, barely a few months in office, embarked upon a transformation of the Venezuelan state: first by sweeping away the old bipartisan *puntofijista* parliament; then drafting the new constitution approved by referendum in 1999. The refounding of the Venezuelan state had begun with formidable vigour, though not without complications. In abstract, the Bolivarianism that is proclaimed in Venezuela is a vague concept. Examined through the prism of the history of the country, however, it begins to make sense. Bolivarian ideology draws its inspiration from the 'Tree of Three Roots': Simón Bolívar, Simón Rodríguez and Ezequiel Zamora. In this case we have the Venezuelanization of politics:

> The reference to Bolívar needs no explanation, and Simón Rodríguez, although little-known in the English-speaking world, was an outstanding Venezuelan intellectual inspired by the Enlightenment who was Bolívar's tutor and mentor. As for Ezequiel Zamora, he was a mid-nineteenth-century liberal *caudillo* who led popular struggles for land and freedom in the 'Federal Wars' of the 1850s and 1860s, a sworn enemy of the landed oligarchy. (Raby 2006a: 147; and see Bolivarian Republic of Venezuela 2007)

This intellectual armoury, which might be problematic to many a theoretical zealot, has produced extraordinary results: the Venezuelan state has undergone so many changes that it has ceased to function as a normal bourgeois state. The armed forces largely identify with the revolution, and are willingly helping to build Venezuelan socialism. The constitution, taken to its logical conclusions, ought to produce a socialist society and economy. Multinational capital in the oil industry has been almost completely expropriated, as has private capital in the electricity industry. Massive amounts of land have been redistributed. Health, education and social spending in general are at historically unprecedented levels. Women have seen their situation improve drastically. Indigenous peoples have been granted special cultural and political rights, as have gay people and, recently, Afro-descendants. Political power is shifting from the state and local government to communal councils.

The commonalities across the region make the collaboration of their progressive movements, parties and governments not only pretty easy but also, in the current context, unavoidably necessary. The intensity of their supranational collaboration is indeed unprecedented: liquidating the US-inspired FTAA (Free Trade Area of the Americas); all manner of regional and bilateral agreements on energy (such as Petrocaribe), health (Mission Miracle), finance (Bank of the South), media (TeleSur) and now defence (creation of a South American Council of Defence). Furthermore, when Colombian troops entered Ecuador in March 2008, their diplomatic united front not only stopped the US war drive, but also gave the empire a bloody nose.

Conclusion

The interconnectedness of the politics of the present with the struggles of the past, which have always existed in the region, has never before made it so intensely important to build hegemonic coalitions that ultimately seek state power in order to make another world possible. This is a complex, difficult and unusual political process which will have, has had and is having ebbs and flows. It is a process strengthened, however, by the inability of the oppositional elite and its imperial mentors to identify or utilize the figures of the region's history as symbolic ideological weapons to legitimize their narrow class interests, unless such figures are emptied of any subversive or emancipatory dimension, and made irrelevant to today's social and political conflicts (as, for example, in the case of the US-run Radio and TV Martí, which uses the name of Cuba's revolutionary hero to endorse its counter-revolutionary purpose). Considering that the inspirational sources of the Bolivarian revolution were nineteenth-century and in the main non-socialist, drawing on them in twenty-first-century Venezuela has revolutionized that society much more in a socialist direction than have other more directly socialist ideological sources. What applies to Venezuela applies also in different degrees to

Bolivia and Ecuador, and in outward concentric circles of contagion across the rest of the continent. The Latin Americanization of the politics of emancipation can feed from an extraordinarily rich history, in which the legitimacy of proposed solutions of the future can be found in the efforts of the past.

Notes

1 Prominent examples include: La Pampa Trágica, La Cantata de la Escuela Santa María, La Matanza, La Sangre y la Esperanza, La Guerra Sucia, La Violencia, La Masacre, Patagonia Rebelde, La Sangre del Condor, El Coraje del Pueblo, Las Venas Abiertas de América Latina. These translate as Tragic Pampas, Cantata of St Marie School, Slaughter, Blood and Hope, Dirty War, Violence, Massacre, Rebel Patagonia, Blood of the Condor, Courage of the People, The Open Veins of Latin America.

2 Others from across the continent have included: Augusto César Sandino, José Vasconcelos, Pedro Albizú Campos, César Vallejo, Miguel Angel Asturias, Ernesto Guevara, Oswald Andrade, Darcy Ribeiro, Carlos Fonseca Amador, Roque Dalton.

3 Including Puerto Rican nationalism in the 1930s, Salvador Allende, Inti Peredo, Víctor Jara, Che Guevara, Hugo Chávez, the US invasion of Panama, Chico Mendes, José Martí, the Argentine workers' movement, Manuela Saenz, the Cordobazo, Fidel Castro, Omar Torrijos, Francisco Miranda, Simón Bolívar, the Gran Colombia, Tlatelolco, Camilo Cienfuegos, the massacre of Santa María de Iquique, Alí Primera, Augusto César Sandino, and the Caracazo (see www.alternativabolivariana.org).

4 See www.alternativabolivariana. org for examples, such as Francisco de Miranda's 'Plans of Government' and 'The Coro Proclamation', Miguel Hidalgo's 'Decree on Land and Slaves', Mariano Moreno's 'Operations Plan', Simón Bolívar's 'Letter from Jamaica', José Artigas's 'Provisional Law on Lands', Bernardo Monteagudo's 'On the Need for a Federal Union of the Spanish-American States and Its Organizational Plan', José Ceciclio del Valle's 'Saint Peter's Abbot was Dreaming and I Can Also Dream', Simón Bolívar's 'Invitation to the Panama Congress', 'The Perpetual Union, League and Confederation', José Martí's 'Our America', and Augusto César Sandino's 'Plan of Implementation of Bolívar's Supreme Dream'.

TWO | **Case studies**

3 | Venezuela: the political evolution of Bolivarianism

JULIA BUXTON

Venezuela's Bolivarian revolution is seen by proponents and critics as a paradigmatic example of the leftward shift in contemporary Latin American politics. The centrality of Venezuela to the hemispheric political realignments of the twenty-first century has some justification. President Hugo Chávez was the first of the 'leftist' presidents to assume executive authority, his election triggering – depending on one's ideological leanings – fears of a domino effect and regional leftist contagion, or evidence that a leftist political alternative was possible in Latin America, a region historically dominated by right-of-centre political forces and neoliberal-inspired economic policies. A decade of *Chavismo* (the term tends to be used interchangeably with Bolivarianism) has produced a truly transformative project in Venezuela, one whose sustainability and capacity for institutionalization are questionable, but which has without doubt seen a significant redistribution of economic and political power from an elite minority to the politically excluded and economically marginalized majority. Outside of domestic politics, the Bolivarian revolution has redefined the regional political narrative, introducing a new language of citizenship, rights, participation, cultural pride and sovereignty. The historical subservience of the South to its neighbour in the North has been fundamentally challenged by the Bolivarian revolution, and new regional institutions that reflect a truly 'Southern' and anti-neoliberal agenda have been inspired and initiated by Venezuela. In 2005, as the contours and popular potential of Bolivarianism became clear, a new end goal was defined by Chávez at the World Social Forum. The Bolivarian revolution was striving to create a model of Twenty-first-century Socialism, a quest that the Venezuelan electorate mandated in re-electing Chávez to the presidency in December 2006.

The Bolivarian revolution should be understood more as a case of socialism by default than design – with the exact meaning of the term socialism ill-defined and contested. It is a revolution that has been in a constant process of change. There are three separate stages in the evolution of Bolivarianism: its moderate social democratic beginnings; its more radical left-of-centre proposition; and the final, third, stage – of creating a model of Twenty-first-century Socialism. This chapter explores the drivers of this change and argues that it has been influenced by factors external to the project itself – specifically the hostile reaction of domestic opponents and the USA, the oil price rise and the leftward shift in Latin America. These exogenous factors led to ad hoc initiatives that have become central to the model of Twenty-first-century Socialism and its identification as a leftist project.

A second, interrelated argument is that the Bolivarian revolution is a specifically Venezuelan phenomenon. Owing to the country specificity of the variables that underpin Bolivarianism (identified as the influence of the pre-Chávez political legacy and the dominance of the oil economy), the revolution cannot be replicated or transposed to other country contexts. Moreover, the extent to which *Chavismo*, Bolivarianism or Twenty-first-century Socialism should be understood as 'of the left' is open to question. Chávez is eclectic in ideology and organizational strategy. The revolution is strongly nationalistic and informed by opposition to the pre-Chávez *Punto Fijo* system that dominated Venezuelan politics for forty years. As such, Bolivarianism should rightly be understood as an anti-*puntofijista* project that evolved a socialist identity rather than as a socialist project per se. This calls into question the homogenizing sweep of the 'rise of the left' thesis, the juxtaposition of a 'good' and 'bad' left that has been used to frame understanding of developments in the region (Castañeda 2006), and the utility of containment strategies, specifically those pursued by the Bush administration in the USA, which are intended to delimit the potency and potentiality of the Bolivarian agenda.

The evolution of Bolivarianism

Hugo Chávez was elected to power in 1998 as an 'anti-party' political outsider. He was propelled to the presidency on the back of deep popular hostility to the two parties that had dominated Venezuelan politics for forty years following democratization in 1958, the Acción Democrática (AD, Democratic Action) and the Partido Social Cristiano de Venezuela (COPEI, the Venezuelan Social Christian Party). The two-party system was highly illiberal and unrepresentative. It operated like a single-party regime, a convergence of the two political parties that was facilitated by their ideological *coincidencia* and agreement through the founding Pact of Punto Fijo (1957) to share control of state institutions. AD and COPEI worked together to exclude party political competitors and to control access to the oil export revenues that flowed to the national treasury from the national oil company PDVSA. These oil rents were divided between AD and COPEI, and distributed to their constituencies through a dense network of corporatist organizations (Buxton 2000; Hellinger 1991).

For decades there was an unwritten trade-off in Venezuela, under which *Punto Fijo* 'democracy' was accepted and legitimate – for as long as it guaranteed popular access to oil rents (Karl 1987). This positive-sum game, in which the state could meet the needs of both business and labour, unravelled in dramatic style in the 1980s. Gross economic mismanagement, declining oil rents, institutionalized corruption and impunity, and rising authoritarianism catalysed popular antipathy towards the parties and the *Punto Fijo* state that they had created and colonized. Despite evidence of mounting popular disaffection, reform was resisted by the increasingly narrow band of elite oil rent beneficiaries and the party leadership, the *cogollo* (Buxton 2000). In 1989, a radical and unexpected effort by the incoming AD government to restructure the economy, turning it away from oil dependence, heterodoxy and state-led development and towards diversification, orthodox approaches and global integration, marked the end of the *puntofijista* social contract. The 1990s was consequently a period of political instability, coup attempts (one led by Lieutenant Colonel Hugo Chávez in February 1992), mass protests and the search for new alternatives as the electorate pressured for the ending of *puntofijista* 'democracy'. It was in this context, and against a background of deepening poverty and inequality, that Hugo Chávez was elected president in 1998.

Bolivarianism phase 1: constitutionalism and moderation

The first phase of the three periods of *Chavismo* was characterized by moderation on the part of the Chávez government. The incoming president and his loose Polo Patriótico (PP, Patriotic Pole) coalition, comprising those previously marginalized from the two-party system – Chávez's own Movimiento Quinta República (MVR, Fifth Republic Movement), Patria Para Todos (PPT, the Country for All) and the Partido Comunista de Venezuela (PCV, the Venezuelan Communist Party) – had an immediate and central objective, namely constitutional reform. This was intended to lay the foundations for the transition to a new Bolivarian Fifth Republic and terminate the institutionalized control of AD and COPEI. At his inauguration in February 1999, Chávez decreed a popular referendum on the constitutional reform proposition. This was supported by a majority of voters, leading to elections to the constituent assembly in July 1999.

Of acute importance to an understanding of the evolution of Bolivarianism, it should be stressed that 'socialism' was not part of the *chavista* political lexicon. This period was dominated by rhetorical vitriol against *puntofijistas* and oligarchs, who Chávez claimed had betrayed and impoverished the country. The new government's primary ideological reference point was Simón Bolívar, the Liberator from Spanish colonial rule, and Chávez pledged to fulfil Bolívar's frustrated ambition of regional integration. According to Chávez, 'Bolívar is not just a man, Bolívar is a complex set of ideas related to politics, society and justice. These ideas remain relevant to the national, South American, Caribbean and world arenas, because Bolívar engendered an international idea. He spoke of what we call today a multipolar world' (cited in Guevara 2005: 11). This vision of a multipolar world, in which the dominance of the USA was balanced by other clusters of influence, was the first of the five elements of the Bolivarian vision and policy agenda. In its original form, however, multipolarism was not expressed as anti-Americanism and, underscoring the pragmatism of the first phase, Chávez prioritized a visit to his US counterpart, Bill Clinton, in 1999.

The *chavistas* looked backwards into Venezuelan history to reclaim national myths, figures and symbols and to legitimize their vision of a new post-*Punto Fijo* nation. Two other nineteenth-century heroes, Ezequiel Zamora, a military leader during the Federal War period, and Simón Rodríguez, Bolívar's tutor, were conjoined with Bolívar to form the *chavista* 'Trinity' of influence and inspiration. It was to this Trinity that Chávez and co-conspirators in the military had first pledged their allegiance, when they founded the Movimiento Bolivariano Revolucionario 200, the forerunner of MVR, in 1983. Bolivarian nationalism was counterposed against the *Adeco* nationalism that had defined the *Punto Fijo* period (*Adeco* being the AD–COPEI consensus). Where *Adeco* nationalism stressed modernity and progress, Bolivarian nationalism looked backwards and emphasized pride in the country's unique history; where *Adeco* culture was predominantly defined by the tastes and interests of the US-acculturalized, ethnically white strata of the population, Bolivarian cultural nationalism elevated indigenous and Afro-Venezuelan traditions and identification with South America (Buxton 2006; Cannon 2008).

In sum, the primary aim of the *chavistas* in this first period was to deconstruct the *Punto Fijo* state and establish a constitutional framework through which the sovereign people, *el pueblo*, and the Venezuelan nation could realize their true potential. The Bolivarian emphasis on *el pueblo* was a point of contrast with the elitism of *Puntofijismo*. It was Chávez's promise to democratize authority and return power to the people which had galvanized popular support for his candidacy in 1998. Leading on from this, the second element of the Bolivarian agenda was the creation of protagonistic democracy, a model of direct democracy premised on routinized popular participation and decision-making. The vision was of a profoundly democratic state, in which power flowed up from the grassroots. This contrasted with *Puntofijismo* and also the liberal democratic model, with its emphasis on insulating the government from the demands of the masses and the importance of intermediary associations mediating between the state and society. Protagonistic democracy looked to forge a direct connection between the people and the people's government (Cannon 2008; Herrera Salas 2007). This was in turn intended to enhance transparency, accountability and the quality of democracy. In line with this, the Bolivarian constitution, which was ratified with majority popular support in December 1999, established mechanisms that included recall referendums for elected officials, including the president (Wilpert 2007).

The third element of the Bolivarian agenda was the creation of a productive economy. In this first phase, this was not framed through an anti-neoliberal narrative. On the contrary, *Chavismo* during this period emphasized respect for private property, the importance of repaying the foreign debt, the role of business in national development and of government engaging the state only when and where the market failed. The British prime minister, Tony Blair, and his Third Way model of socialism was cited by Chávez as an inspiration, and in this context the idea of the productive economy was related to an economy that responded to the need of humans, not the need for profit (Gott 2004). While Chávez stuck with the market fundamentals during this first phase, even retaining his predecessor's economic minister, on the regional stage he assumed a strongly critical position against the proposed Free Trade Area of the Americas. This US- and Chilean-led proposal to create a free trade bloc from Tierra del Fuego to Alaska was denounced by Chávez at the April 2001 Summit of the Americas in Quebec, Canada. He had three points of contention. First, that the planned model of integration between the developed North and developing South was contrary to the economic interests of the latter; second, that integration should encompass only Latin American countries (in line with Bolívar's vision); and third, that integration should not be premised on free markets and free trade. Hence an interesting distinction emerged. In the Venezuelan domestic context, Chávez's anti-neoliberal critique was muted, but he was vocally antagonistic to free trade approaches on the regional stage.

Nationalization was not on the agenda, with one significant exception. The 1999 constitution mandated state ownership of the country's hydrocarbon resources and a PDVSA majority share in any private joint venture. This overturned the part-privatization or *apertura* of the national industry that was undertaken in controversial circumstances and with debatable economic dividends for Venezuela in the 1990s (Mommer 2003). For example, some of the joint ventures permitted private sector contractors to pump oil and sell it back to PDVSA at a fixed rate. When the price of oil collapsed, this increased the profits accruing to the private sector and the price paid by PDVSA. Venezuela was effectively producing oil at a loss. In another scandalous example of the highly prejudicial terms of the process, the information technology division of PDVSA was sold to the US defence contractor SAIC for just $1,000.

In a further break with oil policy, the Chávez government looked to strengthen oil prices through forging a closer working relationship with fellow members of the Organization of Petroleum Exporting Countries (OPEC). There were multiple aims here: boosting prices from the $7 per barrel that they had collapsed to in 1998; ensuring stability of oil prices through coordination of output; shifting the terms of trade in favour of producers over consumers; and building multipolarism. Chávez visited fellow oil-producing countries in 2000, including Iraq, Iran, Libya and Algeria. This laid the ground for Venezuela's assumption of the secretary-generalship of OPEC in June 2000 and the consequent support for Venezuela's proposal to introduce a price band mechanism that coordinated output in order to keep prices within a $22 per barrel (p/b) to $28 p/b range.

Social justice was an interrelated but at this point underdeveloped theme. Social policy initiatives were minimal, and the Chávez government did not demonstrate any grand vision of a social agenda. If anything, Chávez appeared unprepared by the scale of need and popular expectations of his government:

> We had created a government – effectively, a political and constituent-led revolution – in the midst of massive social need. I decided to invite the unemployed to come to Miraflores Palace. They were a veritable army, and during those visits their lines circled the palace several times. They came with expectations we could not hope to fulfil. That was a mistake we made. The process of revolutionary government began in the middle of serious shortages [...] It was a virtual avalanche of poverty stricken people; I barely slept with the torment. (Cited in Guevara 2005: 32)

There was only one significant social policy initiative, Plan Bolívar. This was administered by the military, in line with the Bolivarian vision of the armed forces at the service of the nation (and pragmatically informed by the absence of a functionally effective national bureaucracy), and it focused on infrastructure repair and school building.

The final element of the Bolivarian agenda was national integration. This aimed to overcome three identified problems: the historical fragmentation of the national territory, the lack of transport connectivity, and rural underdevelopment. The grand plan here was to re-energize the rural economy, making relocation attractive to residents of the overcrowded slums or *barrios* of urban areas and to generate food sovereignty. Agriculture had stagnated with the rise of the oil economy at the beginning of the twentieth century. As the oil sector came to dominate the economy, accounting for over 70 per cent of central government revenues from the 1960s onwards, agricultural production slumped. As oil export revenues were accrued in dollars, this led to a significant overvaluation of the Venezuelan currency, the bolívar. As successive *Punto Fijo* governments failed to devise and implement effective macroeconomic management strategies to counter this problem of 'Dutch disease', non-oil exports were expensive and uncompetitive while imports were artificially cheap (Karl 1997). In this context, Venezuela became progressively reliant on basic food imports, and it was this loss of food sovereignty which Chávez was committed to reversing through national integration and rural relocation.

In the schema presented here, this first phase closed with new national elections in 2000 to relegitimize all elected officials, including the president, and the introduction of legislative measures in 2001 which were intended to provide a legal framework for the 1999 constitution, and finalize the overhaul of the *Punto Fijo* state. These included a reform of the corrupt, AD-affiliated main trade union confederation, the Confederación de Trabajadores de Venezuela (Ellner 2007), and forty-nine laws introduced under enabling legislation that, among other things, terminated state funding of religious education, reformed land distribution and raised taxes. Management of the state oil company, PDVSA, which Chávez had criticized for operating like 'a state within a state', was replaced in 2000 and the autonomy of the company was reduced as it was brought under the close jurisdiction of the Energy Ministry.

Bolivarianism phase 2: conflict and radicalization

The next stage in the evolution of Bolivarianism was characterized by the deepening and expansion of the Bolivarian agenda. The administration became definitively pro-poor in its policy and organizational focus. Anti-Americanism and anti-neoliberalism became important elements of the rhetorical and policy agenda. What had originally appeared to be a 'wish list' of ambitions gained programme and policy form, and Bolivarianism took on an increasingly radical hue. During this period, the government introduced an expansive social policy agenda, called the Missions (*misiones*), the financing of which was increasingly dominated by PDVSA. By 2006, the final year of this Second Phase, PDVSA was channelling over $6 billion to the seventeen *misiones*, which operated in welfare fields that included healthcare provision (Misión Barrio Adentro), subsidized food distribution and provision (Misión Mercal), education (Misión Robinson, Misión Ribas, Misión Sucre) and employment training (Misión Vuelvan Caras). The pro-market trend of the 1990s was reversed, as exchange and price controls were restored and private sector foreign partnerships in the hydrocarbons sector were revised in a trend of statization and nationalization that was to gain traction in the Third Phase.

The government's earlier emphasis on partnership with the private sector was replaced by a model of 'socialism with business' that valued state-to-state, public-sector-to-public-sector cooperation agreements. TeleSur, the New Television Station of the South, was launched in 2005, realizing the government's ambition of diminishing US cultural and political influences, and traditional cultures and national cultural values were promoted. Legislation in 2005 and 2006 grounded protagonistic democracy in community-level organizations, the *consejos comunales* and technical water committees (Mesas Técnicas de Agua), and the structure of the productive and social economy gained new definition through the introduction of state support for – and promotion of – the cooperative movement and worker self-management (*cogestión*). At the regional level, the government created the Bolivarian Alternative for the Peoples of Our Americas (ALBA, Alternativa Bolivariana Para los Pueblos de las Américas), which was based on principles of cooperation, social justice and exploitation of comparative advantages. In ideological and organizational terms, the poor and informal sector workers were identified as the vanguard of the revolutionary process, and there was a host of novel and eclectic mobilizational initiatives, including the Bolivarian Circles and Electoral Battle Units (Raby 2006). As a result of this radicalization process, Bolivarianism was seen to become very much a project of the left, a redefinition that Chávez both effectuated and legitimized at the World Social Forum in 2005, when he declared that the end goal of Bolivarianism was to create a new socialist model. This socialism was to be informed by the specificities of Venezuela's historical experience while breaking with the 'failed' socialist and communist experiment of the twentieth century. Venezuela was creating a model of Twenty-first-century Socialism.

It was during this second phase that Bolivarianism came under attack on the international scene from both the conservative right and also from the social democratic left. The causes of right-wing enmity are easy to discern given the policy initiatives outlined above. For the social democratic left, the Bolivarian revolution was particularly problematic because of perceived hegemonic pretensions and authoritarian characteristics. Throughout this second phase, the *chavistas* came to control the National Assembly, twenty of the twenty-four state governors and the majority of municipal governments. Through purges and sackings, they were seen to achieve control of PDVSA management, the judiciary, military and the national electoral council.

The argument of this chapter is that Venezuela arrived at the new end goal of Twenty-first-century Socialism and achieved political hegemony by default rather than design. Four factors are identified as drivers of this radicalization process: the hostile response of domestic opponents to the Bolivarian agenda; the containment and isolation strategies of the Bush administration in the USA; the rise in the international oil price; and the regional political shift away from the right. Each of these variables intersected with and reinforced the others, propelling the Chávez administration in new and unplanned directions. They also altered the coalition of actors and influences around the president and the relative weight and authority of (increasingly conflictive) currents within the PP alliance.

When elected in 1998, Chávez was uncompromising with the traditionally dominant *Punto Fijo* elite. He rejected ministerial proposals made to him by business interests that had courted him in the run-up to his election victory. He bypassed the institutional arrangements that he inherited and which were controlled by AD and COPEI supporters, working through referenda, the constitutional assembly and the military to deliver constitutional, legal and policy change. The *chavistas* broke with the compromise politics of the *Punto Fijo* era and the positive-sum-game framework that had shaped the corporatist and clientelist practices of *Puntofijismo*. Where AD and COPEI had aimed to balance the interests of organized labour and business through subsidies and other privileges, Chávez was clear that the informal sector and the poor should be the singular focus of state support. Zero-sum politics displaced the positive-sum game, creating an adversarial political framework unprecedented in the post-1958 'democratic' period (Hellinger and Ellner 2003).

This *ruptura* catalysed a destabilizing and recurrently anti-democratic response from the AD and COPEI opposition parties and the coalition of *Punto Fijo* interests that coalesced around them, and which included the Roman Catholic Church, business (grouped in Fedecámaras, the Chamber of Commerce), organized labour (in the CTV – Confederación de Trabajadores de Venezuela, Confederation of Venezuelan Workers), the private sector media (which controlled 90 per cent of broadcast output in Venezuela) and the upper classes. AD and COPEI partisan appointments in the judiciary, military, election administration and state bureaucracy worked with these groups to block government initiatives, and roll back the Bolivarian revolution. There were powerful vested interests in restoring the status quo ante, despite its manifest rejection by the Venezuelan electorate. These interests aside, the *puntofijistas* had no experience of being a 'loyal opposition', having enjoyed institutionalized political control for forty years. They were consequently ill-prepared and ill-positioned to serve as a democratic vehicle for the articulation of opposition to the Chávez government.

The AD and COPEI parties manifested their immediate opposition to the Bolivarian agenda by abstaining from elections to the Constituent Assembly in July 1999. This strategy was intended to delegitimize the constitutional reform process, a tactic that was repeated in the 2000 national elections and 2004 regional elections. This had two significant effects. It created a situation of *chavista* electoral dominance by default, and it took organized opposition protest out of institutional spheres and on to the street. This relocation of the politics of protest – from the National Assembly to the street – was also a consequence of AD and COPEI weakness. Both parties, but specifically COPEI, were attenuated as significant electoral forces in 1998, and as a result their capacity to convoke and represent anti-*chavista* sentiment was negligible, particularly in the pre-existing context of potent anti-party sentiment. Fedecámaras and the CTV therefore assumed leading roles in mobilizing and bringing together initially fragmented sectors of opposition. Extra-institutional protest began with a non-payment of taxes campaign led by wealthy groups and business sectors in 1999/2000. This evolved into a strategy of encouraging capital flight (an estimated $30 billion was taken outside of Venezuela during this early period). The referendum on trade union reform in 2000 and the overhaul of PDVSA management structures galvanized CTV opposition to the government, led by the CTV president and head of the FEDEPETROL union, Carlos Ortega.

The confluence of labour and business was strengthened, and gained a civil society dimension with the introduction of the 49 Laws in 2001. The measures affected the interests of the Roman Catholic Church, landowners, industrialists and wealthy families who educated their children at (state-funded) religious schools. Opposition to the measures was manifest through disruptive street 'convocations'. The private sector media played a vital role in publicizing these demonstrations and generating a profoundly anti-government matrix of opinion through studio discussions that were pejorative and unbalanced. In December 2001, the opposition launched the first of its general strikes and private sector lock-outs. Going into 2002, the focus of opposition shifted to the military. Anti-government forces called on the armed forces to intervene to end the Chávez 'dictatorship', a call that was heeded by some sectors in April 2002 when an alliance of anti-government groups launched a failed coup attempt (Golinger 2007). The coup unravelled within a matter of days, after Pedro Carmona, the head of Fedecámaras, assumed the interim presidency and steered the civil–military junta to the far right. Amid massive protests led by the popular sectors, Chávez was restored to power in an event that the private sector refused to broadcast. Following the collapse of the coup, protest shifted back to the street, with a focus on economic sabotage. A sixty-four-day strike at the beginning of December supported by senior management of PDVSA catalysed a deep economic recession as oil exports were halted and production and distribution chains collapsed. Underscoring the national economic impact of these actions, GDP collapsed by 8.9 per cent in 2002 and 7.8 per cent in 2003, reversing the economic recovery of 2000 and 2001, when the economy had grown at 3.7 per cent and 3.4 per cent respectively. During this searing economic contraction, the number of people living in extreme poverty increased from 20.6 per cent of the population when Chávez assumed power in 1999, to 29.8 per cent in 2003.

When the strike finally collapsed, at the cost of $14 billion in lost oil export revenues, the opposition regrouped as the Coordinadora Democrática (CD, Democratic Coordination) and made efforts to reconnect to the portion of the electorate that had not supported the anti-government effort. The strategic focus shifted to removing Chávez through the mechanism of the recall referendum. A leading role was played by the NGO Súmate in collecting signatures to force the referendum, which was finally convened in August 2004. Chávez emerged triumphant with 59.3 per cent of the vote in an election process verified as fair and free by the Organization of American States and the Carter Center, but which was not accepted by Súmate or the CD. The opposition put minimal effort into the state governor elections that were convened at the end of 2004, allowing the *chavistas* to dominate by default. With presidential elections approaching in December 2006, the CD opted to contest the election with the candidacy of Manuel Rosales, the governor of Zulia state. Chávez again emerged victorious with 62.8 per cent of the vote.

A number of factors account for the failure of the anti-government opposition to galvanize the popular support necessary to displace Chávez, either constitutionally or unconstitutionally. Aside from the 'pull' of the ever popular Chávez, the anti-government movement was seen to represent the much-despised *Punto Fijo* regime. Even when the opposition expanded to include 'new' party political organizations such as the youthful and right-wing Primero Justicia (Justice First), Un Nuevo Tiempo (A New Time) and defectors from the PP, it failed to break the impression that it was an opposition movement based on defence of privilege. The neoliberal bent of many groups within the CD and Súmate also failed to commend the opposition to the wider public, and there was a pervasive sense that the opposition was anti-democratic in both organization and ideology. The opposition was also badly damaged by strategic miscalculations such as the December 2002 stoppage, which particularly hurt the interests of the poor. Finally, the opposition was seen as anti-national, and here the link with the USA was particularly misguided.

Hostile bilateral relations with the USA are identified as the second driver of the evolution of Bolivarianism. When the Bush administration assumed office in 2001, it perceived the Bolivarian revolution as inimical to US energy, security and commercial interests and ideologically at odds with the neoconservative world vision. Given the lead role of the Republican Party in isolating the Castro regime in Cuba, the new Republican government could not countenance Venezuela pursuing strong and close relations with the Cuban nemesis. That Bush appointed a number of right-wing hawks who had been instrumental in the bloody anti-communism strategies pursued by President Reagan in South and Central America in the 1980s further narrowed US tolerance of Venezuelan 'deviance'. Key Reaganite officials, including Otto Reich, Elliot Abrams and John Negroponte, were given senior positions in the Department of Affairs for the Western Hemisphere, a move that immediately constrained the opportunities for soft diplomacy and dialogue. Venezuela was viewed through the lens of the cold war and understood as a wayward threat in the North American 'backyard'. Venezuela's decision in 2001 to end a military cooperation agreement with the USA and to ban US counter-narcotics flights over national territory was an invocation of state sovereignty that went against the two-hundred-year-old Monroe Doctrine, which proclaimed South America as part of the US sphere of interest.

There were also more contemporary concerns for the Bush administration. Venezuela occupied a murky grey area in the black-and-white world of the post-2001 'war on terror'. In October 2001, Chávez very publicly condemned the US-led invasion of Afghanistan and criticized the USA for 'fighting terror with terror'. This, combined with Chávez's visit to Saddam Hussein's Iraq in 2000 and later close relations with

Iran and sympathy for the people of the occupied Palestinian territories, fuelled neoconservative allegations of Venezuelan sympathy for 'terrorist' causes which were epitomized by Secretary of State Condoleezza Rice at her confirmation hearing where she declared that Venezuela formed part of a South American 'axis of evil'. Similar statements were made by former Secretary of State for Defense Donald Rumsfeld, who compared Chávez to Adolf Hitler and accused the Venezuelan president of repression, authoritarianism and financing of terrorist activities. In commercial terms, Venezuela's opposition to the FTAA undermined the US economic agenda for South America, while the revision of national oil legislation and Venezuela's proactive role in OPEC ran contrary to US energy and economic interests.

The US response to Chávez was confused; with different state agencies pursuing different agendas, it evolved over time with each successive setback, and it was wholly counterproductive. The principal strategies that were followed were interrelated and they included: efforts to isolate the Chávez government regionally and internationally; the discrediting of the government, particularly in relation to its democratic credentials; and support and assistance (technical and military) for constitutional and unconstitutional attempts to remove Chávez. Arguably the central tactic was a 'skilfully crafted electoral intervention' (Golinger 2007: 20) that was structured around the channelling of financial resources to the opposition through the US State Department to two agencies, the National Endowment for Democracy (NED) and USAID. In the pre-Chávez period, 'democracy promotion' activities in Venezuela through the NED and USAID had been negligible. By 2001, these had been dramatically ramped up. The NED Venezuela budget in 2001 was over $3 million. For USAID the 2002 figure was $15 million, of which an additional $1 million was provided to NED under the State Department's 'Special Funds for Venezuela' initiative. The principal recipients of these monies were anti-government groups and organizations, specifically those that engaged in the 2002 coup attempt, the December lock-out and mobilization for the 2004 recall referendum. The programmes funded by NED, USAID and the principal USAID private contractor in Venezuela – Development Alternatives Incorporated – focused on building a 'democratic' opposition, media training for opposition groups and support in developing party political programmes. In 2003, the US government established an Office for Transition Initiatives (OTI) for Venezuela, in line with its OTI desks for other 'unstable' countries, including Iraq, the Democratic Republic of Congo and Kosovo. Aside from direct financial support to the anti-Chávez opposition, the US government imposed an arms embargo on Venezuela in 2005; decertified the country for failing to comply effectively with the 'war' on drugs; listed Venezuela for people trafficking; and blocked multilateral loans to Venezuela through the World Bank and IMF. The US failed to condemn the coup against Chávez in 2002, it lobbied for OAS support of the Carmona junta, and documents released under the Freedom of Information Act demonstrate that US intelligence was aware of the planned coup (Clement 2007; Golinger 2007).

The impact on the Chávez administration of domestic and US opposition was profound. It was clear to the administration that its survival depended on consolidating support among economically marginalized groups. Social policy and pro-poor economic policy strategies were the immediate response, and this explains the primacy of the Missions in this second phase. Second, because the lock-outs and stoppages impeded production and distribution chains, the government had to step in to ensure basic supply of goods. These interventions were then consolidated in the Missions. Misión Mercal, for example, the network of state-subsidized supermarkets, was a response to shortages of basic goods. It was subsequently retained as a means of ensuring basic nutrition and access to food among the poor. In turn, supply to the Mercal stores came from state-supported cooperative organizations that were intended to build national food sovereignty by boosting domestic output (with land redistribution also accelerated during this phase). Strategies for delivering meaningful change to the poor were also informed by the political component of the Bolivarian agenda. In response to the instability experienced during this phase, the government accelerated application of its protagonistic democracy model, incrementing the power and authority exercised by grassroots communities through the *consejos comunales*.

The US and opposition actions also served to create a situation of *chavista* hegemony by default, with the PDVSA lock-out, military coup attempt and evident sympathy of the judiciary for the military rebellion (those arrested by the government were not found guilty of rebellion by the AD-dominated Supreme Court) legitimizing a purge of state institutions. Loyal *chavistas* were promoted to key positions, a development that was strongly influenced by the government's perception of threat and insecurity. And in the context of US funding for anti-Chávez forces, domestic legislation was introduced to restrict foreign funding of domestic political organizations and NGOs – a move decried by Western social democrats.

Similarly the military doctrine was revised, shifting to a model of asymmetrical warfare in response to fears of US invasion. With the imposition of the US arms embargo, Venezuela turned to China and Russia for long-delayed upgrades to its military capabilities and in order to ensure border integrity. Ties with China, Russia and Iran were deepened in order to balance the negative influence of the USA, and anti-Americanism and anti-Bush rhetoric became pronounced and were used to justify the new anti-imperialist orientation of Venezuelan foreign and regional policy. The instrumental role of the Venezuelan business and private media sectors in directing political events during this phase also convinced the government of the need to build investment relationships premised on public-sector-to-public-sector partnerships, for example with China and Cuba, and to build a public sector media alternative at the national (TVES) and regional level (TeleSur) (Wilpert 2007).

Perceptions of US threat and the ongoing failure of the Bush administration to countenance the legitimacy or democratic nature of the Chávez government were pivotal in driving Venezuelan regional integration initiatives, such as the ALBA and Petrocaribe, first as a defence mechanism intended to insulate Venezuela from US pressure, then during the latter half of this second phase as a means to push back the influence of the USA and US-dominated institutions such as the IMF and the World Bank.

Within the *chavistas* themselves, the events of this second phase reinforced the view that there could be no compromise with *Puntofijismo*. This strengthened the position of more radical left-of-centre elements within the ranks of the PP, in turn undermining moderates committed to a more conciliatory and moderate course. Moderate defections from the PP enhanced the authority of *chavista* currents that identified with communism and socialism, and the core group of advisers around Chávez was increasingly drawn from the PCV, marking an important power shift within the *chavistas*.

Before concluding with discussion of the third phase, two final variables driving this process of radical change should be mentioned. The first is the oil price. It would have been impossible for the government to implement its foreign and social policy initiatives without the strong rise in the international price. By 2004, the price of Venezuelan crude (which trades below the international price) was $32.88 p/b, three times the level of 1999. By 2006, it was $56.45 and was averaging $90 p/b mid-2008. This provided the Chávez government with tremendous fiscal manoeuvrability and negated the utility of traditional tools of US 'control' such as financial embargos and disinvestment strategies. The final key shift related to regional politics. That the electorate in Bolivia, Brazil, Argentina, Chile, Ecuador and Nicaragua all voted for non-right-wing options during this phase was crucial in enabling Venezuela to advance its regional agenda. Had the hemisphere been dominated by the strongly pro-USA, neoliberal orientation of the 1980s and 1990s, Chávez would have been isolated and surrounded by a bloc of ideologically hostile states that would have undoubtedly allied with the Bush administration.

Bolivarianism phase 3: towards Twenty-first-century Socialism

In this third phase, Chávez and his government were identified as a radical left-of-centre proposition. Their policy orientation was seen to elide with traditional socialist programmes of state-led development, nationalization and anti-imperialism. Developments during this phase were the logical culmination of trends in the second phase. Chávez fought and won the December 2006 presidential election on a platform of advancing Twenty-first-century Socialism and launched his presidential term with the unveiling of the Five Motors of the Revolution. These were identified as: the moral struggle (developing popular revolutionary consciousness); a new geometry of power (decentralizing authority down to the communities); the economic role of the state (extending nationalization); constitutional reform (to introduce a strongly socialist orientation into the 1999 Bolivarian constitution); and enabling powers (with the right of the president to introduce change by decree). Running alongside the Five Motors, the government unveiled plans to merge the PP alliance and create a new united socialist party, the Partido Socialista Unido de Venezuela (PSUV, United Socialist Party of Venezuela).

Throughout 2007, the government realized its ambitions in many of these spheres. Chávez was granted enabling powers and used this executive mechanism to nationalize the electricity, telecommunications and oil sectors. But the government hit its first electoral obstacle in December 2007, when voters rejected the proposed reform of the constitution. The scale of the defeat was relatively narrow, just 1 per cent, with 90 per cent of the votes counted, but the referendum débâcle was a psychological boost for the opposition movement, which had effectively gone into retreat following the defeat of Rosales. Despite this setback, the government proceeded, pushing through its policy agenda on a case-by-case basis.

The referendum defeat pointed, however, to some important challenges that the Chávez administration needed to address in its third phase. It was generally recognized that the traditional pro-Chávez sector of the electorate had not come out to support the government, raising questions as to the extent to which the *chavista* grassroots identified with the leftward shift. Further to this, there were seen to be severe policy limitations in relation to the quality of public services delivered though the Missions. While quantity was not in doubt and was borne out in figures for school building, medical consultations and community clinic construction, the nature of need and the capacity of the government to identify and target the most in need became a primary issue. Inflation was rising and shortages of basic goods were experienced. While the government blamed the opposition for hoarding and speculation, there were also non-opposition-related explanations in regard to macroeconomic management. The domestic currency was heavily overvalued and it appeared that the finance team had failed to solve the old problem of 'Dutch disease'. Trying to build a model of socialism in an oil boom posed serious challenges. Domestic agricultural production and the evolution of the cooperative movement were undercut by cheap imports, while the continued reliance on oil export revenues sustained concerns of recession in the event of a price fall. Moreover, PDVSA's central role in the financing of the Missions was seen to come at the cost of underinvestment in the oil sector, raising the possibility of declining output over the longer term.

In terms of the intra-*chavista* impacts of the December defeat, the referendum setback further deepened the cleavage between moderates and radicals, the former arguing that the *chavistas* were not carrying the electorate with them, the latter arguing that disaffection was due to the failure to deliver socialism fast enough. And as the vote of the poor and economically marginalized was seen to be wavering, the labour unions became an increasingly important voice in the *chavista* organization and Chávez himself underwent a Damascene conversion. Having once seen the informal sector as the revolutionary vanguard, and decried union plans for autonomy, by 2008 the president was extolling the importance of organized labour to his socialist project and the administration became increasingly responsive to labour pressure for nationalization. In April 2008, the moderate *chavista* wing of the labour sector, the Frente Socialista Bolivariana de Trabajadores (FSBT, Bolivarian Socialist Workers' Front) was seen to lose ground to socialist and Marxist currents in the pro-government labour confederation after the administration supported the latter's demands for nationalization of the Sidor steelworks. Fundamental questions in relation to preferred models of ownership remained, however, with the unions supporting worker control of state-owned industry and the government seeming to prefer a more limited vision of worker participation in management. To conclude, in the third phase (and the final one for Chávez given the pending presidential vote of 2011) the precise contours of Venezuela's socialist model remained vague and subject to ad hoc and pragmatic change led by Chávez. What will be crucial will be whether he is able to institutionalize Bolivarianism in terms of embedding it in forms and

4 | Venezuela: reinventing social democracy from below?

SARA C. MOTTA

Venezuela's contemporary political process, or *Chavismo*, is characterized in a number of ways: populist, authoritarian, illiberal, revolutionary and socialist. This contested and conflictual terrain of conceptual analysis reflects the dynamic, contradictory and challenging nature of *Chavismo*. A common feature of many of these analyses, however, is their top-down methodology and conceptual apparatus. Accordingly, their analytical focus is the personality, rhetoric and policy of Chavéz, and/or decisions taken at the level of the centralized state by the political elite. This chapter challenges such methodological and conceptual elitism by focusing on the practices, struggles and discourses of popular democratic subjects. With reference to three social/economic programmes based in La Vega shanty town in Caracas, it illustrates how conceptualizations that label *Chavismo* as a form of illiberal populism construct an academic discourse that contributes to the masking and delegitimization of popular articulations of democracy and development.[1] The empirical analysis demonstrates that there are elements of a municipalized social democratic project developing; processes that go beyond social democratic notions of state–society and state–market relationships. Accordingly, counter-hegemonic forms of democracy and development based on popular class rationality and political agency are being forged that challenge the hegemony of elitist liberal democracy and the market economy.

The chapter first considers, and dismisses, the use of the concept of populism to define *Chavismo*, and then introduces the concept of social democracy as an alternative way of evaluating the nature of the political projects within *Chavismo*. Second, an evaluation of the social democratic nature of *Chavismo* is made in relation to three social/economic programmes: Misión Ribas (secondary-school education for those who were unable to complete it originally), Misión Barrio Adentro (a health mission providing basic medical attention in communities) and Consejos Comunales (communal councils). The chapter will conclude with an analysis of the fault lines within *Chavismo*'s political struggle to construct popular forms of democracy and development.

Conceptualizing *Chavismo*

Populism is a term often used to dismiss and delegitimize the contemporary political process in Venezuela (Hawkins 2003; Castañeda 2006; Krastev 2006). Such critics assume that *Chavismo* is a political phenomenon that reproduces traditional, hierarchical and exclusionary political relationships between state and society. This type of politics results in the hollowing out of any of the democratic characteristics of the party system and state, and a concentration of power around the president. Accordingly, it is seen to lead to political and social instability and represents a form of illiberalism verging in some cases on authoritarianism. Krastev is illustrative of this perspective when he argues that 'Liberal democracy is challenged on one side by Hugo Chavéz's revolutionary Venezuela ... unbridled majoritarianism might ride roughshod over constitutionalism and the rule of law ... [He is] freedom's enemy from *within* both democratic discourse and the institutional framework of democracy' (Krastev 2006: 52–4).

Such conceptualizations help to construct an academic and political discourse that delegitimizes any political experiment that presents a popular challenge to the primacy of liberal democracy and the market economy. In academic discourse this is expressed in the discourse of the *two lefts*: one that is realistic and responsible and aware that the only alternative is to work within the hegemonic limits of neoliberal globalization; the other outdated, authoritarian and irresponsible in its challenge to the 'politics of the possible' (Castañeda 2006). This can ultimately lead to the legitimization of new forms of international interventionism in the politics of Latin American states. This raises normative and political questions in relation to the actual, as opposed to rhetorical, limits to people's sovereignty, and their concurrent ability to freely determine their political and economic futures. Illustrative of the potential political consequences of this perspective is Castañeda when he argues:

> but there is a much bolder course, a more statesmanlike approach
> that would foster a 'right left'. This strategy would involve actively and
> substantively supporting the right left when it is in power ... and bringing
> their leaders and public intellectuals into the fold ... The international
> community should also clarify what it expects from the 'wrong left' given
> that it exists ... Europe and the United States have enormous leverage in
> many of these countries. They should use it. (Castañeda 2006: 7)

The concept's applicability to the Venezuelan political process is cast into doubt because, from within the conceptual and methodological assumptions, popular non-liberal articulations of democracy within and outside of the state are excluded from view. Additionally, the popular classes are often labelled irrational, short-sighted, marginal or open to manipulation (Bull 2005: 19–39). As de La Torre astutely notes, 'Modernizing elites have argued that populism's rhetoric and style of mobilization pose dangers to democratic institutions. They have constructed popular subjects as the "Other" – the negation of the "modern and rational" political subjects that they aim to forge' (De La Torre 1997: 13). The concept also posits a notion of modernity bound by the limitations of capitalist rationality, in which the market is assumed as the form of the economy, and the capitalist state the form of organizing power. This raises methodological, empirical and normative problems, as within the framework of analysis the 'other' is denied and the politics of the 'other' is silenced and/or ignored.

Such a conceptualization of *Chavismo* as populist therefore has serious limitations in its ability to accurately capture the dynamics of state–society relationships and the concurrent impact on the distribution of power in Venezuela. It focuses on particular elements of *Chavismo* while ignoring other more substantive political processes and transformations. Noticeable in such accounts is their lack of engagement with, knowledge of or evidence from the popular classes involved within *Chavismo*. A methodological 'turning on its head' of elitist evaluations of *Chavismo* is needed to balance the one-sided analyses that have been developed until now.

Conceptualizing social democracy

The social democratic understanding of 'the political' has a variety of proponents, both historic and contemporary. In general, however, the procedural structures of democratic liberalism are theorized as constituent elements of the political. Accordingly the state is conceptualized as an autonomous entity that can create the conditions to realize the general interest, premised upon the protection and guaranteeing of the individual, who is a sovereign holder of democratic rights. The role of bureaucratic elites and elected elites as the political agents who implement structural change is complemented, especially in contemporary versions, by an emphasis on the inclusion of forms of participatory democracy at the local level (for examples in relation to Latin America, see Panizza 2005; Pearce 2004; Castañeda 1994). The spatial limits of structural change are the nation-state and, in contemporary forms, international institutions (Held 2003).

Social democratic frameworks share with liberal democratic interpretations the assumptions of the compatibility between accumulation and

77

participation and redistribution (de Sousa Santos and Avritzer 2005). This view is premised upon an analysis of society in which different social interests are reconcilable into the general interest and growth is not structurally but politically constrained. The role of the state (or transnational institution) is to enable the formation of a consensus between all major interest groups in order to provide the conditions in which economic growth is combined with social and economic rights. The state working within a capitalist economy to redistribute surplus is assumed as the only and best way of creating social justice, equality of opportunity and substantive democracy. The question of who owns property is therefore of secondary importance. Discussion of different types of control of production is framed in terms of the management of the economy, as opposed to the socialization of production relations or the creation of a different set of production relations. Therefore, equality does not mean sameness, in terms of material possession and control, but rather general welfare.

The organization of popular-class democratic subjects is viewed as a legitimate element of the development consensus. Thus ideology and popular-class organization become premises for progressive structural change (paradigmatic of this is the work of Rueschemeyer et al. 1992; see also Roberts 2002). Party systems therefore gain political significance. Thus a focus on political and non-elected elites is complemented by a notion of mass or popular-class political agency, represented by party and social movement elites. Popular-class political agency is limited to either mobilization so that elites can act within the state, or implementation and formation of policy at the local level and the development of micro-economic projects to enable inclusion into the market (Panizza 2005).

Social democracy is thus distinct from socialism, as it does not envisage a change in the organization of production relations as necessary for the realization of liberty, equality or democracy and the creation of the conditions of the general welfare (Freeden 1988). It is distinct from liberalism, as it embodies the extension of the individual as not only constitutive of society, but constituted by that society. It is also distinct in that it combines the tenets of liberal democracy but extends them to the realm of the socio-economic. It is not only via its differences with both ideologies that social democracy is distinct, but rather by its attempt to bridge the two ideologies and combine them into a force that reforms, but does not transform, capitalism. This ambiguity and amorphous boundary of decontestations opens up a wide spectrum of possible policy approaches for social democratic political parties and governments. Accordingly a municipalized social democracy would attempt to balance the demands of accumulation, distribution and participation by creating an environment for economic growth and state democratization that is enabled by, and fosters, citizenship and individual/community development (see de Sousa Santos 2005 for one of the most sophisticated contemporary accounts).

Popular politics in La Vega, Venezuela

La Vega has a history of nearly fifty years and a population of up to 250,000. Situated on the south-western hills surrounding the valley in which central Caracas stands, it is paradigmatic of the conditions of excluded development that characterized the experience of 60 per cent of Venezuelans during the *Punto Fijo* period (1958–98). The *Punto Fijo* was a pact between the political elites of Acción Democrática (AD, Democratic Action) and the Partido Social Cristiano de Venezuela (COPEI, the Venezuelan Social Christian Party) which maintained a formal power-sharing democracy fuelled by oil rents. It ensured the exclusion from government of other political forces between 1958 and Chávez's election in 1998. This experience was comprised of economic informality, political delegitimization, social exclusion, territorial illegitimacy and historical invisibility. La Vega is also, however, a site with a rich history of struggle from below to transform social conditions into relations of dignity, liberation and democracy. Such struggles were characterized by the rejection of political parties and suspicion of the state; traditions of direct democracy and community-led change; and the politicization of the everyday, community and family (Ruiz 2006). This helps us explain the passion with which a project (*Chavismo*) that seeks to break the *Punto Fijo* system based upon popular participation has been embraced. The community's experience and relationship with *Chavismo*, while containing particularities related to its political, social and economic history, also express the general trends of the political dynamics at the heart of the struggle to define and give direction to the Bolivarian revolution. The exploration of this particular case study seeks, therefore, to provide insights into the nature of the political project that is developing within contemporary Venezuela.

As in other poor communities in Venezuela, many of La Vega's inhabitants have benefited from the social policy of the Chávez government. Such social policy consolidated around the concept of social programmes (*misiones*), which were implemented from 2003 onwards. The aim of the *misiones* was to provide social and economic rights to excluded communities and individuals in a localized and participatory manner (author interview with Marta Harnecker, January 2006). Thus communities would not only be recipients of rights and services but would be involved in the structuring, organization and realization of social policy. This was understood as a means of creating the conditions for the inclusion of the excluded by a process of empowerment. In their outlines and logic, their objectives fall within a social democratic understanding of development and democracy, combined with forms of local participation. The content and rationale of the *misiones*, however, are not of necessity the same as their implementation on the ground. It is in their implementation and interpretation that a struggle over a municipalized social democracy and a reinvented anti-capitalism is occurring.

Mission Barrio Adentro aims to provide basic healthcare to those who have historically been denied such services. This involves the setting up of a community health committee (Comité de Salud) in order to organize and facilitate a local GP office, and community health services such as midwifery and immunization services. In La Independencia, the politicization of health had a long history, with community organization around access to decent healthcare and water services. Thus the call to set up a local health committee was met with enthusiasm. Community members occupied an empty property and began to decorate and furnish it. As Isabella recounts, 'Myself and Marisol went to all our neighbours asking for resources for the health centre. When we had collected enough to initially set up the centre we stayed up all night painting the building and sorting out the chairs, table, and putting up the curtains.' The Cuban doctors who arrived in Venezuela in 2003 were sent to shanty towns such as La Vega and one was placed in La Independencia. As Mercedes recalled, 'I was there to greet them and housed two Cuban doctors for two years. At first there was a lot of suspicion of them and the programmes they began implementing. But gradually the community came to trust the doctors and to realize the importance of immunizations, for example for their children.' Women such as Isabella were trained in basic nursing skills, employed by the *misión* and offered the opportunity to continue with higher-level training. Mercedes laments the decrease in organization and participation in the health committee, however: 'There are basically only the two of us in the health committee now. Everyone has returned to their own lives.'

This experience of Misión Barrio Adentro illustrates the potential and limitations of a municipalized local participatory social democracy. Communities that have struggled for decades for decent health services have been recognized as citizens with rights to health. Their invisible informal struggle has been granted visibility and legitimacy. They have been empowered to organize community health with funds and training.

Providing decent healthcare is one element in ensuring equality of opportunity and the development of citizens able to participate in a democratic society. As in classic state-centric social democracy, however, there is a trade-off between the autonomy and mobilization of popular-class communities, and their institutionalization (Przeworski 1985). This leads to the depoliticization and fragmentation of struggle. Thus health can become a particular issue solved in a functional manner that undermines the community's organization and therefore the development of a participatory social democracy. Individuals who were once organizers of their communities become functionaries of the state. These processes result in a form of debilitated inclusion which curtails and limits the community's development as autonomous political and social agents. This in turn undermines the socio-political conditions that could ensure that a social democratic project is implemented at higher levels of the state and universally across localities.

Meanwhile, Misión Ribas, which began in late 2002, enables mature students to complete their secondary-school education. It is organized in local communities and run by individuals either trained in secondary-school education or who are ex-students of the *misión*. The curriculum is set out centrally and applied locally. There is a relative amount of flexibility in the way that the curriculum is applied. It is in the flexibility of local application that different interpretations of education, and different consequences of this *misión*, become apparent. One of these is the extension of the social right of education, as a means of empowering individuals and communities and providing them with the skills to facilitate inclusion in the political and economic system and participation in the development of solutions to their local problems. This in many ways constitutes a form of municipalized participatory social democracy. The second is the use of the space provided by Misión Ribas to develop a process of collective critical reflection, based on the tenets of popular educationists such as Freire, and viewed as a means of creating the conditions for emancipatory knowledge able to fuel a process of self-government (Freire 2000). While self-government has no necessary content, it often involves a questioning of the market economy and the liberal state as the economic and political boundaries within which popular participation can occur. Both types of implementation of Misión Ribas can be found in the communities of La Independencia and Las Casitas in La Vega.

In La Independencia, Misión Ribas is organized in a local building occupied by the community and used as a space for the education *misiones* and other community assemblies. Mario, himself a graduate of Misión

Ribas, works three times a week giving classes to a group of between twelve and fifteen individuals. The curriculum involves two-hour sessions in which students watch a video dealing with a particular subject and then have half an hour to reflect and discuss the subject, guided by their teacher. Completion of the course involves two years of classes with the objective of learning and implementing a methodology of diagnosis. The latter has four stages: a census to gauge the number of inhabitants, the condition of housing and the provision of water, education and health; identification of the problems confronting the community; prioritization of the most urgent problems and possible solutions to them; and, finally, individual students in conjunction with their local community deciding which problem they will focus on in their project and developing an action plan for the project's realization. As Elizabeth recounts, 'We have organized all over La Vega. Many of the students are women. It has been an emancipatory experience for me and many others who have begun to believe in their ability to solve problems in the community.'

Through this process, students develop reflexive skills, political knowledge and practical experience. Learning is embedded in the realization of social development and justice, and recognition is given to members of communities as agents able to develop solutions in reaching these goals. The development of Misión Ribas in La Independencia provides a form of secondary education that challenges neoliberalized learning, and develops the conditions for a social democracy based on active, educated and participatory citizens in their local communities. The understanding and citizenship developed are, however, within the confines of the local. It seeks to enable the student to find solutions for particular problems, such as inadequate housing, within the limits of broader structures of power. In doing so it attempts to democratize these broader structures, but not transform them. The central strategy of learning (via class videos) maintains the passivity of the student and conforms to traditional methodologies of learning and knowledge acquisition which represent a non-reflexive, depoliticized and hierarchical conceptualization of education (Canaan 2002). This prevents an educational process in which community rationality and collective historical experiences are at the heart of political agency and analysis. It maintains an individualized relationship between learner and teacher, reinforcing hierarchies of power that limit the formation of a qualitatively more developed collective consciousness of the problems facing the community.

In the neighbourhood of Las Casitas, Misión Ribas is being developed in a very different way. Students told me that they dropped the watching of the video which they found boring and uninstructive, as it left little time for discussion. Instead they began to organize classes around collective discussion and reflection about the problems they faced in their community, such as delinquency, unemployment and impoverishment. Depending on the issues and ideas raised, the facilitators will suggest particular texts that will be useful to the students to continue and deepen their reflection. As one student commented, 'I had no idea about the history of resistance in Latin America. Nor did I understand what caused our impoverishment and exclusion. Now I have read and thought about issues I have changed the way I view the world and my life.' The issues covered have included a popular history of the neighbourhood, the history of resistance and domination in Venezuela and the continent, and why their community is characterized by unemployment and underemployment, delinquency and lack of schooling. While fulfilling the requirements of the curriculum, they develop it in a way that is not constrained by an understanding of education as providing the conditions to create participatory citizens that democratize the state and market. Rather, the objectives of social change are open-ended, and the methodology of education developed is premised upon developing a holistic understanding of the problems facing their community, and a valuation of the process of change in which communities become agents of their self-government. This evolution was not spontaneous. Rather, it was grounded in the community's history of self-governing popular projects organized around a media collective that uses the method of popular education as a means of social transformation.

Thus, educational practice is not limited to the improvement of contemporary power structures but to broader social processes. Solutions proposed for particular problems are not just specific but also involve a general questioning of the organization of social relations and the development of students' knowledge based on their reflections about their political and social struggles. Knowledge does not come from outside in the form of either 'experts' or political leaderships. Therefore the forms of education developed do not maintain the passive status of the student who learns from the wisdom of the teacher but rather construct a practice in which the student (collectively) becomes the agent of social rationality and change.

The struggle between a municipalized social democracy and self-governing anti-capitalism is occurring in the implementation stage of this *misión*. The type of educational and political space that is opened up by Misión Ribas is not, as these two examples have shown, solely determined by the centralized structure of the *misión*'s curriculum and organization. Rather, the political history and culture of the communities

83

influence its content and form. It is often argued that the decentralized nature of social policy reproduces traditional clientelistic power structures and reconstructs a dependent popular participation not based on citizenship (Hawkins 2006). While this is a reality of some social policy implementation, these two communities' experiences and development of the *misión* illustrate the multiplicity of spaces of experimentation and political participation that are also opened up by the localized and decentralized nature of this policy.

Finally, the popular political project that is developing in Venezuela is perhaps paradigmatically captured in the development of the Consejos Comunales, which were introduced in January 2005 as a response to sections of the governing coalition's attempt to create a new state institutionality based on a process of the localization and regionalization of executive, legislative, juridical and financial power. The organization and exercise of such power are through a combination of deliberative, direct and representative procedures. As the Consejo Comunal Law states (Ministerio de Comunicación e Información 2006: Art. 2, 8):

> Within the constitutional framework of a participatory democracy, the Consejos Comunales are instances of participation, articulation and integration between the diversity of community organizations, social groups and citizens. They enable the organised 'people' to directly exercise the management of public policy and projects orientated to respond to the necessities and aspirations of communities involved in the construction of a society of equality and social justice.

The process of constituting a Consejo is coordinated by a team of eight, working in the Presidential Committee of Popular Participation. The first stage of the team's work is to travel to communities in order to explain their purpose, objectives and organization while the second is to authorize their creation in particular communities. If a community wants to organize itself into a Consejo, it is legally obliged to create it in accordance with the framework specified in the law. A community encompasses from 200 families in urban areas to 400 in rural areas and indigenous communities. The citizens' assembly is where power is exercised within a Consejo, and all members of the community over the age of fifteen are entitled to participate on an equal basis. The work committees (Comités de Trabajo) are staffed by elected and unpaid *vocero/as* (spokespersons), and their job is to develop a programme for the implementation of projects agreed by the citizens' assembly. *Vocero/as* are elected for a maximum of two years, although they can stand for re-election. A communal bank is organized which receives funds from central and regional government and also any profits made from the cooperative economic projects approved and developed by the community (Ministerio de Comunicación e Información 2006: 33–8).

Consejos are an attempt to create a new set of state institutions that bypass the traditional state, and distribute power in a democratic and participatory manner. Some view them as a means of strengthening a new popular state based on participatory social democracy (Bonilla-Molina et al. 2005). Others see them as part of a process in which the state is dissolved and a process of self-government develops that challenges contemporary structures of power (Denis 2006). At the Fourth National Meeting of the Mesas Técnicas de Agua (MTA, Water Committees) held in Caracas, 4–6 August 2006, delegates from the states of Apure and Sucre complained of the power of state bureaucrats, governors and mayors over Consejos. These traditional political elites have created a regional framework that seeks to control their development and prevent them from becoming a parallel 'popular' set of institutions able to challenge the former's institutional and political power. This framework sets out specific provisions for the formation of a Consejo Comunal in which legal authorization must come not only from the Presidential Committee of Popular Participation but also with an official stamp from the mayor and governor. This has meant that Consejos have been set up to undermine and sideline popular power, participation and autonomy and, thus, have been used as a form of reproducing traditional power relations.

At the same workshop there was a detailed and heated discussion which dealt with the relationship between MTAs and Consejos. The main conclusion that came out of the discussion was the importance of articulating forms of local organization and political agency at regional and national levels. This, it was agreed, would take place through a process of critical reflection, dialogue and mutual support. As one of the conclusions of one of the Mesas de Trabajo (working groups) stated: 'We must obtain the tools to be able to struggle against the bureaucracy and search for a way to get rid of leaders that want to control us, look to maintain their own power and who divide the community.' Such a process of collective reflection and deliberation is a novel form of constructing social knowledge, especially in light of the dominant political history of communities in which the state related to them as clients without rights, knowledge or capacity. It is based upon communities understanding their common problems and suggesting solutions shaped by their histories of struggle. This process is not an insular practice but rather is shaped by communities exchanging their accumulated experience, critically reflecting on that experience and forming new levels of collective knowledge. This social knowledge and the process of its construction are signs of the creation of a new political culture and practice based on participation and popular rationality. As Edenis Guilarte explains, 'What we are doing is training, creating consciousness, which is a process that goes beyond repairing a road, obtaining a service, enabling access to water, it's a macro process, a process of social change, a fight over ideas and practices.'

The politics of the process of constitution of Consejos Comunales is one institutional space in which the struggle between old and new politics, the formation of new state–society relations and the formation of a new popular democracy is occurring. There are no guarantees that more participatory forms of organizing power, authority and government will succeed. Indeed, the Consejos could play a role in channelling and controlling the development of innovative forms of popular politics. It could be argued that the way in which they have been developed, from above via a presidential decree, contradicts the idea of popular self-government and/or participatory government. Accordingly, there is little room for community experimentation and involvement in the design and development of institutions of government.

Nevertheless, the granting of local rights to housing, health and economic development is compatible with the development of a localized social democracy, one that democratizes the state and market so as to radically transform both. The difference from a classic social democratic policy framework is that the management and organization of local community development are not undertaken by a technocratic or political elite but rather through a partnership between local community and state officials. It is believed that the tensions between creating economic growth, ensuring redistribution and enabling political participation will be overcome by the institutional structure, which is embedded in political participation linked to social policy and economic development (Harnecker 2007a; de Sousa Santos 2005). The institutional framework and justification for the Consejos therefore contain the seeds of a counter-hegemonic practice of democracy, which challenges elitist liberal democratic assumptions that mass mobilization acts to undermine institutionalization, elites are necessarily pro-democratic and governance can be organized and implemented only by them and other experts. In this case, conversely, mass mobilization helps to create new cultures and practices of democratic institutionalization, and efficient governance is being created within a framework that is embedded in community rationality and understanding.

Critics, however, argue that the localized nature of this institutional structure could reinforce a fragmented popular political analysis and practical resolution of socio-economic problems. The resolution of health issues could be separated from that of housing problems, thus impeding universal access to basic services, creating an environment conducive to the flourishing of traditional clientelistic politics. The localized nature of the democratic process could also encourage community divisions both within and between communities, as they compete over scarce resources. As communities' political struggles become institutionalized in the fight for resources, their political and ideological capacity diminishes and this undermines their autonomous political agency. What we witness therefore is the potential for the trade-offs within classic social democracy between institutionalization and mobilization and autonomy, which reassert themselves on the local level, compounding the traditionally fractured nature of Venezuelan popular socio-political articulation.

The potential drawbacks of the centralized nature of the Consejos Comunales are perhaps offset by the possibilities that are opened up by the national nature of these new institutions of popular power. The scale of this institutional experiment creates possibilities for the development of new forms of state power: a state power that bypasses the corrupt and illiberal centralized state and decentralizes power to a multiplicity of linked-up local 'states' (Denis 2006). This re-creation of the state is territorialized in particular places, but these local sites are not insular and exclusionary. Indeed, there are provisions within the law for Consejos to work together on projects such as cooperatives and social development. This institutional structure creates the possibility of local participation that, while embedded in community needs, does not reinforce political, social and ideological fragmentation. The connections between local communities perhaps also open up the possibility of the sustainability of participatory forms of governance and economic development which do go beyond the liberal state and market economy. What has characterized many movements' experiments of this sort has been the difficulties encountered in scaling up their activities and in ensuring their viability (Motta 2008). This institutional structure creates a framework that could help to overcome these problems in the development of a counter-hegemonic project. The provision of funds, constitutional legality and implementation of an institutional structure are, however, not the same as the construction of a new form of state, and new forms of political and economic power. This depends upon the political struggles and creative developments of communities, and the political struggles within state institutions. As the example of Misión Ribas illustrates, the Venezuelan poor are not a homogeneous mass but rather have different and often conflictual political histories, cultures and ideas about alternatives, all of which shape the developing national political project.

Consejos Comunales are an institutional space in which the content and direction of *Chavismo* are being politically and practically struggled over. Tendencies that reproduce 'old' politics that disarticulate the poor coexist with forms of a municipalized social democracy and elements of a self-governing anti-capitalism. These political and ideological fault lines are reflective of the different histories and levels of organization of poor communities and the relative power and political orientation of politicians in the local and national state. As Andres Antillano explained, 'The Consejos Comunales could be an institutional space to develop a popular project that totally transforms Venezuelan society or they could become a site of inclusion that nevertheless localizes communities and de-mobilizes them.' The political struggle therefore revolves around the question of whether they become an institution that channels the demands of poor communities to a localized social democracy (with all the possibilities and limitations that this entails) or whether they enable the expansion of demands for community self-management that challenge capitalist social relations.

Conclusion: beyond liberal democracy and markets in Venezuela – counter-hegemony in action

This chapter has sought to contribute to the debate on the nature of *Chavismo*. It has done this by focusing on those poor communities which are providing the momentum for Venezuela's present political evolution. Concentrating upon popular politics does not imply ignoring ongoing struggles within the state between competing political factions within *Chavismo* or the relationship between the Venezuelan state and the international economy, or the tensions with the political opposition (national and international). Rather it is a lens through which we can construct a nuanced and complex picture of the political dynamics and fault lines of *Chavismo* and in this way develop analysis in solidarity with ordinary Venezuelans' struggles for human dignity and social justice. In this context, solidarity is understood in terms of mutuality, accountability and the recognition of common interests as the basis for relationships between diverse communities. Rather than assuming an enforced commonality of oppression, the practice of solidarity foregrounds communities of people who have chosen to work and fight together. Solidarity is thus always an achievement and involves an active struggle to construct the universal on the basis of differences (Mohanty 2003: 7).

Analysis of Misión Barrio Adentro demonstrated the importance of ensuring community health provision as a right rather than a political gift, thus challenging traditional clientelistic relationships between the local state and community. The institutionalization of this process has, however, demobilized a community that in the past undertook collective struggle for healthcare, and has also co-opted key leaders and organizers as the providers of basic services. Thus, the granting of rights in this localized, participatory manner has undercut the political autonomy of the community, resulting in its fragmentation. This in turn undermines the socio-political conditions necessary for the development of a more consolidated participatory social democratic project.

Study of Misión Ribas demonstrates that the constitutional underpinning of a *misión* is not the same as its implementation on the ground. La Independencia has experienced the development of an educational practice that is linked to the resolution of local community problems rather than one that adopts a marketized and individualized neoliberal curriculum. Use of traditional methods of teaching ensures the passivity of the student in relation to the teacher, however, and creates fragmented, and potentially localized, political and social understanding. This could restrict poor communities to improving their own conditions but not challenging macro-structures of power and inequality. In contrast, where the banking method of teaching has been abandoned and a model of popular education introduced, a new knowledge has begun to emerge, one able to challenge both micro- *and* macro-structures of power. This is part of the process of creating self-governing communities. Social transformation becomes linked to the production of emancipatory knowledge constructed through the communities' own practice and based in their own historical experience. The educational mission reflects the struggle between a participatory social democracy and a project that potentially transcends the structures of liberal democracy and the market economy.

In the case of the Consejos Comunales the reproduction of traditional political relations is accompanied by an institutional structure that is framed within a municipalized social democracy. This is contested by certain 'politicized' communities whose praxis develops forms of self-government beyond the limits of this institutional structure. They therefore challenge both the liberal state and the market economy. There are potential drawbacks in localized governance: competition between communities could be created, as well as fragmentation in the resolution of community problems. This could result in an institutionalization of the poor's political agency at the expense of their autonomy and mobilizing capacity, thereby accentuating the potential trade-offs in classic social democracy as opposed to ensuring their resolution. These problems may be overcome at the national level, however, with initiatives to implement inter-local projects. Again, it is community political agency and creativity which will shape the direction that the political struggle takes and the type of state that is produced as a result of this institutional experiment.

An analysis of Misión Barrio Adentro, Misión Ribas and the Consejos Comunales illustrates first the simplicity and arrogance that characterize those that seek to disqualify *Chavismo* as a form of illiberal populism. The experiences of the communities involved in these projects demonstrate that popular politics are criss-crossed by a political rationality and creativity that is masked by dominant elitist conceptualizations of the ideal of political evolution – liberal democracy – against which Venezuela is implicitly compared in such characterizations. It is clear that while there are tendencies that reproduce traditional illiberal relationships between state and society and within popular political culture, there are other tendencies that mirror a municipalized and participatory social democracy and the nascent development of paths to anti-capitalism. Thus there is a clear shift away from rule over subjects to rule by citizens, defined and practised in ways compatible with, but also contesting of, political liberalism and the market economy. Tensions between institutionalization and mobilization and between representation and autonomy which are characteristic of classic social democracy are at times accentuated by the localized nature of social and political policy, and at other times creatively overcome by a focus upon popular rationality and practice as the basis of new democratic cultures and institutions. The forms of democracy and development that are being created by Venezuela's popular classes demonstrate the counter-hegemonic practices that are the progressive kernel of *Chavismo*. This reinvention of utopias challenges the discourse of the 'two lefts' which seeks to disqualify, debilitate and silence political projects that rupture the 'end of history' dystopia of political and intellectual elites.

Note

1 The author wishes to thank the inhabitants of La Vega and particularly Andres Antillano and Nora Machado for their assistance with this project. Unreferenced quotations are from interviews.

5 | Bolivia: playing by new rules

JOHN CRABTREE

We can carry on talking about our history. We can continue recalling
how our predecessors struggled: Tupac Katari to restore Tahuantinsuyo,
Simón Bolívar who fought for the greater fatherland, Che Guevara who
fought for a new world with equality. This struggle for cultural democracy, this democratic cultural revolution is part of the struggle of our
predecessors, it is a continuation of what Tupac Katari fought for. That
struggle and these results are part of the legacy of Che Guevara. That's
where we are, brothers and sisters of Bolivia, of Latin America. We will
continue until we attain that equality in our country; it only takes the
concentration of capital in few hands for the many to die of hunger.
Such policies have to change, but they have to change in democracy.
(Evo Morales, inaugural speech to Congress, 22 January 2006, author's
translation)

It was with such words that Evo Morales Ayma addressed his Congress
and people for the first time as president. Rarely in Bolivian history had
the person of Tupac Katari, executed in truly gruesome colonial style in La
Paz in 1781 (Hylton and Thomson 2007), been invoked in this way by the
country's president; still less Che Guevara, who met his own violent death
at the hands of the Bolivian military more recently in 1967. Morales's
speech configured the country's historical legacy as one of fighting for
autonomy and social justice, and it conjured up a new beginning in the
country's politics, in particular a new deal for the country's indigenous
majority, long excluded from the political mainstream.

His extraordinary electoral victory, in which nearly 54 per cent voted
for Morales and his vice-presidential candidate, Alvaro García Linera,
underscored that mood of optimism and change. Morales's party, the
Movimiento al Socialismo (MAS, Movement towards Socialism), had won
a substantial majority in the Chamber of Deputies, and only narrowly
missed a majority in the Senate. Evo's victory broke with the traditional
pattern of fragmentation in elections over the previous quarter-century,
leading to governments bereft of support and legitimacy. The three main
parties that had dominated since the restoration of democracy in the
1980s, the right-of-centre Movimiento Nacionalista Revolucionario (MNR,

Revolutionary Nationalist Movement), the Movimiento de la Izquierda Revolucionario (MIR, Movement of the Revolutionary Left) and Acción Democrática Nacionalista (ADN, Democratic Nationalist Action), were relegated to the margins. The MAS had even won substantial backing in the more conservative eastern part of the country, in places such as Santa Cruz, where its opposition was most entrenched.

The importance of the changes did not go ignored elsewhere in the world. Evo's victory was seen as a clear rejection of the economic liberalism espoused by the international financial community in the previous twenty years, and a reaffirmation of the primacy of the state. It was seen as further evidence of the leftward shift in Latin America that began with the election of Hugo Chávez in Venezuela in 1998, followed by the presidential elections of Luiz Inácio Lula da Silva in Brazil in 2002 and Néstor Kirchner in 2003 in Argentina. There had been few more strident critics of the neoliberal model than Evo Morales and, as head of the *cocaleros* (coca farmers) of the Chapare, few more outspoken opponents of the role of the United States in Latin America. Moreover, the fact that Evo was the first pro-indigenous president in this indigenous country struck a strong chord internationally.

The achievements of the years since the inauguration of Morales have been substantial, although the full impact will take longer to assess. As one would expect, the opposition to his agenda was not long in making itself felt, taking full advantage of the democratic spaces open to it. As Latin America had shown before, the problems of conducting a revolution in a democracy are not to be underestimated. The size of the task of redesigning institutions and reframing policy had also become more apparent, heightening the problem of weak state institutions. Still, the country had entered a new phase in its history which, like it or not, would not be easily reversed (Crabtree and Whitehead 2008). The first part of this chapter places the Morales government in its context, while the second examines the main policy orientations adopted by the new government and some of their immediate consequences.

Political legacies

Bolivia's political development since independence from Spain in the early nineteenth century has been characterized by two key influences (Whitehead 2001). The first of these is a tradition of constitutionalism that goes back to its initial constitutional assembly in 1825/26, when its republican institutions were established. Like other Latin American countries, perhaps more than most, Bolivia has seen its constitution repeatedly revised to adapt its institutions to new social and political realities. The constituent assembly of 2006/07 was but the most recent of a long and well-grounded historical tradition of constitutional assemblies and conventions (Barragán 2006).

The second powerful tradition is that of popular mobilization within a state whose authority and capacity to resist or absorb dissent has, historically, been limited. This is a history of rebellion and protest against the constituted order, often led by unruly *caudillos*. By far the most important in recent times was the 1952 revolution, which produced nationalization of the mines and agrarian reform. Key protagonists in the revolution were the mineworkers, a highly politicized section of the workforce whose union, the Federación Sindical de Trabajadores Mineros de Bolivia (FSTMB, Federation of Bolivian Mineworkers), formed the nucleus and vanguard force of the newly constituted Central Obrera Boliviana (COB, Bolivian Workers' Confederation) (Dunkerley 1984).

One of the legacies of the 1952 revolution was a concept of political organization in which autonomy and unity were key principles. In spite of the fragmentation among the parties of the left, the COB managed to maintain its unity and programmatic principles. Peasant unionization was also a corollary of the agrarian reform. Although peasant unions were more dependent on the state, and more easily co-opted by it, they too maintained a degree of autonomy, especially where pre-Columbian forms of social organization subsisted in the basic political unit known as the *ayllu*. The Popular Assembly of 1970, with its notions of dual power, was perhaps the high-water mark of that spirit of syndicalism. Although unions faced repression during the Banzer dictatorship (1971–78), it was in part the spirit of resistance in the mines which forced the return to some sort of democratization.

A second important strand to develop at this time was indigenous politics or *indigenismo*. The *Katarista* movement (Albó 1987), which evolved in the late 1970s, challenged the pre-eminence of the mineworkers in the union movement, creating a blend of ethnic politics with *clasismo*, class politics. Rooted among the Aymara population of the *altiplano*, the *Katarista* movement heightened the political salience of more in-dependent peasant politics within a new confederation, the Confederación Sindical Unica de Trabajadores Campesinos de Bolivia (CSUTCB, Confederation of Bolivian Agricultural Workers). Following the virtual collapse of the FSTMB with the closure of most public sector mines in 1985, the CSUTCB became one of the main arenas of independent union organization. By the 1990s, sections of the CSUTCB, especially in the *altiplano*, were embracing ethnicity as a form of identity politics (see Van Cott 2003; Yashar 2005). The *cocaleros* were among the more organized groupings within the CSUTCB, especially in the Chapare, where successive governments sought to eradicate coca cultivation. The second Banzer government (1997–2001), encouraged by Washington, pursued eradication with special zeal: the so-called 'zero coca' policy. This period saw the rise to influence of Evo Morales. Since many Chapare *cocaleros* were recently displaced mineworkers, that strong tradition of left-wing unionism persisted.

Economic liberalization and its critics

In the late 1980s and early 1990s, Bolivia became a testing ground for some of the neoliberal economic policies then in vogue. The economic stabilization programme initiated in 1985 began the liberalization of one of Latin America's most statist economies (Morales, J. 2001). It was during the Sánchez de Lozada government (1993–97) that many of the most ambitious reforms were enacted to promote a market economy with a stronger private sector. Perhaps the most conspicuous element was the privatization programme, known as 'capitalization' in Bolivia, which sought to attract foreign investors, notably into the key oil and gas industries. Bolivia, indeed, became something of a showcase among international financial institutions for the success of liberalizing policies of 'structural adjustment' (Wolfensohn 1999).

Economic liberalization was sold to public opinion as the way to create employment through export-led growth, but its effects were disappointing. Although an increase in investment and exports followed the privatization of hydrocarbons, this did little to improve living standards for the vast majority; indeed, it appears to have accentuated inequality, both socially and geographically (Crabtree 2006). The economic downturn between 1998 and 2002, accentuated by economic crises in Brazil and Argentina, only compounded the sense of pessimism. It became increasingly clear that the export-led model of growth, focused on capital-intensive, foreign-owned extractive industries, was not meeting the country's development needs or dragging it out of poverty (PNUD 2005).

The privatization policies of the mid-1990s sparked sometimes violent opposition from the COB and others, but did not postpone implementation. Closing the state mining sector had eroded the industrial and political power of the union movement. But this lack of effective resistance was not to last. It was the Banzer government's attempts to privatize water in Cochabamba, Bolivia's third-largest city, which provoked a widespread, though largely unexpected, popular reaction.

Social movements and their efficacy

The so-called 'water war' in Cochabamba involved a broad alliance of interests opposed to the privatization of water in and around the city. It forced the Banzer government to abrogate a contract with the US corporation Bechtel that had triggered a sudden and substantial increase in water prices. Moreover, the 'water war' prefigured a succession of mobilizations by social movements that gained momentum in those years. They included the *cocaleros* of the Chapare; landless peasants in Santa Cruz; indigenous groupings in the highlands and lowlands; the urban residents of El Alto; and even old-age pensioners in the former mining camps (Crabtree 2005). The government's about-turn on water privatization therefore demonstrated its weakness under coordinated pressure from a variety of social movements.

Two common interconnected elements underpinned this new tide of opposition. The first was a new concern about the exploitation and ownership of natural resources. Oil and gas privatization raised new questions about the extent to which ordinary Bolivians would be the beneficiaries rather than transnational corporations. The discovery of large gas reserves in Tarija in the late 1990s highlighted this problem, generating a polemic about how this wealth would benefit the national economy. The Cochabamba water war highlighted the problem in a rather different way: how was it, the farmers of the valley of Cochabamba asked themselves, that such a gift of nature as water could be traded for the benefit of a foreign transnational? In Santa Cruz, too, unbridled soya cultivation was producing personal fortunes for agribusiness at the expense of other claimants to land, as well as producing severe ecological damage.

The second element was the increased salience of ethnic politics in Bolivia. First enunciated by the *Kataristas* in the 1970s and 1980s, this agenda was given new force by ethnically based protest in the *altiplano*. Particularly notable here was the figure of Felipe Quispe, who, as leader of the CSUTCB, proclaimed himself the *mallku* (leader) of the *Nación Aymara*. A new organization, CONAMAQ (the Confederación Nacional de Markas y Ayllus de Q'ollasuyo), came into being to defend the interests of indigenous communities. In the jungle lowlands, too, ethnic groupings had been organizing themselves politically, ever since a successful march from Trinidad to La Paz in 1990 first put them on the national political map. The 2001 census proclaimed that the country's indigenous peoples represented a substantial, 62 per cent majority of the country. The first big political breakthrough for indigenous organizations was the 2002 elections in which these won substantial weight in Congress for the first time ever (Van Cott 2003: 89).

95

This coming together of ethnic identity, external pressure and the exploitation of natural resources took a particular form in the Chapare. Coca, whose cultural and religious significance runs deep in traditional Andean society, became the symbol of the struggle against outside impositions of one sort or another. The rise in the political profile of Evo Morales was a consequence of opposition by the six *cocalero* federations of the Chapare to the policies imposed on Bolivia by Washington through its embassy in La Paz. The Chapare also provides a particularly telling case study of an area where the predominant unit of socio-political organization was the union or *sindicato*, but where images of ethnicity also became part of the campaign to halt eradication. Evo, an Aymara from Oruro who had migrated as a young man to the Chapare, personified this blending of traditional *sindicalismo* with nationalism and the new politics of ethnicity.

The next major milestone in the story of social mobilization was the protests in El Alto and elsewhere in 2003 against the Sánchez de Lozada government's plans to export Bolivian gas to the United States, through Chilean ports in territory that Bolivia lost to Chile in the War of the Pacific in the 1880s. Perhaps inevitably, this came to be known as the 'gas war'. The tight social and ethnic organization of El Alto, the sprawling township that abuts La Paz, provided the social basis for political action that eventually brought down the government (Lazar 2006). The geographical location of El Alto, commanding key routes into the city, gives it a strategic stranglehold. The government's decision to send in troops to clear roadblocks, causing numerous deaths, resulted in a social conflagration that culminated with Sánchez de Lozada's ousting on 17 October 2003. The so-called 'October Agenda', a list of political demands including renationalization of hydrocarbons and the convening of a constituent assembly, became the yardstick by which subsequent governments were judged.

Social movements of one kind or another provided the base for a new political party that eventually became known as the MAS (Zegada et al. 2008). The success of social movements in Cochabamba and then in El Alto in forcing governments to yield to pressure had a multiplier effect all over Bolivia. In 1999, the MAS, and in particular Evo Morales, who was first elected as a deputy for the party's forerunner organization in 1997, became a new sort of political party, with its roots firmly embedded in civil society. It had first emerged in the mid-1990s as the political expression of the Chapare *cocaleros*, who understood the need to match social activism with winning space within the existing political system (Crabtree 2005: 38–9). Because of his ability to project the MAS beyond the ethnically narrow agenda of the *Katarista* parties and Quispe's rival Movimiento Indígena Pachakuti (MIP), Morales was able to turn the MAS from a regional force, with its support limited to Cochabamba, into a national political movement. The general elections of June 2002 were a breakthrough for the MAS, converting it into the main opposition in Congress. It won twenty-seven seats in the Chamber of Deputies and eight seats in the Senate. For its part, the MIP won six seats in the Chamber, its geographical outreach confined mainly to the department of La Paz.

Party implosion

The growth of the left was also aided by the decline in the legitimacy and popular support of parties associated with the status quo, namely the MNR, the MIR and ADN. Between them these parties had ruled the country in pacts of one sort or another for most of the twenty years since the restoration of democratic institutions in 1982. Of the three, the MNR had the longest history and the most influence. This was the party that had pushed through the 1952 revolution and which had governed the country until displaced by the military in 1964. It was also the party most frequently in office after 1985, occupying the presidency both under Víctor Paz Estenssoro (1985–89), and during Sánchez de Lozada's two terms (1993–97 and 2002–03). Buttressed by electoral pacts and coalition governments, there was a good deal of policy continuity, despite alternation in government, with a strong penchant for technocratic top-down styles of government.

Political parties therefore became primarily governing rather than representative entities, and the interface with the electorate was largely confined to periods of electoral contests. They also acquired an unhealthy reputation for clientelism and corruption (Domingo 2001). Indeed, increasingly, their relationship with their constituencies acquired highly patrimonial features, with various forms of office and preferment becoming the rewards for political loyalty. While it was a system that helped foster political stability, it led to a growing divorce between elected politicians and their grassroots constituencies. Public attitudes towards political elites thus became increasingly negative, particularly when the economy went into the doldrums during the Banzer presidency of the late 1990s.

The stability of the party system was, however, protected by the institutional proviso that only registered parties could participate in elections, with barriers to other entrants to the political system. The difficulties that the MAS had in achieving electoral registration for the 1999 municipal elections underlined this point. Of course, this was not an entirely closed system: other parties were able to enter electoral contests, such as Carlos Palenque's Conciencia de Patria (Condepa), and Max Fernández's Unión Civica Solidaridad (UCS), but they were quickly enveloped by the clientelistic politics of alliance formation, and became absorbed into the mainstream.

The monopoly enjoyed by recognized parties was finally broken in 2004, leading to fears that the system would be atomized between competing social movements. This, however, did not happen. In the elections of 2005, social movements rallied behind the new party that seemed to provide them with a powerful political voice, the MAS. Bolivia was clearly entering an era of a new politics in which grassroots interests, rural as well as urban, would find strong representation at the level of the state. The danger, it seemed, was that this new alliance of social movements would lack the unity of purpose and understanding to run the state in an effective way. It was also unclear whether the MAS would be able adequately to reflect the interests of people beyond those social movements that had provided its constituency up to that point.

The MAS in office

The scale of the MAS's electoral victory came as a surprise to friend and foe alike. It revealed the degree of public expectation generated by the campaigns of the MAS and its allies in the foregoing few years. Bolivia was anxious for change, but the exact direction that this change would take was much less clear. In its desire to maximize dissatisfaction with the status quo, the MAS had presented itself as its antithesis, but its programme of government was vague at best.

The challenges of moving from critical opposition to government, from *protesta* (protest) to *propuesta* (policy proposal), were thus formidable. Not only was the nature of the project unclear, but the new administration also lacked the administrative experience and, indeed, the bureaucratic machinery required for planning and executing policy. Furthermore, the political movement that was the MAS was little more than a loosely structured coalition of social movements, and far from being the disciplined and hierarchical chain of command needed to spearhead a process of speedy and radical change. From the outset, therefore, there was always the danger that the new government would fail to satisfy the demands and expectations it had helped to kindle, while antagonizing those vested interests that it had identified as the authors of the country's problems. Evo Morales was well aware that, initial triumphalism apart, he would be walking a difficult tightrope.

At this stage it is not possible to provide a comprehensive evaluation of the MAS government, its achievements and limitations. The focus here is more on its initiatives and some of their immediate effects across a range of policy areas: the attempt to reassert state control over the economy, particularly in the field of hydrocarbons; the more overtly political terrain and the story of how the 2006 Constituent Assembly sought to reconfigure political institutions; initiatives in the area of social policy; and Bolivia's new relations with the rest of the world, most notably with Venezuela, Brazil and the United States.

Reasserting the primacy of the state

On 1 May 2006, troops took control of Bolivia's principal gas fields in a show of force that hit world headlines. The move was designed to demonstrate the new government's determination to push ahead with the October Agenda demand of reasserting national control over the main source of the country's export revenues. The self-styled 'nationalization' of oil and gas was less a nationalization in the traditional sense of the word, rather a unilateral requirement that existing foreign investors sign new contracts to replace those that they had signed with the first Sánchez de Lozada government in the 1990s. The new contracts reasserted the primacy of the old state company Yacimientos Petrolíferos Fiscales de Bolivia (YPFB, Bolivian State Oilfields), proclaimed national ownership of reserves up until the wellhead, and changed the tax regime so as to substantially raise foreign investors' tax contributions. These and other points had been the subject of a referendum held in 2004, in which the vast majority of voters upheld the need for greater state control over these industries. In future, the contractual relationship with foreign companies would be on the basis of service contracts.

This was, of course, not the first time that Bolivia had 'nationalized' its hydrocarbons. The first nationalization took place in 1937, when YPFB was set up following acquisition of assets previously in the hands of Standard Oil of New Jersey. This was two years before the nationalization of oil in Mexico and the establishment of the state-owned company Pemex. Bolivia's second nationalization took place in 1969 during the left-of-centre military regime of General Alfredo Ovando, when YPFB took over the Bolivian assets of Gulf Oil. The main companies affected by this, the third 'nationalization', were those which had assumed operational control of the industry in 1996 with the 'capitalization' of YPFB, of which the most important were Petrobras, Repsol, British Gas and Total. As we have seen, the capitalization of YPFB and other changes in hydrocarbons legislation became controversial when major new discoveries were made in Tarija that underlined the importance of gas to the country's economic future.

The takeover of the gas fields brought positive short-term results, both politically and economically. Politically, it revived the long-standing tradition of economic nationalism that had stemmed from the 1952 revolution. The move was widely welcomed as helping to protect the country's resource base, and introducing a tax regime that would enable gas rents to be fed through into wider economic development. Hostility was muted even in those departments, such as Santa Cruz and Tarija, which had done best from the gas bonanza of previous years. The government's strategy seemed vindicated when, six months later at the end of October, the foreign companies all signed up to the new contracts, thereby avoiding any danger of Bolivia being taken to international arbitration. Economically, the new fiscal terms greatly increased the funds available to the state, facilitating greater spending in other areas. In 2006, for the first time in living memory, Bolivia achieved a substantial fiscal surplus, enabling it also to wriggle free of dependency on IMF conditionalities.

In the longer term, the key issue for the gas sector is whether foreign investors will increase their investment in the industry, or simply bide their time. Some companies, like British Gas, have made clear their unwillingness to invest more. Without continued investment, Bolivia's reserves are threatened with continued depletion, with the country poorly placed to meet its contractual commitments to supply gas to both Brazil and Argentina while having sufficient supplies to meet its own needs at the same time. Others, however, including Petrobras, made promises that they would speed up the process of investment to avert the possibility of energy shortages in Brazil, which is Bolivia's main market for natural gas and, in the short term, remains highly dependent on Bolivian supplies. Important discoveries of Brazilian offshore gas in 2007 and 2008 will, however, reduce that dependency substantially.

In the mining sector, the MAS government also sought to raise the tax yield. Again, and without much conspicuous success, the Sánchez de Lozada administration aimed to attract new investment into the sector by reducing the tax payable by mining companies. Historically, the mining industry had been the mainstay of government revenues. In 2006, however, the industry as a whole contributed a mere US$58 million in tax, in a year in which minerals exports, boosted by high international prices, were worth in excess of US$1 billion. Among the beneficiaries of low taxation were the mining operations owned by the Sánchez de Lozada family, for long the largest private mine owners in Bolivia. The nearest the new government came to nationalization in the mining industry was the renationalization of the Vinto smelter near Oruro. This previously belonged to Comsur, whose largest shareholder was Sánchez de Lozada. In 2005, Sánchez de Lozada sold his interest in Vinto and various mines to Glencore International of Switzerland. But the government's attitude to private investment has been pragmatic; it is aware that it lacks the capital to push ahead with new projects. One of the largest-ever mining operations in the country received the go-ahead in 2007, following the signing of a contract with Jindal of India to exploit the iron ore reserves at Mutún in the department of Santa Cruz close to the Brazilian frontier.

Another area where the government advocated greater state regulation in order to comply with the public interest was in agribusiness. The 1953 agrarian reform was never implemented in the eastern lowlands of Bolivia, and recent years have seen growing conflict over access to land between large landowners on the one hand and small peasants, landless peasants and indigenous communities on the other. Legislation was introduced in 2006 to impose limits on landholding where this serves neither a social nor an economic purpose. It brought immediate protests from the landowning classes, particularly in Santa Cruz and the Beni. Implementation of the law was suspended in 2007 following devastating floods in the Beni department. This suspension of the law appeared, at least in part, to be a tactical decision to avoid a possibly violent confrontation with the agricultural elites of the eastern departments.

The Constituent Assembly and the vexed issue of 'autonomism'

Among the first decisions of the new government was to convene elections to an assembly to rewrite the country's constitution. The Constituent Assembly was duly elected, and took office on 6 August 2006. The Assembly hoped to 'refound' the country, changing the entire relationship between the state and civil society (see Monasterios et al. 2007; and for an incisive assessment of state–society relations, PNUD 2007). It was given a year to come up with a draft, which was then to be put to a referendum for approval. Again, this had been one of the main demands of social movements during the previous decade, and had been a key point on the October Agenda. Among the main objectives of the Assembly was to extend indigenous rights.

Progress on rewriting the constitution ran almost immediately into a concerted effort by the opposition to stymie the initiative. Although reduced to a fairly small group in both the 2005 elections and the July 2006 Constituent Assembly elections, right-wing opposition groups proved skilful in frustrating the objectives of the MAS majority. Much of the first nine months of the proceedings was taken up by angry debates over procedure: the exact voting margins for each decision adopted. The MAS majority were obliged to make significant concessions. When it became clear that the Assembly would be unable to reach a concerted agreement within the twelve-month deadline, the time limit was extended to December 2007. Then proceedings were halted by opposition-organized protests in Sucre, the city where the Assembly was sitting, in support of Sucre's erstwhile claim to be acknowledged as the full capital of Bolivia. Sucre had been the capital of Bolivia until 1899 when, after a brief civil war, La Paz became the seat of the legislative and executive branches of government, although Sucre remained the seat of the Supreme Court. With the final deadline fast approaching in 2007, the MAS majority took matters into their own hands, and proceeded to withdraw the sessions to a military-protected base in Sucre, and then to Oruro, to approve its preferred constitutional text. For their part, most opposition members chose to boycott the final sessions, thereby seeking to undermine the legitimacy of the final document.

The new constitutional text, at the time of writing still due to be submitted to a referendum, sought to introduce a number of important changes in the institutional structure of the country. A document with 411 articles, it upheld the 'plurinational' and 'communitarian' nature of the Bolivian state; the introduction of a 'plurinational' assembly to replace the existing Congress; and the introduction of a system of direct, participatory mechanisms for decision-making. It thus responded strongly to the need to improve methods of representation and participation, thereby enhancing ethnic inclusion. It also removed the constitutional bar on immediate executive re-election, while introducing the concept of recall for executive authorities that lose the confidence of those who elected them. Also, controversially, it introduced a system of decentralization or *autonomías* designed to counter the proposals advanced by opposition-controlled prefects and civic committees to increase their own power at the expense of the central government.

The issue of autonomies lay at the centre of the increasingly bitter power struggle between the government and the opposition. In a referendum, held at the same time as the elections to the Constituent Assembly, four departments had voted 'yes' to a proposal mandating the Assembly to consider a regime of autonomies for those departments where the 'yes' was in a majority. These were the lowland departments of Santa Cruz, Tarija, the Beni and Pando, often referred to as the 'half moon', the *media luna*. The prefects of these departments were all prominent opposition figures, and they worked in close coordination with the civic committees representing largely the elites of the departmental capitals. The most powerful of the latter, and with much the longest history of anti-centralism, was the Comité Pro Santa Cruz (Committee for Santa Cruz), representing the region's main business organizations and renowned for the conservatism of its views (see Prado et al. 2007; and Sivak 2007). At the point at which the MAS members of the Assembly approved the new constitutional text, the departments of the *media luna* unveiled their own de facto statutes of autonomy, documents not far removed from outright secession. They also rejected the constitutional text and threatened not to abide by its provisions. At the same time, the civic committees sought to swing two other departments, Cochabamba and Chuquisaca, behind their campaign for autonomy. The first of these had elected as prefect in 2005 a leading opposition figure, Manfred Reyes Villa; the second became estranged from the MAS as a result of the refusal of the MAS leadership to support the demand for Sucre to be restored to its former rank as Bolivia's full capital.

Matters came to a head in May 2008, with the holding of a referendum on autonomy in Santa Cruz, the first of a number of such referendums in the *media luna* departments. The statute of autonomy advanced by the *cruceño* (Santa Cruz) elite was a particularly radical document, designed to exacerbate the contradictions between the department and the central government. Its pretensions went considerably beyond the norms of federalism in other countries. The 'yes' majority achieved in the referendum in Santa Cruz thus increased the political stakes, opening the way for ever more overt forms of conflict with the government in La Paz. So, relegated to the political margins in 2005, the right-wing opposition thus managed to use the opportunities open to it to rally against the government. In June 2008, 'yes' votes were also recorded in the departments of Beni, Pando and Tarija. As well as being able to use regionalist sympathies to rally public opinion in the *media luna* departments against the government, the opposition also exercised a powerful influence over the mass media and was able to use its majority in the Senate to block government legislation. In response to an opposition attempt to build on this groundswell of support in the east, Morales responded to the main opposition party's attempts to force a recall referendum by challenging the opposition prefects to such a referendum in which both they and he (as well as the vice-president) would submit their future to a political duel. The date chosen was 10 August 2008, and the outcome was a triumph for Morales, who secured over 67 per cent of the vote, considerably higher than the 54 per cent he won in his 2005 election victory. He also increased his support in all but one of the nine departments. On the back of this new and stronger national mandate, Morales sought to make progress in the delayed construction of a new national constitution. Rising opposition culminated in a massacre of Morales supporters in Pando department in September 2008, followed by the imposition by Morales of a state of siege in the department and the arrest of its prefect. Within days an international mediation effort was under way, led by Unasur, the recently constituted union of South American republics, to secure a national pact between the national government and the opposition prefects.

The social agenda

In its five-year development plan for 2006 to 2011, published in June 2006, the new government mapped out some of its socio-economic aspirations, and put emphasis on the need to forge a fairer, more equal and democratic society. The plan was premised on the perhaps optimistic assumption that growth would reach at least 7 per cent per annum and that increased investment would raise the country's productive potential while reducing poverty levels substantially. At the same time, the government promised to introduce social policies that would enable the people of Bolivia to 'live well', 'vivir bien', a somewhat hazy concept but one designed to enhance indigenous people's ability to enjoy a reasonable livelihood (if not live prosperously) within their specific environment.

While the economic policies of the MAS administration represent a conscious attempt to reverse previous neoliberal macroeconomic concepts, social policy has represented less of a break with the past. There have, however, been a number of innovations in this area, and policy has sought to steer clear of the traditional sources of foreign aid, which provided the financial basis for social spending in the past. Particular policies include:

- The Bono Juancito Pinto. This is a transfer of 200 bolivianos (around US$25.70) to 1 million schoolchildren, financed from the extraordinary revenues generated by the 2006 'nationalization' of hydrocarbons. To a large extent, this policy runs along similar lines to the conditional cash transfer schemes implemented in Mexico (*Oportunidades*) and Brazil (*Bolsa Familia*). As elsewhere, one of the main problems here lies in the poor quality of public education in Bolivia.
- The introduction of a universal health insurance scheme. This covers all those under twenty-one, provides specific services for women between twenty-one and fifty-nine (reproductive health, pregnancy and birth) and a system of consultation for all other groups. It builds on a successful mother and child coverage scheme, widening the numbers involved. Also in the health sphere, some 1,700 Cuban doctors have

been collaborating with eye operations and other surgical necessities in areas where there is a chronic shortage of health professionals.

- The Renta Dignidad pensions scheme for the elderly. Again this builds on and expands the coverage of an earlier scheme, the *Bonosol*. It aims to increase the pensions payable and to make them available to all over the age of sixty. The *Bonosol* scheme, introduced in 1996 as part of the capitalization scheme, was paid only to those over sixty-five. It was highly valued by recipients and their families. The government's attempts to fund this programme from budgets previously earmarked to departmental prefects proved highly contentious.
- A programme of subsidized house construction in both urban and rural areas. This was programmed to benefit 15,000 families in 2008.
- A programme to reduce levels of illiteracy, especially in rural areas.

Many of these schemes were only at an initial stage at the time of writing, so it is difficult to evaluate their impact. But by building on earlier successes, it seems probable that these success stories can be reproduced and amplified. In the longer run, however, social benefits will depend also on the government's success in the wider management of the economy, particularly in controlling inflation and increasing employment through GDP growth. It will also depend on the amount of remittances repatriated to the mother country from the Bolivian diaspora, equivalent to 4.6 per cent of GDP in 2006, mostly contributions sent from Argentina, Spain and the United States.

Bolivia and the outside world

In his foreign policy, too, Evo Morales has sought to redirect his country's traditional allegiance away from the United States and to build new relationships with new partners. His itinerary on his first trip abroad after his election in December 2005 was illustrative: Cuba, Venezuela, France, Belgium, Holland, China, South Africa, Brazil and Argentina. Although he has visited the United States, he has focused his attention on visits to the UN General Assembly in New York, and shied away from direct contacts with US officialdom.

Considerable media attention has been directed towards Evo and his relations with Cuba and Venezuela and the creation, in ALBA (Alternativa Bolivariana Para los Pueblos de Nuestra América, the Bolivarian Alternative for the People of the Americas), of a sort of socialist axis within Latin America, including latterly Nicaragua and Honduras. Of these, by far the most important economic relationship is with Venezuela, which, while also a co-founder of the Andean Pact, has traditionally had relatively little economic contact with Bolivia. Evo Morales has been a frequent visitor to Caracas, while Hugo Chávez has returned the compliment on a number of occasions. Venezuela has offered Bolivia valuable economic assistance, as well as military assistance at various points. It would be wrong, however, to portray Evo as some sort of junior partner in a Venezuelan project within the wider world, or Bolivia as condemned blindly to follow every Venezuelan initiative. The relationship with Chávez was sometimes a source of embarrassment and even friction: for example, Chávez's effusive support for Bolivia's maritime claims against Chile caused Bolivia more problems than it resolved. Furthermore, the Bolivian opposition has been quick to latch on to all links with Chávez as evidence of Bolivia's dangerous subservience towards Caracas.

Far more important than Venezuela in economic terms are Brazil and Argentina, Bolivia's main foreign trade partners and the markets for almost all its gas. Morales maintained a close personal rapport with both Lula in Brazil and Kirchner in Argentina. In the case of the former, this overrode the problems created by forcing Petrobras to revise its contractual relationship as Bolivia's most important foreign investor. In the case of the latter, Argentina was prepared to sign a gas purchase deal under which it pays Bolivia more than does Brazil for the gas received over the next few years. As an associate member of Mercosur, Bolivia understands the importance of building economic linkages with these and other Mercosur member countries. In 2008, Bolivia became a founder member of Unasur, based on the states of Mercosur and the Andean Pact, and it was Unasur, prompted by its Chilean presidency, that intervened in September 2008 to attempt to mediate tensions between Morales and the opposition.

So far as relations with the United States are concerned, it is not surprising that Bolivia under Morales has adopted a critical stance. The role of the United States in seeking to eradicate coca and defeat the *cocaleros* is well known, as was the poignant warning by former US ambassador Manuel Rocha on the eve of the 2002 elections that Bolivians should think twice about the consequences before voting for the MAS, which many commentators say greatly helped Evo's almost victorious election campaign that year. Despite periodic verbal spats, however, including repeated accusations from Morales about US ambitions to destabilize his administrations, the relationship has been one typified by a degree of caution on both sides. The positions adopted by US ambassador Philip Goldberg have generally sought to ease tensions and look for diplomatic solutions to bilateral problems. On the Bolivian side, there has also been a degree of realpolitik, especially with regard to the need to maintain the regime of trade preferences for Bolivian exporters in the US markets under the Andean Trade Preferences and Drug Eradication Act. These preferences are particularly important for businesses working in El Alto, where textiles, clothing and other factories are highly dependent on the US market. As tension and violence in opposition departments rose in September 2008, however, suspicion of US involvement with the opposition culminated in a serious diplomatic rift as Morales expelled Ambassador Goldberg, accusing him of conspiring against democracy.

Conclusion

In many senses, the politics of the first two years of the Morales administration represent an abrupt change to what had gone before, even though some continuities were present. As always in Bolivia, the future was hard to predict with any great certainty, but one thing seemed sure: Bolivia would not return to the status quo ante.

In embarking on this new agenda, Bolivia revealed some of the conditions that had led elsewhere in Latin America to increased disenchantment with the decades of economic and political liberalization. First, the economic reforms of the 1980s and early 1990s had failed to meet expectations, particularly among the majority of Bolivians who are indigenous and poor. 'Trickle-down' had been negligible, and problems associated with unemployment became worse. And second, democratic government had been found wanting as representative institutions, especially political parties, conspicuously failed to articulate grassroots demands at the level of the state.

In other respects, however, Bolivia represents a rather different panorama to other countries in the region, especially in the way in which social movements emerged as a defining factor in politics, in many ways replacing the traditional parties. The force of ethnic politics in Bolivia, in particular, has few parallels elsewhere in the region. Bolivia is also somewhat exceptional in terms of its political traditions and how these validate the politics of mobilization, exploiting areas where the state is weak or non-existent. The election of Evo Morales and the MAS in 2005 was indicative of these peculiarities. Evo was able to make enormous political capital out of his claim to be the first indigenous president of his country. At the same time, the MAS was an organization without parallels elsewhere in Latin America, a movement rather than a party, but one that could lay claim to be effectively providing new linkages between civil society and the state in ways that traditional parties simply could not.

The difficulties in running the country along new lines became clear early on, however. The MAS lacked a clearly articulated programme; it lacked experience in government; the machinery at its disposal for administering change was largely absent; and it was in no way a tightly disciplined political party. Moreover, it revealed a penchant for polarizing politics that swiftly energized powerful economic interests disinclined to accept many of the proposed changes and keen to challenge the new-found power of the social movements and a left-wing party. By the autumn of 2008, as tension and violence increased, anxious neighbouring states launched an attempt to secure a settlement between Morales and the national government, and opposition leaders based in the wealthy departments. Still, as this chapter has sought to show, important new policies were developed under Morales that contrast markedly with those characterizing the previous two decades. While turning points in history frequently turn out to be more illusory than real, 2005 would seem to mark an important new departure in Bolivia's pattern of development; as important perhaps as 1952. Time alone will tell.

6 | Nicaragua: the return of Daniel Ortega

DAVID CLOSE

From 1979 to 1990, the Frente Sandinista de Liberación Nacional (FSLN, Sandinista Liberation Front) governed Nicaragua. It took power via revolution, overthrowing the Somoza family's dictatorship in 1979. After 1984, the revolution turned to electoral and pluralistic methods. In 1990, the FSLN suffered the first of three electoral defeats, losing to a conservative but essentially democratic coalition. For sixteen years, the right governed Nicaragua. Two of the three administrations, those of Violeta Chamorro and Enrique Bolaños, followed the rule of law and continued the Sandinistas' commitment to political pluralism. The other, Arnoldo Alemán's, did not. When the FSLN regained the presidency in 2006, its leader, Daniel Ortega, the party's only presidential candidate ever, followed Alemán's path. This was not surprising, because in 2000 Ortega and Alemán sealed a pact to restructure Nicaraguan politics so as to make *caudillo*, boss-style politics the order of the day.

Daniel Ortega has been a leading figure in Nicaraguan politics since 1979. He has been a Commander of the Revolution and the FSLN's representative on the junta that governed from 1979 to 1984. He was elected president in 1984 and was the party's losing candidate in 1990, 1996 and 2001. In 2006, he regained the presidency and the FSLN became the largest member of the National Assembly, though without a majority. Ortega's strength is his tactical and strategic political sense; his weaknesses are administration and policy development.

Understandably, nearly thirty years in politics have changed both Daniel Ortega and the FSLN. The party has changed from a revolutionary movement to an office-seeking political machine, while Ortega has evolved from being one member of a radical collegial leadership to emerge as the unquestioned boss of the FSLN (Close and Deonandan 2005). The heady, hopeful days of 1979 are long past, and of the great accomplishments of the revolution – extending education and healthcare to the poor, carrying out agrarian reform, granting autonomy to the Atlantic Coast, where Nicaragua's Afro-Caribbean and indigenous minorities are concentrated, and making Nicaragua a functioning electoral democracy – only the last remains fully in force. Although the Sandinistas are the only party in Nicaragua to talk about the poor, building socialism has given way to negotiating with the World Bank and IMF, and Sandinista entrepreneurs have joined Nicaragua's economic elite.

During the FSLN's spell in opposition, 1990–2006, Ortega did whatever was necessary to strengthen his and his party's hand. Sometimes confrontation was the chosen method; but he also negotiated and bargained with the administration of the day. Whichever he chose, Ortega's political acumen gave the party an importance beyond its numbers. This chapter examines how he built the FSLN's power in opposition and came back to take the presidency in 2006, what he did in his first year back and what this means for Latin America's contemporary left.

Building power in opposition: 1990–2006

Opposition is always part of political life. In a democracy, a party can expect to spend much of its time out of power. In fact, voters often punish parties that lose touch with them or become arrogant or corrupt with a period in opposition. Thus opposition is where parties and politicians rebuild, relearn their skills and reconnect with their fellow citizens. This is what happened to the FSLN and Daniel Ortega, the only person to lead the party into an election.

Between 1990 and 2006, the Front suffered serious splits, came to be dominated by its leader, sealed a pact with bitter foes, made peace with the Catholic Church, which had once vehemently opposed it, and embraced, surreptitiously, neoliberal economic and social policy (Close 1999; Close and Deonandan 2005; Perez Baltadano 2009). It also combined extra-parliamentary tactics, including encouraging violently confrontational strikes in the transport and the university sectors, with support for whichever party of the right was governing or had lined up

TABLE 6.1 Sandinista electoral performance, nationwide elections, 1984–2004

Year	Election	FSLN	Leading opponent
1984	President	67.0	14.0
1990	President	40.8	54.7
1996	President	37.8	51.0
2000	Municipal	40.4	41.6
2001	President	42.3	56.3
2004	Municipal	43.8	37.3

Note: Only municipal elections held independently of presidential-legislative elections are included. Atlantic Coast elections are excluded as they are regional, not nationwide
Sources: Adapted from Close (1988); Political Database of the Americas (2008)

with it. In three straight national elections, however, four straight Atlantic Coast regional elections and, after 2000, in local elections, the party was rejected by over half the nation's electorate (see Table 6.1). Despite this, the Front and its leader were able to hold on until their opponents split and left the FSLN an opening to return to power.

Four things combined to let Ortega and the FSLN thrive in opposition. First, since his initial term as president (1984–90), Daniel Ortega was concentrating power in his own hands. The party opted not to hold a leadership review after losing power and this gave Ortega time to consolidate his position. Since then, those who challenge Ortega generally find themselves ex-Sandinistas. Ortega's authority is unquestionable. A second step was to turn the judiciary into a Sandinista stronghold (Martinez Baharona 2009). This meant ensuring there were enough Sandinistas trained to be judges. But even more important was putting Sandinistas in the Supreme Court, and that required the Pact.

The Ortega–Alemán Pact was Ortega's crowning achievement in opposition. Literally an ad hoc alliance between the FSLN and Alemán's Partido Liberal Constitucionalista (PLC, National Liberal Party) to pass a series of constitutional amendments and amendments to ordinary laws, the Pact was crafted to give the two parties permanent control of the Nicaraguan polity. Normally non-partisan state institutions – courts, the Controller General and the electoral authority – became party strongholds, divided between the PLC and FSLN according to their electoral weight. The Pact allots quotas of power and guarantees government posts that assure the two parties a presence in state institutions, letting them defend their interests and shape the national agenda. Unlike earlier pacts between the Somozas and the Conservatives, however, this one accepted that elections would be freely competitive (the Somozas used to offer the Conservatives a substantial block of legislative seats in order for them to turn a blind eye to the government's rigging of successive elections).

Although they started from a subordinate position, the Sandinistas managed the Pact better than did the Liberals. The FSLN first gained control of nearly half of the country's judiciary. With its partisans well ensconced in the courts, the FSLN has been able to secure politically favourable decisions whenever necessary. Further, the Frente became the dominant force in the National Assembly, again with only the second-largest caucus. Additionally, a change to the electoral law that the FSLN insisted be part of the Pact gave Daniel Ortega a first-round win in the presidential contest of 2006.

Finally, the FSLN benefited from President Enrique Bolaños's (2001–06) decision to prosecute Arnoldo Alemán, whom he had served as vice-president, for corruption. Sandinista judges assured Alemán's conviction (Liberals would have acquitted him) and gave him a twenty-year sentence (Dye 2004; Dye and Close 2005). These same judges later charged Bolaños with electoral finance irregularities when he stopped working with the FSLN. They also ordered that Alemán be held under house arrest instead of in prison, which led the PLC benches to vote with the FSLN through much of Bolaños's term. As long as the PLC cooperated with the FSLN, Alemán was allowed increasing freedom of movement until May 2007, when, presumably to ensure that the PLC's legislative votes stayed with Ortega, he received permission to travel throughout the country. This was interpreted as keeping the Pact alive and paving the way for Alemán to run in 2011 and ensured that the PLC benches voted with the FSLN through much of Bolaños's term. This did not prevent the new Ortega government threatening Alemán again with house arrest in December 2007 when the PLC was showing signs of voting with the anti-Sandinista majority in the Assembly. Controlling 90 per cent of the votes in the Assembly permitted Ortega to secure the adoption of constitutional amendments in 2005 that made most presidential appointments subject to approval by a 60 per cent congressional majority, enough to ensure that the Sandinistas had a say.

The return to power: a saga in several parts

Daniel Ortega understands the significance of getting state institutions right. Though no policy wonk, he appreciates the importance of formal structures and processes, and the informal institutions that arise alongside them. Among those informal institutions, he particularly values the Nicaraguan tradition of quotas of power. Like many another Nicaraguan leader, including his pact partner yet bitter opponent Arnoldo Alemán, Ortega has concentrated on setting rules that give him and his FSLN the biggest edge possible. On being re-elected in 2006, he shifted his theatre of operations from opposition to government.

Since 1979, Daniel Ortega has shaped Nicaragua's political system. It is polyarchic, has substantially free contestation and completion rein and elections are the only road to legitimate power (Dahl 1971). Nicaragua qualifies as a delegative democracy, because political leaders, at least of the FSLN and PLC, consider electoral victory as a ticket to five years of unaccountable rule (O'Donnell 1994). Finally, electoral competition and oversight-free government exist in a highly conflictive, two-party system in which Sandinistas and anti-Sandinistas struggle for hegemony. There has never been agreement on the basic governing model, beyond the role of elections, a powerful executive and, in the two major parties, an acceptance of *caudillo*-style, one-man rule. The result is what Thomas Carothers (2002) labelled a 'feckless democracy', but it still worked.

Going into 2006, momentum favoured Ortega and the Sandinistas. Municipal elections in 2004 gave the FSLN its best results in twenty years: nearly 44 per cent of the vote and control of 87 of Nicaragua's 152 municipalities, including Managua. Ortega took this as proof of his leadership; though a more cautious reading suggests that the FSLN was known for honest and efficient municipal management (Grigsby 2004). Either way, Ortega was the country's most powerful politician. Although every Nicaraguan national election since 1984 has seen a number of parties run, there had never been a race where the winning ticket did not have majority support. From 1990 until 2006 Nicaragua had polarized, the two-party system pitting the Sandinistas against the anti-Sandinistas in 1996 and 2001. The Pact, however, together with the Alemán government's corruption and the determination of Ortega and Alemán to retain control of their parties, produced fractures that gave Nicaragua a real four-way race in 2006.

The process began in 2005 when both the PLC and the FSLN expelled leadership hopefuls who later ran against their old parties. In the case of the Liberals, it was Eduardo Montealgre who left. A banker and a conservative technocrat, Montealgre had been a minister in both the Alemán and Bolaños administrations. He ended up leading the Alianza Liberal de Nicaragua (ALN, the Nicaraguan Liberal Alliance). On the Sandinista side, it was Herty Lewites who was ejected. Lewites had a long history of service with the Frente: gun-runner and treasurer for the guerrillas; tourism minister and developer of the Diplotienda hard currency shops in the 1980s; and FSLN mayor of Managua from 2000 to 2004. Pragmatic and patient, Lewites stayed loyal to Daniel Ortega but wanted to run for president. Thus, like Montealgre, he formed his own party: the Alianza-Movimiento de Renovación Sandinista (the MRS – the Sandinista Movement of Renovation had been formed in 1995 by FSLN dissidents led by former Vice-President Sergio Ramirez). As both Alemán and Ortega regularly showed low public approval ratings (CID-Gallup 2006), their parties could have justified a new standard-bearer, but instead they dismissed the challengers. In the end, since Alemán's status as prisoner precluded him from standing, the PLC chose Jose Rizo, Bolaños's vice-president and long-time Liberal influential. The Frente went again with the only man to carry its colours in an election, Daniel Ortega.

Initially it seemed that the outsiders would do well. For the first several months of 2006 Lewites and Montealgre led the polls (Table 6.2). Then, on 1 July 2006, Herty Lewites died of a heart attack, and without the popular

TABLE 6.2 Voting intentions, Nicaragua, 2006

Candidate/party	April	June	August	October
Ortega/FSLN	16	26	29	33
Montealagre/ALN	22	22	23	22
Rizo/PLC	13	13	14	17
Lewites/Jarquin/MRS	18	21	14	13
Don't know/n.a.	33	16	19	15

Source: Adapted from CID-Gallup (2006)

ex-mayor heading its ticket, the Alianza-MRS began to decline. By that point, the split in the Liberal Party had caught up with Montealgre, who lost the lead in polls to Ortega. By October, everyone ceded first place to the latter. The only question was whether he could avoid a run-off, which he would almost certainly lose. The Sandinistas' 37.99 per cent of the vote put him ten points ahead of Montealgre, however, not just the legally stipulated five, and gave Daniel Ortega his second term as president after a hiatus of sixteen years.

A look at the results of the polls and the election reveals two unexpected patterns (Table 6.3). First, summing the FSLN and Alianza-MRS votes gave the left its best result since 1984 (44.3 per cent), despite the FSLN having its second-worst showing ever. Further, the combined Liberal vote was higher than the PLC tallied in its two victorious campaigns (55.4 per cent). Having minor parties in the race is the probable explanation. Equally interesting, the combined Sandinista preferences, Daniel Ortega plus Alianza-MRS, led the Liberals even into October (Table 6.2). Nicaraguans wanted change.

As in 2001, the Frente was part of an electoral alliance: the Con-

TABLE 6.3 Nicaraguan national election results, 2006

Candidate	Presidential vote %	Party	National Assembly seats
Daniel Ortega	37.99	FSLN	38
Eduardo Montealegre	28.3	ALN	22
Jose Rizo	27.11	PLC	25
Edmundo Jarquin*	6.3	MRS	5
Others	0.28	Others	0

Note: * Became Alianza-MRS candidate when Herty Lewites died
Source: Adapted from Political Database of the Americas (2008)

vergencia Nacional in 2001, the Alianza Unida Nicaragua Triunfa in 2006. What converged in the Convergencia and allied in the Alianza Unida were the FSLN and an array of political figures from the right and centre-right. In 2001, Ortega's running mate was Agustín Jarquin, an active anti-Sandinista in the 1980s but also a bitter foe of Arnoldo Alemán. Indeed, Jarquin had been jailed by both pact partners. Although Jarquin ran for the Alianza again in 2006, he was replaced as vice-presidential candidate by Jaime Morales Carazo, a leader of the Contras in the 1980s whose house had been expropriated and was now occupied by the Ortegas. There were other significant radical anti-Sandinistas from the 1980s in the alliances, such as Miriam Argüello, whose distaste for Alemán and the Liberals led them to join their old foes.

What prompted the Frente to accept its former enemies was its campaign of national reconciliation, the centrepiece in both 2001 and 2006. This excerpt from a campaign speech by Rosario Murillo, Ortega's wife, in Chinandega during the last week of the campaign, gives a sense of the mood:

> In Nicaragua we will install a new culture of Love, of Reconciliation, of Peace, because it is the only way for us to go forward and because it is the wish and promise of the Frente Sandinista de Revolución Nacional. It is the will of the Nicaraguan people and for us the will of the people is sacred: it is the will of God. (Murillo 2006; capitalization in original)

This is not the historic discourse of the Sandinistas. Having been burned in the past, especially in 1996 (Close 1999), by opponents waving the bloody shirt of revolution and frightening voters into the arms of the right, Ortega and the FSLN did not just reach out to their old nemeses, they expropriated their language and concepts (Perez Baltadano 2009). Their government programme (Alianza Unida Nicaragua Triunfa 2006) repeatedly invoked the Lord's blessing, while talking about respecting the rights of private property; redistributing land without occupations or confiscations; addressing poverty, illiteracy and inequality; and installing a form of direct democracy the FSLN calls citizens' power. As well, Ortega benefited from donations of fertilizer and diesel fuel from Hugo Chávez. Although the materials were eventually distributed through official channels, Ortega's links to an international and wealthy ally would have been noted.

The clearest shift from the old Sandinista political path, however, came on 26 October 2006, ten days before the elections, when the FSLN joined the other parties in the National Assembly to outlaw therapeutic abortion (abortion performed to save the mother's life). This was not a bow to public opinion, because polls have shown majorities of between 55 and 69 per cent of Nicaraguans favouring therapeutic abortion (CID-Gallup 2007; Reed 2006). Rather, this is best seen as part of Ortega's strategy to placate old adversaries. In the case of the Church, this began in 2005 when he and his wife renewed their vows, first exchanged in Costa Rica in 1978, before Cardinal Obando y Bravo (Envio 2005).

Although the Catholic Church embraced the prodigal Ortega, the US government still saw him as a pariah. At first, Washington's treatment of the Sandinista leader was sophisticated, labelling him and Alemán old-style leaders, while pointing to Montealgre and Lewites as leaders who understood that the world had changed. After Lewites's death, however, the State Department moved firmly into Montealgre's camp and pressed the Liberals to unite and defeat the FSLN (COHA 2006). Although there were suspicions that the PLC refused to back Washington's choice in order to hand Ortega the election, the Liberal split occurred because Alemán wanted Montealgre out of his party and that, as much as any plot to divide the anti-Sandinista vote and let Ortega win, made a fusion ticket impossible.

After taking barely three-eighths of the vote, and winning by a feat of electoral engineering his own party had performed six years earlier, Daniel Ortega appeared unlikely to begin a significant transformational process. Further, the FSLN's campaign had promised reconciliation, peace and love, which implied negotiation and compromise. True, Ortega did promise to fight poverty and illiteracy and to bring in new forms of citizen participation, yet commentators did not see these as inconsistent with a moderate Sandinista administration. This applied particularly to the president-elect's foreign policy, which showed a willingness to work with the United States (Contreras 2006; Ikeda 2007).

As the two months between election and inauguration passed, signs appeared that Ortega's aims might be different to what had initially been thought. One of these was the appointment to key positions of individuals who had held influential posts in the revolutionary government of the 1980s. Not that Bayardo Arce (financial adviser), Samuel Santos (foreign minister) and Paul Oquist (transition team coordinator and coordinator of a presidential advisory council on public policy) are not competent or are bent on revenge. Their appointments suggested, however, that Ortega's views on how best to govern had not changed much since 1990. Harder to miss was the presence of Hugo Chávez and Evo Morales at Ortega's inauguration as guests of honour, with Arnoldo Alemán also among the new president's invitees. If having the two Bolivarians there indicated that Ortega wished to be identified with that group and presaged

Nicaragua's entry into ALBA (Alternativa Bolivariana para los Pueblos de Nuestra América, Bolivarian Alternative for the Peoples of the Americas), Chávez's economic integration scheme, Alemán's inclusion showed that the Pact still functioned.

Up to Ortega's inauguration, things were quiet. In the weeks that followed his assuming power the outlines of his vision for Nicaragua emerged rapidly. Some of what he did was expected, such as reorganizing ministries, but there were also striking new initiatives. The latter included: Hugo Chávez's promises of extensive assistance, including a multi-billion-dollar oil refinery; the visit of Iranian president Mahmoud Ahmadinejad and promises of increased aid (critical in a country where 45 per cent of the population lives in poverty; UNICEF 2008); talk of a constitutional amendment to permit a president to serve two consecutive terms; the first hints about the role 'people's power' would have; the fusion of party and state; and a crucial if not quite constitutional role for Rosario Murillo. Since January 2007, these plans have dominated Nicaraguan politics. We can divide them into questions that affect the structure of the state and Ortega's broader policy agenda.

All political leaders surround themselves with trusted confidants. In Latin America there is a tendency to rely on family that seems stronger than in Canada or the United States. When family is involved, it is usually a brother or male cousin or son who fills the adviser's role. The Ortegas have changed that, as Rosario Murillo, Mrs Ortega, shared top billing with her husband during the campaign – which she managed – and then became de facto prime minister in his administration. Two generations of dictatorship from the Somozas led Nicaraguans to place consanguinity rules in the constitution in 1995 to keep a president's close relatives out of public office. Twelve years later the Sandinista president and his wife were skating around those provisions, if not plainly breaking them.

Controversy engulfed Murillo when Ortega named her coordinator of the Consejo de Ciudadanía y Comunicación (Citizenship and Communications Council) in January 2007. This council was one of several formed in a presidential decree (3-2007) amending Law 290, which covers the organization of the executive branch. Most of the councils are conventional consultative bodies bringing together stakeholders and the state, such as those on public policy, the Atlantic Coast and reconciliation, the latter headed by Cardinal Obando y Bravo. Murillo's organization is distinct, however. The citizenship part of the council is concerned with devising ways to implement people's power, and it is not surprising that it is in the president's office and headed by a person of confidence. The communications side controls government advertising, however. This put

Murillo in charge of deciding how advertising funds would be spent and thus able to punish unfriendly media. Commentators soon spoke of an '"Ortega-Murillo" government. ... A regime of personal power in which the Frente Sandinista is solely an executing instrument, a transmission belt, whose institutional identity as a party is subject to the will of the presidential couple' (Chamorro 2007: 2). Murillo's defenders quickly accused critics of anti-feminism. They carefully avoided issues related to the personalization of executive power, however.

Nevertheless, it was only when the president proposed giving the coordinators salaries that the storm broke. This proposal violated Law 290's provision that such councils should not spend public funds. And in Murillo's case, the matter was even more serious as naming a presidential spouse to a paid, executive position violates Article 150 of Nicaragua's constitution. Eventually this crisis was resolved by making the coordinators' jobs unpaid. Left unaddressed was whether a post as key as Murillo's should go to the president's spouse. Such centralized, personalized political power evoked unpleasant memories of the Somozas.

Sandinista Supreme Court magistrate Rafael Solis declared the councils that the Ortega government was constructing to be the advance guard of a new political system (Pantoja 2007). Indeed, the judicial system itself – in contrast to most around the world – was becoming extremely politicized and considered the second most corrupt in Central America (Martinez Baharona 2009; Dye 2004; Cruz Sánchez 2007). The councils themselves were created by decree, not legislation, and thus without debate. Most are consultative bodies, whose job is to give the president more direct access to and knowledge of specific policy areas. This is not novel and scarcely points to a new political system. Only the Consejos de Poder Ciudadano, the Councils of Citizen Power (CPC), should be regarded as innovative. They are the instruments for making *El Pueblo Presidente*, the People as President, operational. Rosario Murillo describes the two concepts in this way: 'The political will of President Daniel is to share the presidency with the people. We are the servants of the people, because it's the people who are really in the presidency. And how does this translate into daily life? Through the creation of the Councils of Citizen Power!' (quoted in Rogers 2008). Moving from the rhetoric of press conferences to the language of public policy produced an organization that belonged to the executive branch and was dominated by the FSLN (Arroliga 2007). The logic was simple: set up a mechanism to let citizens make demands directly to mayors and ministries. In this system, the people shape legislative decisions through their participation in the budgetary process and by being able to articulate specific policy demands.

The CPCs' structure is complex: base committees (a neighbourhood or its rural equivalent) feed into municipal cabinets which can themselves represent several towns as well as unincorporated rural areas. These then feed into departmental cabinets, which send their material on to the national cabinet, headed by the president. At each level the cabinet has a coordinator, most often an FSLN professional, for example a local party secretary, who turns citizens' input into policy proposals. In total, there are 272 officials (Alvarez, W. et al. 2007). Besides territorial divisions, there are functional specializations within the three senior cabinets. These cover citizens' rights, publicity and public security, as well as sections corresponding to conventional line departments: health, transport and infrastructure, education and culture. All these lines converge at the top in the president's hands. Thus the CPC looks like a parallel government centred in the office of the president.

The Consejos are also controversial. They were suspended early in September 2007 when the Assembly voted to delink them from the executive, leaving them just another consultative council. Ortega vetoed this but the Assembly overrode his veto in November. At that point, the Court of Appeals for the Managua district stepped in with an injunction (*decreto de amparo*) before the veto was overridden. It was also about that time that the judiciary began speaking of returning Alemán to prison. Then, to give the CPC a stronger claim to legality, Ortega moved them under the CONPES (Comité Nacional de Planificación Económica y Social), which is established by the constitution (Article 150.13). As a result, it now requires a constitutional amendment to change the CPCs' status (Tunnerman Bernheim 2007). As well, the CPCs acquired a new function: distributing cheap food in poor *barrios*, which should raise their public profile (Galeano, L. 2007). All this manoeuvring ended in January 2008 when the Supreme Court, composed of eight Sandinistas and eight Constitutional Liberals, declared unconstitutional the law giving the president the authority to create the CPCs, in their current form, but also held that the organizations could continue to exist if they got no state funding (Marenco 2008). Coincidently, talk of jailing Alemán ceased.

Why the president fought so hard for the CPCs can be explained by the chance they offer him, as coordinator of the national cabinet of the CPC, to present a view of citizens' demands that corresponds to his values and not the Assembly's. That this could provoke a conflict between executive and legislature that would bring government to a halt would not be bad from Ortega's perspective, as it would allow him to push for a new constitution. In 2007, Ortega floated two proposals for constitutional changes that would not make him leave power in 2011, when

119

his term ends. The first of these would permit immediate presidential re-election (Loasiga Lopez et al. 2007); the other posits a parliamentary system, which would let President Ortega give way to Prime Minister Ortega (Galeano and Miranda 2007). Daniel Ortega's tailor-made state has him staying at its helm; but not controlling the legislature makes realizing his dream harder.

There are other elements that suggest how Ortega wants to redesign the state to keep himself in power. One is the fusion of party and state. This is seen most clearly in the Ortegas' refusal to live in the presidential mansion; they prefer to stay in their own home, the one the revolutionary government expropriated from the current vice-president. The compound where the Ortegas live, however, is also the seat of the FSLN's secretariat. Thus the president has his residence and office at the address of his party's headquarters. Another factor is the iron control that he and Murillo are imposing on the FSLN. This led to a well-known Sandinista intellectual, Oscar Rene Vargas, having his appointment as ambassador to France revoked after giving an interview to a paper that the administration viewed as unfriendly (Juaréz 2007). It also generated a running dispute between the Ortegas and Dionisio Marenco, mayor of Managua and another long-time, high-ranking Sandinista, over the couple's continuing usurpation of the mayor's prerogatives. As well, there are tensions within the Alianza, whose non-FSLN members have scant presence in the government. Further, one could look at Ortega's control of off-budget funds in the form of 40 per cent of the yearly revenues derived from sales of subsidized Venezuelan oil by Petronic, the state oil company, and see him arrogating unaccountable power (Olivares 2008). President Ortega's behaviour is not that of a prudent leader respectful of the majority that opposed him in the elections. He has gone for broke and up to now is winning his bet.

To round out this analysis of the first year of the Ortega presidency we turn to its policies, beginning with foreign policy. It is in foreign policy that the administration has had greatest success. Daniel Ortega managed to cultivate warm personal ties with Hugo Chávez and Evo Morales, Mahmoud Ahmadinejad and Mu'ammer Gaddafi, and of course Fidel Castro, while maintaining good relations with Washington. And in one of the surprises of 2007, Ortega retained diplomatic ties with Taiwan while Oscar Arias, the centrist president of Costa Rica, embraced Beijing. Ortega's accomplishments here reflect his native political sense and skills honed during thirty years in public life.

It is natural that Ortega would ally Nicaragua with like-minded states, since these offer political support and reinforce the FSLN's self-image as a revolutionary organization. Choosing Taipei over Beijing, however, is a clear attempt to advance Nicaragua's national interest, as Taiwan seemed more ready to finance projects. There has been speculation that a Hong Kong firm is involved in upgrading the Panama Canal and a Taiwan one might be willing to finance a competing dry canal (a rail line) in Nicaragua. Even his embrace of the Iranian leader has a pragmatic side, as Tehran, unlike donors from western Europe and North America, places no strings on its assistance. And Hugo Chávez is more than Ortega's greatest political ally, for he serves Nicaraguan interests very well by promising massive aid (Rogers 2007). So it is not surprising that Ortega dusted off his anti-USA speeches and joined Chávez and Ahmadinejad in denouncing Washington, as there is currently little else Nicaragua can offer its international friends.

Ortega's domestic agenda has been less successful, perhaps reflecting his lack of interest in policy details. It is still early days but economic progress is slow, with 1.1 per cent growth per capita in 2007 and inflation for the first eight months of 2008 reaching 23 per cent (EIU 2008). His administration's economic policy initiatives have centred on renewing Nicaragua's accord with the IMF and diversifying the country's heavy dependence on foreign donations by shifting away from traditional donors to Venezuela, Iran and Libya. Specific social policies are working. Reports indicate that the government's lifting of school fees has increased enrolment (Sabo 2007). The star attraction, however, *Hambre Cero* (Zero Hunger), which targets the poorest rural families, has got off to a slow start, reaching only 5,481 families in its first year of operation, instead of the projected 15,000. It will now be financed by Venezuela, instead of by a combination of Nicaraguan government funds and foreign donations (Observador Económico 2007; Rugama 2008; Loasiga Lopez 2008). It does appear, though, that the policies are applied impartially, and it is unlikely that the Liberals would have implemented these redistributive programmes.

Overall, the early policy initiatives of Daniel Ortega's second government are interesting but tentative. Aside from the CPCs, there have been no dramatic moves to restructure the state. Indeed, the FSLN's most radical social policy initiative, criminalizing therapeutic abortion, came before the election and remains unchanged.

Learning from Nicaragua

Much of Daniel Ortega's activity in his first year back in office was geared towards building a framework for political reconstruction, but what is he building? The FSLN describes itself as revolutionary and Ortega calls his opponents counter-revolutionaries (Confidencial 2008), but compared to the projects of Chávez, Morales or Correa, his policies appear generally incremental. There are important successes. In foreign policy, the administration is far more open to the left than its three predecessors, and Ortega also has better relations with Washington than did Alemán. Further, domestic social policy is far more redistributive. Only the Committees of Citizen Power, however, a cross between radical democracy's mass organization and liberal democracy's civil society, look able to bring dramatic change. At the level of policies, then, Ortega's government may not need constitutional or institutional change to achieve its goals.

Looking at Daniel Ortega's governing style and how his administration works one sees movement towards hyper-presidentialism, personalistic politics, a ruling family clique and designs to lay the bases for hegemonic rule. Those are staples of Latin American political history that have seldom benefited ordinary citizens. Unfortunately, they are also staples of recent Nicaraguan politics, since Arnoldo Alemán pursued much the same objectives (Close and Deonandan 2005). That leads to the uncomfortable conclusion that although Daniel Ortega is moving policy-making to the left, his constitutional legacy may be a refinement of the Pact that makes his Frente the dominant force, not Alemán's Liberals.

That does not mean that Nicaragua's experience since 1990 does not offer useful lessons to Latin America's new left. Ortega has shown, first, that the left can play brokerage, log-rolling politics to its advantage, even while out of office. Further, he and the Sandinistas have demonstrated that electoral defeat is not the end of the world and that opposition parties of the left really can use conventional electoral politics to win power: elections are not the monopoly of the right. The South American Bolivarians understand the value of elections and Hugo Chávez tasted defeat in his 2007 referendum. The left that does not seek massive state reform (Lula, Bachelet, Vazquéz and probably Colom and Lugo) grasps the need to make deals and knows that defeat at the polls will come some time.

Daniel Ortega obviously wants to avoid further electoral losses, three straight defeats being enough. Yet trying to build a hegemonic project, one sure never to lose, in a pluralistic framework seems chimerical. The FSLN's experience in the 1980s certainly points that way. Ortega should bear in mind that vanguardist attempts at transformation, such as the Soviet or Chinese communists, did not produce lasting results either. Pluralism may have to be an acceptable bet for those who want to change the world.

its welfare internationalism. Cuban medical and literacy brigades appeared all over the Third World, plugging the vast gaps in provision being exacerbated by the neoliberal medicine prescribed by the USA.

This last cold war, against the Cuban people, was actually intensified in the 1990s. New US blockade legislation now sought to punish non-US firms doing business with Cuba (Morley and McGillion 2002). Pressure increased in G. W. Bush's second term, and in 2008 at least two British banks closed Cuba-linked business accounts, under threat of US fines. In the twenty-first century, the US government still produced 400-plus-page reports, 'Plan Bush' to Cubans, on regime change in Cuba, how to privatize its health service, put a US marshal in charge of law and order, and give the descendants of Batista's thugs their properties back (US Department of State 2004, 2006). Cuba continued to intercept Miami terrorist groups infiltrating its territory. In 1998, after an Italian tourist was murdered in a hotel bombing, Cuba supplied evidence of terrorist activities to the FBI. The US response was to use the information to arrest Cuba's undercover anti-terrorism agents, try them in Miami, and jail five for espionage against the USA, using a conspiracy charge in the absence of credible evidence (Dávalos Fernández 2006; Ludlam 2009). Perhaps an Obama presidency will bring change. The business lobby that persuaded Clinton and Bush to permit food exports to Cuba may open more doors. Divisions in the Cuban-American electorate suggest new political openings, which may one day break the hold of Cuba-America on US policy (Wilkinson 2008). Cubans are not holding their breath.

Cuba's international position has changed in spite of US diplomacy. It now features a multiplicity of trade links, reflecting a determination never again to become dependent on a single linkage. Chinese and Canadian investments in nickel and oil mirror earlier European and Latin American investment in tourism. The formation of ALBA (Alternativa Bolivariana para los Pueblos de Nuestra América, Bolivarian Alternative for the Peoples of the Americas) has given Cuba valuable trade with Venezuela, Bolivia and other ALBA states, and thereby with the wider world (Monreal 2006: 466). ALBA has already produced dozens of economic projects for Cuba, on top of Venezuela's sale of discounted oil, restoration of the Cienfuegos oil refinery, and construction of undersea cabling to increase Cuba's Internet capacity. Hugo Chávez's prominent support of Cuba, and the multifaceted reintegration of Cuba into Latin American life, has transformed the island's status across the continent, and improved morale in Cuba. Many non-ALBA Latin American and Caribbean states are also resisting US pressure and normalizing bilateral relations. In 2008, for example, Cuba became Brazil's second-largest trading partner in Latin America. Cuban academics and other professionals are attending each other's events and advising each other under a plethora of bilateral arrangements. Cuba's historical defence of the Latin American left during the dictatorships, and Fidel's personal relationships with leaders such as Lula, Chávez and Evo Morales, certainly helps. So too does Cuba's deployment of its unrivalled medical and education resources to support social justice programmes across the region. The Cuban-staffed primary health service in Venezuela's slum *barrios* and its illiteracy eradication systems are dramatic examples of the island's 'internationalist' missions. Its continental Misión Milagro (Mission Miracle), the eye surgery programme backed by ALBA finances, had restored sight to 1.2 million people by 2008. The question arises of whether Cuba, leader of an earlier 'red tide' and enthusiastic spectator of the 'pink tide', and a keen participant in the accompanying new regionalism, will now be drawn politically away from its socialism and towards the radical social democracy of the left-wing presidencies.

Cuban exceptionalism: regime change and retail therapy?

After *el triunfo* in 1959, the revolution became the process of building a new society, based on the social and racial justice and anti-imperialism that the national 'apostle' José Martí died for in 1895, in Cuba's final war of independence against Spain. The preamble to Cuba's constitution declares that it 'should be presided over by the profound desire of José Martí, at last achieved, "I want the first law of our Republic to be the worship by Cubans of the full dignity of humanity"' (Republic of Cuba 1992: 2–3). The fog of the cold war long concealed this authentic radical tradition, but it has inspired what Cubans call their *conquistas*, the conquests of their revolution: the world-renowned health and education systems, the access to culture, the right to work and to land, civil equality – the programme set out in Fidel Castro's 1953 courtroom defence of his armed rebellion (Castro Ruz, F. 1987: 106–14). It was the unending US 'dirty war' after 1959 that turned many radical liberals and social democrats towards their socialist comrades. *Cubanía rebelde*, rebel Cubanness, was turning into *cubanía revolucionaria* (Kapcia 2000). Cuba was propelled into the Soviet bloc, where it lived for a generation. For all its bureaucratism and continued dependence on sugar exports, this was a period of belief in a future of growing prosperity and equality. The future, however, as has been observed since the collapse of the Soviet bloc, is not what it used to be. Nowhere was the post-Soviet loss of certainty more traumatic than in Cuba. The rapid loss of some 80 per cent of trade and 40 per cent of national income was compounded by the intensification of the US blockade. As Cuba entered its emergency 'Special Period Not in Time of War', international debate focused on how quickly the revolution would collapse. Domestic debate focused on how much marketization and external business collaboration was compatible with saving the revolution (Suárez Salazar 1997; Vilariño Ruiz 1997; Bell Lara 2004). Sympathetic analysts concluded that Cuba was 'a nascent class society' (Landau 2004: 626); and on 'an ineluctable drive towards a capitalist future' (Gott 2004: 324). Academic surveys were similarly pessimistic: Cuba was coming back from the future 'with no prospect of reversal' (Eckstein 2003: 242); the end of Cuban 'exceptionalism' after its decades as a haven of social justice in Latin America was predicted (Centeno 2004; Hoffman and Whitehead 2007).

Renewed foreign interest in Cuba was prompted by Fidel's retirement. His illness in 2006 forced him to step aside, initially temporarily, but in February 2008, with the newly elected National Assembly preparing to elect the president, he withdrew and Raúl was elected. This was not the 'regime change' the US government's multi-million-dollar 'transition studies' industry had been planning. The rusting tools of Kremlinology were soon being wiped down with an oily rag, to identify hardliners and softliners. In Raúl's case this was complicated: in the early years Raúl had been seen in the USA as the hard-line communist, Fidel the flexible pragmatist. Now Fidel was seen as the inflexible ideologue, Raúl the pragmatist who had pioneered the decentralization of Cuban business in the 1990s. Raúl's instantly rejected invitations to the USA to reopen dialogue were, for example, interpreted as a new softer line, although they simply repeated long-standing policy. The notion that Raúl would follow the Chinese road to capitalism was based on little more than his willingness to experiment with markets, and on growing commercial links with China. It certainly did not mean, as in China, charging for healthcare or welcoming multi-millionaire capitalists into the leadership of the Communist Party. Nevertheless, a study of the different possible forms of social ownership was launched, amid expectation of an extension of the agricultural cooperative model to other sectors. The catastrophic impacts of Hurricanes Gustav and Ike in 2008, while prompting a tremendous effort in central planning, may also open more doors to small-scale private enterprise as the state focuses on restoring core areas. Indeed, the allocation of state agricultural land to self-employed farmers and farm cooperatives was accelerated in the wake of the destruction of crops.

Fidel's retirement was always going to unleash debate inside Cuba, if only because no other leader had such charismatic authority to augment the government's legitimacy in difficult times. A change of leadership was always likely to mean a less personal, less mobilization-based and more institutionalized style of leadership. Raúl's government has earned popular support by focusing on everyday frustrations, especially food prices and salaries. Fidel had already tackled the infuriating power cuts, driving through an 'energy revolution' in 2006 which installed a new network of electricity generators, and distributed low-energy lighting, kitchen and ventilation appliances to homes. By 2006, most other capital investment was in housing, transport, water and hospitals. Having promised to remove 'outdated limits and prohibitions', Raúl's administration not only lifted restrictions on selling consumer electronics, but addressed a range of irritating bureaucratic procedures in housing allocation (Castro Ruz, R. 2007b). To judge from media coverage, Cuba was rushing headlong into consumerism. Images flashed around the globe showing Cubans leaving *el shopping*, the hard currency shops, with newly available commodities: bundling colour TVs and DVD players into taxis, driving off on new mopeds, and waving mobile phones. If they had the money they could now use international hotels and tourist hire cars. The revolution was getting what it really needed: retail therapy!

Such perceptions were superficial compared to more significant economic and politics changes. Bureaucratic inefficiencies, along with corruption, identified by Cuban leaders as having destroyed the Soviet bloc, are being addressed at several levels. The structure of ministries is being reformed in 2008 'to reduce the enormous amount of meetings, coordination, permissions, conciliations, provisions, rules and regulations etc etc' (Castro Ruz, R. 2008a). The administration of key policies, such as the new land distribution programme, has been decentralized to municipal authorities. The Communist Party (PCC) established new municipal groups specifically to monitor food production, reflecting the government's top policy priority. This priority is very popular indeed, when prices, quality and availability of foodstuffs in the supply-and-demand-priced agro-markets are major issues. Cuba is rich in land, but imports 70 per cent of its food at rapidly increasing prices, much of it from the USA. Such changes have to be understood in the economic context. By 2005, the economy, as measured by GDP, had recovered from the post-Soviet crisis, though Cuban society was far from having recovered. The economic recovery was based on strategic investment in tourism, nickel production, and the knowledge-based sectors that became Cuba's main hard currency earner (Morris 2007). Strong growth, at around 10 per cent per annum, continued in 2006 and 2007, enabling a move away from crisis management and towards a more balanced recuperation of the whole economy. This, though, demands increases in productivity that in turn require the resolution of the social damage of the Special Period, above all more of a reliance on legal salaries, and less on the informal and illicit activity that undermines day-job motivation and results in theft of state materials. It was a sign of the underlying confidence and openness of Cuba's political leaders that in his first big set-piece domestic speech, on 26 July 2007, Raúl launched a classic Cuban *consulta pública*, public consultation on economic problems, which produced over 1.5 million proposals from over 200,000 meetings (Castro Ruz, R. 2007a, 2007b).

Political change might be accelerated if the US blockade and 'transition' threats were lifted. With the external threat removed, pressures for greater political and media pluralism would be harder to resist through recourse to defence of national unity. The popular identification of all dissidents with the groups that collaborate with US agencies would lose its meaning. Without a US volte-face, though, Cuba's political system is unlikely to change rapidly. Although Raúl has demanded deeper institutionalization of politics, a fluctuation from crisis-led mobilization to more orderly institutionalization is far from novel in the revolutionary era (Castro Ruz, R. 2008a, 2008b). The convening of the long-overdue Communist Party congress in 2009 similarly signalled a return to more normal politics, and suggested that the leadership believed it could present a package of viable and popular policies for the coming period. The 95 per cent turnout and 91 per cent 'united ticket' vote in the January 2008 National Assembly elections reinforced political confidence. The encouragement of self-criticism in public life, described by Fidel as having 'practically fossilized', has taken many forms – the *consulta pública*, Internet blogging, the shift of Cuban journalism (attacked by Raúl for its triumphalism and complacency) to more critical habits, and the publication in *Granma* of readers' letters, which have included calls for the media to represent the people, not just the state (Castro Ruz, F. 2007; *Granma*, 18 April 2008). Further, it is a commonplace that Cuba's electoral system had already become more democratic and its civil society more autonomous in the 1990s. In the diplomatically hypersensitive area of civil rights, Cuba signed up in 2008 to two legally binding covenants of the Universal Declaration of Human Rights, on freedom of expression and association, and the right to travel. The UN had dropped a long-standing US demand that Cuba submit to a special inspection regime. And in a highly symbolic move, given the country's outdated but damaging reputation on lesbian and gay rights, the National Centre for Sexual Education, directed by Mariela Castro, Raúl's daughter, proposed enacting equal rights to civil marriage for gay and lesbian Cubans. Cuban society, while it remains under the real and threatening siege that makes it easy to equate unity with conformity, is loosening its collective tongue, and no one has so far died of fright. For most Cubans, though, what threatens support for the political system is far more mundane.

Equality

In Fidel's own words, 'The Special Period gave rise to profound inequalities' (Castro Ruz, F. 2007: 598). Now, as the Special Period is ending, both the availability of electronic goods in *el shopping* and the lifting of the cap on bonus payments for production workers (discussed below) have been interpreted as signalling a 'tolerance for inequality', and in the case of bonuses, as knocking away one of Cuba's 'pillars of socialism' (*Guardian*, 13 June 2008). On closer examination both measures can be interpreted differently. Given that Cuba's 'new rich' can easily pay for DVD players, etc., imported privately, and that such items carry 240–270 per cent value-added tax, selling them in Havana may increase visible inequality but is also a redistributive fiscal measure. And if the 'new rich' are buying such goods instead of every onion they encounter, then Cubans on ordinary salaries benefit. The effect of the lifting of the bonus cap on salaries, and focusing bonuses on individuals rather than groups, is also presented as strengthening the 'socialist principle of distribution' (Pérez Navarro 2008). Cuba's 'socialist principle of distribution' provides a rationale for individual material incentives; raising national productivity provides another. Trade unionists in capitalist societies treat such rationales with caution. The difference in Cuba is that the benefits are reallocated by the political process to the benefit of Cubans, not whisked away by 'market forces'.

This brings us to a consideration of how change in Cuba, before and after Fidel's retirement, has impacted on equality and socialism. A preliminary note on terminology is needed. Cuba's constitutional 'socialist principle of distribution' is linked to a position adopted by Marx in a debate in the 1870s with German socialists, and later adopted as the basis of salary policy in the Soviet bloc. In his vision of communist society, Marx foresaw distribution of wealth on the basis of the formula 'From each according to his ability, to each according to his needs'. But, when addressing the value of wages in the period of socialist transition from capitalism to communism, he insisted that the second clause should be 'to each according to his work'. This reflected Marx's proposition that, in the socialist stage, the material basis for equality based on needs would not exist, so while that basis was created, work should be paid on the basis of time worked, and effort and skill invested (Marx 1974: 346–7). Hence in Cuba, unlike civil equality and equality of access to universal services, material equality is rejected as implying equal rewards for unequal effort, and *igualitarismo* (egalitarianism) in this respect is condemned. In this chapter, however, egalitarianism is used simply to describe a desire for greater equality. Similarly in Cuba, the perception of social democracy is negative, reflecting its history during the cold war, and role in promoting neoliberalism in several Latin American states. In the remainder of this chapter, however, the concern is not judgement of history elsewhere, but the political essence of social democracy (egalitarianism) and socialism (egalitarianism plus social control of the economy) in contemporary Cuba.

Equality of access

The Special Period had many negative social effects (Ferriol Muruaga et al. 1998). The crisis exacerbated gender inequalities, as Cuban women, still subject to the double burden of work and housekeeping, had to spend even more time managing households (Caram León 2005). Race equality became an issue again. Lack of access to hard currency remittances, and signs of discrimination in employment, reminded black Cubans that legal reform does not change society overnight (Saney 2004: 108–21). Universal provision of free health, education and other social services, however, was not sacrificed, as sources from varied viewpoints attest (Erickson et al. 2002; Alexander 2005; Martínez Puentes 2004). Infant mortality rates and life expectancy remain astonishingly high, even in First World terms, and continue to improve. Education indicators regularly place Cuban children in the top ranks in the continent and, in some subjects, the world. One Cuban sociologist has summed up why such gains have to be sustained: 'The Revolution was made in order to solve social problems from which its strength is derived, losing these conquests would be losing the meaning of the Revolution because these forces materialize socialism for the masses' (Bell Lara 2002: 114).

Measures since the turn of the century have thus included radical reduction of class numbers in schools; teacher training and school building programmes; the universal introduction of television and computing resources into classrooms, with new educational television channels and educational software; the reform of secondary-school teaching to support the most disadvantaged students; the universalization of higher education access, through municipalization of delivery and university television programming, and new educational IT networks; and the extraordinary mushrooming since 2000 of Cuba's University of the Third Age. Similarly, modernization of hospitals, polyclinic health centres and family doctor services has been funded. Over seven thousand public service projects have been implemented under the banner of the 'Battle of Ideas', a programme that cuts through bureaucracy, mobilizing political support and voluntary labour to remind Cubans, especially young Cubans, of what the revolution gives them in spite of material shortages.

Equality of income and wealth

The impact on material equality, though, has been very serious, prompting debate on social stratification and the emergence of new elites (Lievesley 2004: 166–7; Carmona Báez 2004: 206–13; Dilla 1999; Landau 2004: 626). In a society whose official basic salary scale limits the highest salaries to around three times the lowest, the impact of differential access to hard currency through crisis measures such as dollarization, legalizing remittances, self-employment, informal sector work and access to tourist spending has been immense. *El shopping*, hard currency shops opened originally to farm dollars from foreign diplomats and businessmen, offer the most visible sign of income inequality. One Cuban survey estimated that while 4 per cent of households had no hard currency income at all, relying on official salaries whose average value in hard currency terms is about 20 CUC (convertible pesos) a month, some 30 per cent had incomes above 200 CUC, ten times the average, and 8 per cent of Cuban households had incomes exceeding 1,000 CUC a month, fifty times the average salary (Espina et al. 2006). Even assuming three or four incomes per household, these are striking inequalities.

In confronting these deformations of the Special Period, the government has been taking a variety of redistributory measures to reduce inequalities in income and wealth, both by pressing down on high incomes, and dragging up low salaries. Steps have been taken to bear down on illegal and informal incomes by both fiscal and police actions, notably since a keynote Fidel speech asking, in a much-cited passage, 'Just how many ways of stealing do we have in this country?' (Castro Ruz, F. 2005). Measures to curtail illicit acquisition of hard currency were introduced in 2004, to reduce unauthorized currency activities in Cuban enterprises, and in 2005, to control corrupt relations between managers and foreign companies. Breaches of Cuba's managerial Code of Ethics are more severely penalized. In 2005, action was taken against the theft of motor fuel, which apparently stopped the theft of half of Cuba's motor fuel, a key black market commodity (Castro Ruz, F. 2007: 598–9). Such action has intensified, along with action against petty and not-so-petty workplace theft, often rooted in getting hold of materials to resolve some immediate problem, or in just having something to trade in the informal sector. Campaigns in the press, in editorial material and

Cuba

readers' letters have begun to expose short measures and adulteration in the retail sector and other service sector failings.

At the same time, indirect tax measures have been introduced, with more likely in future if new forms of self- or cooperative employment emerge. In 2004, 'de-dollarization' ended legal circulation of US currency. The substitute hard currency, the CUC, gave the government the immediate option of imposing a special 10 per cent fee on dollar exchanges. In 2005 the CUC was then revalued against the dollar, by 8 per cent. In effect the government was now taxing remittances and tourist dollars at 18 per cent, a highly redistributive measure. It also revalued the CUC against the national peso (CUP) by 7.5 per cent, making it slightly cheaper for CUP holders to buy CUCs for *el shopping*, and again slightly devaluing the CUCs that wealthier Cubans held. The level of value-added tax in *el shopping* is between 240 and 270 per cent. In 2007 a measure to tax CUC gifts to workers in mixed foreign–Cuban companies was announced. The government's ambition is to restore a single currency regime, but fears of inflation will make this a gradual process in which every adjustment will be greeted as a gain for equality. The legal redefinition of salary in 2005 to include all plus payments, thus raising sickness, unemployment and holiday benefits, also makes the national insurance tax, levied at between 1 and 5 per cent according to income, more progressive. A more progressive tariff of electricity prices came into effect in 2006 to reduce the subsidy to heavier users in small businesses and wealthier households, and this has been presented as a model for progressive indirect taxation, and an approach that will eventually enable Cuba to dispense with the ration book with its universal distribution of highly subsidized goods (Soberón Valdés 2005; Castro Ruz, F. 2007: 601).

It is much easier to bear down on high incomes than it is to raise low ones. The latter in Cuba's situation requires higher productivity, and wages had actually been rising faster than productivity. Nevertheless, as the macroeconomy recovered to pre-crisis GDP in 2005, modest salary increases across the board followed more generous increases to the poorest, with the minimum wage more than doubling, and tripling the minimum pension. The impact for workers, though, was offset by rising prices in the CUP sector, not least in the food markets (Nova Gonzáles 2006: 231). Some trade union leaders are clear that unless salaries once again become adequate to live on decently, the revolution cannot survive. Dramatically, at the annual commemoration of the 26 July attack on the Moncada barracks, Raúl Castro, then acting president, called for an open national debate on recovering the economy noted above, and set an example with a public admission:

We are equally aware that in the midst of the extreme objective difficulties that we face, salaries are still clearly insufficient for satisfying all necessities, so that in practice they do not perform their role of assuring the socialist principle that everyone contributes according to their capacity and receives according to their work. (Castro Ruz, R. 2007a; author's translation)

In 2008 further pension increases of up to 20 per cent were announced, as were salary increases in some sectors. Given the productivity problems, however, a further legislative reform was announced in Resolución 9/2008. The new law lifted the cap from productivity bonuses for production workers, and was quickly reported in the world's media as the end of Cuban socialism. This was typical of the overdramatization of news coverage from the island after Fidel fell ill. At one level, the change simply rewards 'each according to his work' based on the 'socialist principle of distribution'. At another, although it shifts the emphasis towards individual 'material incentives', it is simply trying to universalize a process of introducing performance-related pay, often with hard currency bonuses, that grew rapidly and haphazardly in the 1990s, mostly in the companies in the Sistema de Perfeccionamiento Empresarial (SPE, System of Business Improvement) scheme originating in 1980s reforms in defence ministry factories (Casas Regueiro et al. 1990; Klepak 2005). By 2005, within SPE companies, salaries rose by 30 per cent in around two-thirds of such companies (*Trabajadores*, 25 April 2005). More generally, as early as 2001, over 1.25 million were receiving bonuses in hard currency, and by 2004 nearly 1.5 million workers (out of 4.6 million in work) were receiving payment-by-results bonuses, according to the minister of labour (Morales Cartaya 2001, 2005). If higher legal incomes reduce black-marketeering, more not less income equality will result, and Cubans' equal access to universal services can only benefit from higher national productivity. Both effects would strengthen Cuba's social democratic egalitarianism.

Economic democracy

By contrast, the fundamental indicator of Cuba's socialist 'exceptionalism' is economic democracy. Two elements are central here: social ownership and government control of the economy; and workers' rights and participation. Despite all the reforms, state ownership and regulation have not been fundamentally weakened. As Carmona Báez demonstrates in detail, state economic supremacy is 'the one pillar of the Revolution that remains constant' (2004: 228). Since he wrote, there have been signs of tighter control of foreign trade by Cuban enterprises, and numbers of foreign trading firms and of mixed enterprises have been reduced (Frank 2005; Marquetti Nodarse 2006: 316). The scale of licensed self-employment has also declined after an initial surge, although unknown numbers work full time in the unlicensed informal sector. The preservation of macro-economic control does not mean, of course, that Cuban workers will not become more alienated or exploited as market forces intrude, but that outcome would result from a political choice by the state. It is likely, as noted above, that Cuba will continue to permit more plural forms of economic activity, but these need not be capitalist forms. An extension of worker cooperatives from agriculture into small-scale manufacturing such as clothing and shoes and motor workshops has been mooted by some Cuban economists (Davis 2007). ALBA agreements on economic integration with Venezuela and Bolivia may require novel relations with private capital from those states. But these would hardly dent Cuba's economic democracy and state regulation. Here the evidence points to the impact of the Special Period as having been just that, special, and limited. As one prominent trade unionist and parliamentarian insists:

> The central point is that we can have different forms of economic activity, as we do, but the role of the state must remain central. ... We can have indirect regulation of different forms of activity but that is not enough, the state must direct the economy. The state is the agent of our democracy in the economy, not market forces. (Interview with Leonel González González, 16 January 2007)

A second touchstone of Cuba's economic democracy is workers' rights. As most of Latin America has simply expelled workers into the informal sector, how has Cuba, facing its own restructuring crisis, treated its workers? Cuba's 1984 Labour Code of fundamental employment rights has become outdated, owing to periodic complementary laws, and to the wider range of enterprise forms and employment relationships introduced. Hence a radical reform of employment relations has been taking place, including an as yet unfinished reform of the Code itself. Given the constitutional right to work, much recent labour legislation has been designed to protect workers from the crisis. Since 1997 there have been new worker grievance procedures, whose first stage is an elected panel of workers (Evenson 2001). Health and safety at work suffered in the crisis, not least because of shortages of equipment and clothing. Legislation in 2002 introduced much tougher obligations on managers, and unions have been running an extensive training programme. The overall number of accidents has fallen, although serious accidents remain a concern.

Resolución 8/2005, the major piece of general labour legislation of recent years, codified protection in redundancy and redeployment situations. No worker can be discarded in redundancy or lay-off situations. This followed the position adopted in the severe contraction of the sugar industry in 2002, which was preceded by negotiations with unions and meetings involving all 900,000 workers; 170,000 went to new jobs, 33,000 took up study and about 4,000 took enhanced early retirement. Restructuring must be agreed with unions and workers' assemblies, and managers must find alternative work or continue to pay salaries. The alternative can be another job, or 'study as a form of work' with workers retaining salaries and employment rights while at college. Laid-off workers receive 100 per cent salary for thirty days, then 60 per cent until alternatives are agreed, and salary was redefined to include plus payments. A culture of training is seen as central. As Elio Valerino, CTC head of labour affairs put it, 'No-one can be made unemployed for lack of training in the face of current or future changes. We have an ageing population facing technological changes but we are training them, not sacking them' (interview, 28 January 2008). Resolución 8/2005 also codified more flexible forms of employment contract, such as part-time, home-working and fixed-term contracts. Individual managers, not just company entities, are now accountable for violations of employment rights.

Cuba is implementing a new model of human resources management, embedded in law and the national standards systems. These are seen as crucial to increased productivity, now that Cuba can plan growth rationally again. Resolución 8/2005 thus provided for annual performance and promotion reviews; the national grade structure has been reformed, and thousands of new job descriptions issued; comprehensive work study, generalized performance-related pay and training systems have been introduced. Other reforms underpinning the new HR system include the use of comprehensive work study. In capitalist societies, such reforms are associated with intensified exploitation and insecurity, and attempts to neuter trade unions. On the latter practice, Dr Francisco Guillén Landrián, Labour Ministry legal director, commented, 'Anyone who did that in Cuba would have to be suicidal or mad' (interview, 17 January 2007). Further, the benefits of increased productivity do not pass to private investors but to Cuban workers, in both personal salaries and public investment. This is fine in theory, but our perspectives on the gaps between constitutional generalities in socialist states and the realities on the shop floor have been conditioned by the experience of 'actually existing socialism' in the Soviet bloc and China. Do Cuba's workers and unions exercise adequate power and influence to make the constitution's 'socialist state of workers' real, in the more complex world of labour that the Special Period heralded?

The 'political power of the workers'

At its 2006 Congress, a CTC resolution enumerated the damage done by the crisis. 'Nevertheless,' the resolution insisted, 'the principal conquests of the Revolution have been preserved, first of all, the political power of the workers' (CTC 2006). Two aspects are addressed here, the making of labour law, and its implementation. Even in the depths of the crisis in the mid-1990s, over two million workers, in specially convened 'workers' parliaments', discussed proposed emergency laws and reported to the National Assembly. Some proposals were then shelved, including proposals to levy income tax for the first time, and to allow mixed-investment firms to employ workers without the full protection of the Labour Code (Evenson 2001). The constitution requires that unions are consulted on new or amended labour law. Although the unions clearly accept a responsibility to help rationalize the economy, they do have an effective veto on labour law proposals. They are also careful not to lose their authority as workers' representatives. In the consultations on reforming the Labour Code, for example, the unions rejected initial proposals to limit their membership of company boards to employment issues, and to limit the right to stop unsafe work to individuals only, removing it from unions. When, in 2008, the government published a plan to reform the retirement age legislation, the National Assembly called on the CTC to organize a *consulta pública*, a mass consultation during a six-month discussion period. The CTC organized over eighty thousand meetings to ensure all workers could participate directly in the debate, and composited workers' opinions for presentation to the legislature.

At the level of implementation, a new law places an explicit obligation on management to implement all labour law, backed by sanctions. More to the point here, labour legislation repeatedly specifies the requirement for union and worker participation and agreement, sometimes specifying new workplace committees for the purpose. Participation in salary system management was set down in law, such that a system of payment by results could not be introduced, even with official union support, if the workers' assembly rejected it. As a senior ministry official insists, 'You must remember that we do nothing, absolutely nothing, until we reach agreement with our comrades in the unions' (interview with Francisco Guillén Landrián, 11 January 2007). When Resolución 9/2008 attracted brief worldwide attention to the lifting of the bonus cap, there was no comment on the fact that the new law, throughout its provisions, specified the requirement of union and worker agreement. And new labour law has to be incorporated into workplace collective bargaining agreements, the *Convenio Colectivo de Trabajo* (CCT).

CCT legislation, which covers all workplaces and all aspects of working life, has also been updated to cover the various new forms of economic entity. The CCT agreement is produced by management and unions, but it has to be approved by the workers' own assembly, providing, in theory, a fundamental guarantee of worker participation and control. An important example emerged in 2006, in a controversy picked up in the world press, over the sensitive area of workplace discipline. As part of the post-crisis drive to renormalize work and raise productivity, legislation was announced on timekeeping and fulfilling the normal working day. During the Special Period, lack of transport, materials and electricity often made normal work practices pointless. Faced with these new discipline proposals, workers pointed out that transport remained too unreliable for normal timekeeping; and shops and offices worked the same hours as other workplaces, so how could workers access them except during their normal working day? After discussion with unions, the ministry delayed implementation for three months. The government announced transport improvements, and negotiations began on changing opening hours in key services. The key protection for workers, which illustrates the persistence of elements of workers' control, was, as the CTC provincial secretary for the City of Havana pointed out, that the new measures had to be incorporated into the workplace collective bargain. Implementation was subject to union negotiation and a final vote in the workers' assembly. Hence, he said, 'Unless the conditions exist, we cannot apply the Resolutions mechanically. The application is flexible. ... Like everything else in Cuba we discuss with the workers' (interview with Raul Hodelín Lugo, 17 January 2007). Collective bargaining has been the subject of a national union training programme to raise participation levels after the process atrophied in the Special Period (CTC 2004; Valdés Mesa 2008). A recent factory-level participation survey found evidence of this training in the workplace (Evenson 2006). The recognition that new levels of trade union expertise and workplace activism are needed in the post-crisis world has also produced a restructuring and refocusing of union resources on workplaces. In 2007, both the government, through a Council of State notice to employers to improve the quality of information provided, and the unions, through a major national programme, prioritized the reinvigoration of monthly workers' assemblies. Raising levels of worker participation is seen as crucial to Cuba's economic recuperation, and to giving life to the constitutional assertion that that workers are the owners in Cuba.

Conclusion

Lawrence Whitehead has argued that Cuba's need to integrate internationally is incompatible with its revolutionary legacy (Whitehead 2007: 8). The argument of this chapter is that the prospect of economic support from Venezuela and China, noted by Whitehead, has since become a reality. Cuba's growth now rests on a variety of trade deals, not least in 'pink tide' Latin America, despite the US blockade. The world fuel and food price crisis emerging in 2008 could not come at a worse time for Cuba, but its people – all, not just some of them – will enjoy as much protection from the effects as any government will deliver, and more than most. This chapter also suggests that, for all the damage to society triggered by the Soviet collapse, there is a determination to preserve what has been called here social democratic equality, equality of access to services, and sufficient equality of wealth to make equality of opportunity real.

The social foundation of popular universal welfare services makes it possible to hypothesize that in the future Cubans might decide to relax state ownership of the economy, and settle for indirect regulation and taxation to sustain their egalitarian *conquistas* – settle, in other words, for some version of radical social democracy or Venezuelan-style twenty-first-century, mixed-economy socialism. There is no sign of this happening. Indeed, Cuba's most profound 'exceptionalism', its socialist economic democracy, its state regulation and workers' rights, not only remains in place, but is the subject of a sustained programme of recovery. Without a restoration of a sense of popular ownership of the revolutionary process, economic recovery alone will not guarantee socialism's survival. This restoration has been going on for some years, and appears to be accelerating under Raúl. For all the disruption and corner-cutting of the Special Period, for all the spread of individualism in the informal sector, underlying commitments to the idea of workers' power in society have not gone away. Change in Cuba remains a process of debate and negotiation, between partners with different roles in a collectivized society, not a life-and-death conflict to impose, or avoid, the private consequences of neoliberal market forces. This is the result of nearly half a century in which, for all the frustration and privation, Cuban workers have come to regard themselves not as subordinate wage slaves, but as the collective partners in a 'socialist state of workers'.

Note

1 This chapter incorporates work supported financially by the Nuffield Foundation and the University of Sheffield. Work for this chapter was made possible by the assistance of many CTC staff. In 2005–08, interviews or multiple interviews were conducted with CTC officers including Raúl Hodelín Lugo, Elio Valerino Santiesteban, Ernesto Freire Cazañas, Luis Manual Castanedo Smith, Ada Benítez Coloa; and with Leonel González González of the National Assembly of Cuba, with Francisco Guillén Landrián of the Ministry of Labour and Social Security; and with specialist labour lawyers including Antonio Raudilio Martín Sánchez, Lydia Guevara Rauniez, Lydia Guevara Rauniez, José Carbonell García, Marta Martinez Navarrao, Francisca Proenza Naranjo and Georgina Cambet Torres. I want also to acknowledge the help of the CTC interpreter, Eddy Brown; and I have also benefited greatly from conversations in Havana with Debra Evenson, whose research prompted my own interest in Cuban labour relations. None of them is responsible for the views expressed above.

8 | Mexico: political parties and local participation

VALERIA GUARNEROS-MEZA

In the 2006 national elections, for the first time since 1989, the Partido de la Revolución Democrática (PRD, Party of the Democratic Revolution), the main left-wing party in Mexico, became the second political force in the country. This outcome was achieved by means of the PRD's coalition with two smaller parties, the Partido del Trabajo (Labour Party) and Convergencia (Convergence) under the banner Por el Bien de Todos (PBT, For the Good of Everyone). The 2006 elections revolved around two leading political forces, the conservative Partido Acción Nacional (PAN, the National Action Party) and the PBT. Almost two months after election day, and following serious criticism of the electoral process, the electoral tribunal finally declared Felipe Calderón (PAN) the new president. This result was not accepted by the PBT and particularly not by its presidential candidate, Andrés Manuel López Obrador, who denounced the electoral process as fraudulent.

The 2006 elections were very tense and competitive. This can be seen not only in the close result of the ballot, with the PAN winning nearly 36 per cent of the votes and the PRD 35 per cent, but also in the 'negative' campaigning strategies that the parties employed. An example of these negative strategies was the television and radio propaganda sponsored by the PAN, which suggested that López Obrador posed a danger to Mexico, as his policies while mayor of Mexico City had incurred public debt and resulted in economic crisis. And, vice versa, propaganda sponsored by the PRD declared that Calderón and his party promoted fascist policies. The electoral tribunal responded slowly to the media struggle between the parties, and this provoked criticism from intellectuals and the general public, who felt the negative campaigning was propelling voters towards abstention. In the end, electoral turnout reached 58.5 per cent, five percentage points lower than in 2000 and twelve lower than the average turnout between 1978 and 2004 (Latinobarómetro 2006: 12). The tribunal's reputation as a strong democratic institution was also adversely affected when the PRD declared on the day after the election that the vote count at many polling stations did not correspond to the official results and asked for a recount of 40 per cent of ballot boxes.

The electoral tribunal decided, however, to recount only 2 per cent, and Calderón was confirmed as the victor. The PRD's appeal may not have changed the electoral results, but it highlighted the need for reform of polling station practice and the elimination of negative political campaigning. Over the next two months, the PBT responded to the recount results with demonstrations and the organization of public sit-down protests in central Mexico City with close to one million supporters taking part. The PBT finally ended the occupations in response to the massive traffic problems they created. These demonstrations marked the emergence of a new social movement comprising urban and rural popular groups and unions, represented by the three-party coalition which, in September 2006, formed the Frente Amplio Progresista (FAP, the Broad Progressive Front) led by López Obrador. In November 2006, the latter declared himself the 'legitimate' president of Mexico, while a few weeks later Calderón took office as the 'legal or institutional' president.

The mobilizations led by López Obrador shifted from an electoral to a social focus with the aim of keeping the issues of poverty, inequality and human rights on the political agenda. Although a diverse range of groups comprise the FAP, it is worth mentioning other groups that did not support the PRD during the election and continue not to endorse López Obrador's leadership. These groups are composed of independent, middle-class citizens who are aware of Mexico's weaknesses in consolidating a democratic state, and who are concerned about the country's unequal distribution of wealth and poverty. These citizens stopped supporting López Obrador, however, because of his personal stubbornness, and his intolerant and contradictory declarations against democratic and republican institutions. Furthermore, radical groups such as the Ejército Zapatista de Liberación Nacional (EZLN, the Zapatista Army of National Liberation), the Ejército Popular y Revolucionario (EPR, the Popular Revolutionary Army) and the Asamblea Popular de los Pueblos de Oaxaca (APPO, the Popular Assembly of the Peoples of Oaxaca) have publicly distanced themselves from López Obrador's campaign, claiming that it is immersed in political intrigue and corruption.

This chapter argues that one of the reasons for the lack of support given to López Obrador by some citizens and radical groups is the PRD's inability to distinguish itself from the centre-right policies of the PAN and the former governing party, the Partido Revolucionario Institucional (PRI, the Revolutionary Institutional Party). This is not to underestimate the PRD's local achievements in, for example, Mexico City or Zacatecas state, which have been its strongholds since the mid-1990s. Indeed, what the chapter seeks to show is the discrepancy between its national and local agendas and, particularly, its failure to incorporate its municipal innovations at a national level. The first part of the chapter provides a brief discussion of Mexico's democratization and decentralization processes and the PRD's involvement in them. This is followed by a discussion of the different approaches to governance and how these can be applied to the Mexican case. The final section compares the PRD's record in promoting citizen participation at the municipal level with the strategies followed by the PAN and the PRI.

Mexico's democratization and decentralization processes

Analysts have identified parallel processes of democratization and decentralization in contemporary Mexico (Aziz-Nassif 2003; Levy et al. 2001; Rochlin 1997). With regard to the electoral system, it has been argued that Mexico has followed a positive path in so far as political pluralism has been observed in the national legislative bodies since 1997. In 2000, the transfer of power from the authoritarian PRI to the right-wing PAN was seen as another step towards democratic consolidation. In the July 2006 general election, the closeness of the result indicated strong political competitiveness, although there were serious doubts about the system's integrity.

At the sub-national level, democratization is demonstrated by the political diversity of local governments in contemporary Mexico. From the early 1980s, some of these were captured by political parties that opposed the PRI; this was particularly the case in the northern and central areas of the country. By 2005, the PRI controlled only 27 per cent of municipal governments, a huge drop from the 90 per cent control it had in 1994. Between 1994 and 2005, municipalities governed by the PAN increased from 4 to 21 per cent and those by the PRD from 4 to 12 per cent (Porras 2005).

Apart from facilitating alternation in government by political parties, the democratization process has also strengthened the checks and balances that structure relations between local executive and legislative bodies (Rodríguez et al. 1999). Local vested interests and political rivalries can, however, threaten the effectiveness of democratization (Cornelius et al. 1999; Aziz-Nassif 2003). Among the latter's positive effects have been the introduction of new actors emerging from the democratic social movements of the 1980s, accompanied by neoliberalism's legitimization strategy of citizen incorporation in the delivery of basic services and policy-making in the 1990s (Foweraker 1995; O'Toole 2003; Ramírez-Saiz 2003). The involvement of new actors has created a series of collaborative arrangements, not only across different tiers of governmental bodies, but also with non-governmental organizations. A series of decentralizing reforms in the fiscal and administrative sectors has sought to make sub-national stakeholders more responsible for promoting local development, and has had the result of improving the administration and delivery of public services, especially in large urban areas. Municipal authorities face a number of challenges, including an increasingly urban population, limited fiscal resources and economic problems that do not directly fall under the competencies of municipal governments (such as unemployment and investment). Such challenges have prompted local governments to look for new forms of organization in which the public, private and community sectors can collaborate. In Mexico, multi-sector collaboration is realized in areas such as the contracting-out of public services, but most of all through the creation of citizen councils or committees which implement national and sub-national legislation (such as the Law of Fiscal Coordination and the Law of Participation).

Neoliberalism and the PRD's political trajectory

The institutionalized left in Mexico has developed an anti-neoliberal, although not an inherently anti-capitalist, discourse (Stolowicz 2004). Although there are other organizations, since its creation in 1989 the PRD has dominated the left's political landscape. Since then, it has striven to unite left-wing groups through a series of alliances, the most recent being the PBT and FAP. The political demands behind these initiatives have been the strengthening of the judicial system and national security, the enhancement of human rights (including political participation), and the reduction of income inequalities. Although the FAP represents diverse left-wing groups, its common objective is to fight the elitist and conservative policies implemented by the neoliberal PAN and the neoliberal faction of the PRI, and to achieve progress in areas such as poverty and inequality; national sovereignty (especially with regard to energy and other natural resources); an end to oligarchic governance; access to public information; and profound reforms to the systems of justice and electoral representation (Nueva Izquierda 2007). The social mobilization that facilitated the FAP's emergence highlighted once again two challenges that have preoccupied the PRD since its foundation, and which are reflected at both the national and local levels (González 2003). These are the unification of the different left-wing currents within the party and the balance between social movement interests, and the need to institutionalize the party (Prud'homme 1997; Nueva Izquierda 2007). The latter issue has created an institutional crisis because López Obrador both leads the political front, which itself is supported by a social movement, and maintains his PRD membership. There was, for example, a period of confusion in late 2006 when PRD state governors had to decide whether to support the traditional, constitutional institutions, and thus recognize Calderón's presidency, or support López Obrador's claim to be running an alternative presidency.

With regard to intergovernmental relations, the challenge that the PRD has encountered is the creation of an integrated national strategy, reflected at state and municipal levels of government (Nueva Izquierda 2007; Prud'homme 1997). It has had considerable experience in local government and has developed innovative policies and programmes, but these have tended to be shaped to suit specific local conditions. This is the case, for example, with the participatory budgeting initiative in Tlalpan, Mexico City, and the inter-municipal collaboration promoting public–business partnerships in Zacatecas state (Flores 2005; García, G. 2003). These innovations have not had an impact on the party's national political strategy.

Among its local policy innovations, the PRD has promoted citizen participation through plebiscitary initiatives, participatory budgeting and citizen councils. It has designed inclusive participatory systems at the neighbourhood level, and has introduced management reforms that secure financial and service delivery efficiency. Both the PAN and the PRI have, however, also implemented local strategies that target participation and the improvement of public management and services. Some scholars argue that the PRD has been more flexible than the other parties in incorporating citizens' views within the decision-making process, although it is still unclear how any party balances the priorities of citizens with those of politicians (Morales, M. 2005; Porras 2005).

As a result of the political, economic and social changes that Mexico has experienced since the 1980s, the PRD has been made aware of the multiple dimensions of action and negotiation that the country's commitment to neoliberal democracy has entailed. This awareness is reflected in party literature on international relations, including publications on the left in other countries, social forums against neoliberalism, the dominance of the USA over Mexico, and the role of international organizations in promoting neoliberal policies (Nueva Izquierda 2007). Although the PRD is thus aware of international stakeholders, there is little discussion of local stakeholders (for example, municipal associations and local government officials) in its publications, with the result that the party's awareness of local initiatives and the institutional capacity required to sustain them remains vague.

Governance in Mexico

The liberalization of trade and interest rates, the implementation of structural adjustment policies and the re-regulation of certain trade and fiscal policies have required interactions between multiple organizations and stakeholders and have also stimulated new forms of political organization. There has been an increasing tendency for government to play the role of manager rather than that of provider. As result, a greater interdependency has developed between organizations from different social sectors (for example, the private and voluntary) and on different levels of action (the transnational, national and sub-national). This complex interdependency has been characterized by three features: overlapping responsibilities between the organizations providing common goods and public services; formal and informal methods of agreement to achieve specific goals; and a tendency to create public–private and public–civil relationships.

In Mexico, the promotion of federalism and the implementation of decentralization policies since the 1990s have involved a multiplicity of actors belonging to different tiers of government. Furthermore, different organizational models of governance have been developed through the promotion and creation of public–private partnerships for regenerating a public place, for example historic centres (Guarneros-Meza 2006); the change of land use from rural to urban purposes (Jones and Pisa 2000); the provision of basic services (Porras 2005); and the creation of metropolitan agencies across capital cities (Rodríguez-Acosta and Rosenbaum 2005). Municipal authorities, the business sector, professional groups and citizens have all collaborated in these processes. Multi-actor and multi-tier forms of organization have been part of the institutional reforms promoted by democratization and decentralization since the 1980s. Public–private relationships have helped to break with the legacies of the past: ending clientelism; dismantling bureaucratized public administrations; promoting civic awareness of government performance in service delivery; and improving the accountability of public administration (Ramírez-Saiz 1998, 2003; Bolaños and González 2004; Méndez-Ortíz 2005). Reform has created an environment in which diverse channels of participation have emerged for different citizens and interest groups. The political parties have, however, paid scant attention to issues that affect popular participation, such as inclusion, the distribution of power within decision-making, and capacity-building for sustaining multi-collaboration. All the parties have failed to reflect the importance of these issues in their national programmes (Morales, M. 2005; Porras 2005; Nueva Izquierda 2007). If the PRD hopes to distinguish itself from the PAN and PRI, it must incorporate

145

local initiatives that address inclusion, power and capacity-building into its national participatory agenda.

The different discourses of governance

Different forms of governance create an opportunity for the direct participation of non-state actors in policy decisions and may facilitate the inclusion of individuals and groups that would have been marginalized by authoritarian regimes. The potential inclusion of civil representatives into policy-making has created a normative stance for governance, what the World Bank and the United Nations define as 'good governance'. 'Good governance' may not be achievable, however, if existing national and local structures and vested interests undermine efforts to promote participation and accountability. Although the implementation of governance has the potential to promote inclusion and participation, it may fail to do so if social and political processes depart from genuine democratic principles. For example, the existence of public–private relationships raises questions about who is being involved in these sorts of arrangements, their transparency, and the nature of coordination and collaboration within these new channels of participation. Lack of clarity on these questions has led to the identification of three types of discourse observed within governance models: the managerialist, the consociational and the participatory (Skelcher et al. 2005). The conflation of discourses is the main cause of the PRD's lack of distinctiveness.

The managerialist discourse emphasizes the efficiency, effectiveness and economy of public services and focuses mainly on user satisfaction. In Mexico, the implementation and delivery of local services have been provided mainly by the public sector. As previously discussed, it is unclear how the priorities of citizens and managers are balanced and how citizens' influence over the policy-making process is achieved under PRD, PAN and PRI administrations (Morales, M. 2005; Porras 2005). The PRD's efforts to promote better public services have been observed in at least two different ways: the simplification of bureaucratic processes – for example, citizens' payment of taxes and fees in the municipality of Nezahualcóyotl, State of Mexico (Arzaluz 2002); and the enhancement of municipal governments' capacity-building as a consequence of decentralization, such as the provision of electricity in the city of Acapulco using the municipality's own resources (Gómez 2002). Both of these strategies have helped to reduce corruption, but unsurprisingly have also been adopted by the PRI and PAN.

Population growth and scarce public resources, particularly within urban municipalities, have prompted authorities to look for innovative ways of providing public services. Privatization – for example, of water in the city of Aguascalientes – has been suggested but it has not been an option popular with many Mexican municipalities. The creation of local public–private relationships in the form of citizen councils and commissions, where non-governmental representatives of professional and expert organizations sit together and negotiate the delivery of a service, is a more widespread strategy. The creation of these councils and commissions has occurred in municipalities governed by all political parties, but the PRD has included a more diverse range of civil groups, from social movement representatives to small rural or urban businesses – for example, local popular groups in Nezahualcóyotl and the Municipal Association of Local Development in Zacatecas (Arzaluz 2002; García, G. 2003). In contrast, the PRI has recruited from traditional sectoral entities such as unions and student groups while the PAN has selected professional, middle- and upper-class individuals. These are general tendencies; in practice, they are often not so rigorously delineated (Arzaluz 2002; Cabrero 2005; Porras 2005).

The consociational discourse provides an environment for coalitions among a variety of social groups in a population, but the coalition can then employ an elitist decision-making structure. In the case of the PRD, the members of the coalition tend to represent communities in addition to unions and business groups such as chambers of commerce and industry. The PRD's inability to keep these divergent interests united has often lost it electoral support, from both moderate and radical groups (Nueva Izquierda 2007). The case of Mexico City has been exceptional in that PRD administrations since 1997 have demonstrated an ability to maintain a diverse coalition composed of business, including Carlos Slim's consortium (Slim was the world's second-richest man in 2008, www.forbes.comm/2008/03/08), non-governmental organizations and moderate popular groups for the purpose of regenerating the historic city centre.

In the cases of the PAN and the neoliberal faction of the PRI, the local elite leadership has been characterized by its members' middle- or upper-class background. These local elites have secured the social recognition and respect of the rest of population over a period of decades. These characteristics seem to be reflected in middle-size, conservative cities governed by both the PAN and the PRI, such as Puebla, Querétaro, Guadalajara, León and San Luis Potosí (Cabrero 2005; Guarneros-Meza 2006; Jones and Varley 1999; Ramírez-Saiz 1998). Their class nature results in coalition meetings being held in private, rendering them publicly unaccountable. Public–private relationships concerned with city-centre

regeneration programmes have proved to be the arena where the maintenance of social order, security, economic development and exclusive
citizen participation have been promoted (Guarneros-Meza 2006). Of the
three political parties, the PRD has encountered the greatest challenges
in reducing internal conflicts within its consociational forms of organization. The challenge arises from the incorporation of a variety of left-wing
grassroots groups and groups from a conservative and liberal stance
within specific governing coalitions, such as Mexico City's regeneration
programme.

The participatory discourse extends policy-making authority to wider
community actors in order to achieve a more sustainable alternative to the
dominant market-oriented managerialist political economy. It is based on
participatory democratic principles with local communities collectively
identifying impediments to the achievement of a better quality of life and
as a result working together to create long-term sustainable solutions. In
several municipalities where the PRD has governed, participatory forms
representing this discourse have been observed through referenda, community fora, neighbourhood committees and citizen councils (Flores
2005; Porras 2005). A distinctive characteristic of the PRD's strategies
has been the promotion of fora as spaces where minority groups such
as women and children have a voice to promote human rights, such as
the Women's Forum in Nezahualcóyotl and the Children's Council in
Acapulco (Arzaluz 2002; Santín and Tapia 2006). In contrast, local administrations run by the PAN have created innovative forms of citizen participation through flagship programmes in municipalities in central and
northern Mexico, such as 'Citizens' Days' and the Institutes of Municipal
Planning (Cabrero 2005; Guarneros-Meza 2006; Porras 2005). Over time,
the former have become spaces for citizens' voices while the latter have
grown into more formal institutions which collate the views of 'expert'
citizens and thus facilitate planning procedures. Case studies have found
that participation in citizen councils in PRD municipalities has allowed
people to have greater influence than in those local governments run by
the PRI or the PAN – examples include the citizen councils in Zacatecas
City and participatory budgeting in Mexico City (Flores 2005; Porras 2005).
The decision-making process, however, remains opaque in all cases. The
mode of operation of these citizen councils and the way in which they
arrive at decisions are unclear. Many questions have arisen regarding
the following issues: relationships of power between politicians and
citizens; the frequency with which community groups have influenced
policy decisions; and the representativeness of individuals or leaders
of community groups participating within the councils. Furthermore,

none of the three main political parties seems to be promoting citizen participation as a means of achieving political change or of strengthening deliberative forms of participation (Morales, M. 2005).

Finally, PRD local administrations have also been characterized by their promotion of assistance programmes to marginalized citizens and communities. These combine municipal financial and administrative resources with citizens' resources, mainly labour or skills. This characteristic is not unique to the PRD, however, as it has also been promoted by the PRI through the legacies of the 1992 Solidarity Programme and, in the past six years, by PAN administrations which have focused upon social policies to alleviate poverty (Morales, M. 2005). Governmental strategies revolving around accountancy rules and performance benchmarking underpin the meaning of liberal democratic governance (Swyngedouw 2005). Managerialist and consociational discourses contribute to this meaning. As the PRD was founded at the same time as neoliberal democracy was emerging, the party adopted these governance discourses but also challenged them. This ambiguity is reflected in the PRD's institutionalized structures and relations. Thus, it is not surprising that the party struggles to maintain a balance between ideals of communal trust and support which characterize grassroots forms of organization, and ideals of managerialism and consociational negotiation. This struggle has been reflected in its internal divisions at the national level with the emergence of two main factions since the 2006 general elections: these are the groups that support López Obrador, Izquierda Unida (United Left) and Nueva Izquierda (New Left). The former stresses the importance of popular support while the latter focuses on discourses of accountancy-based discipline and performance.

In practice, the three governance discourses can exist at the same time in the same municipality, being used for different policy projects (Arzaluz 2002; Flores 2005). Thus, it is common to find a managerialist discourse, in which an organizational relationship exists between municipal government and the local business sector with the aim of improving the quality of local administration processes. At the same time, it is possible to observe a consociational discourse where a public–private partnership promoting the city's development exists, but which only experts and professional groups are invited to join. Finally, one can encounter a more participatory discourse in neighbourhood partnerships with local government where 'ordinary' citizens can get involved in the improvement of their living areas, using methods based on the Brazilian participatory budget model. This combination of discourses is discernible in several municipal policies implemented in Querétaro, San Luis Potosí, León and some municipalities in Mexico City's metropolitan area, all of which have been run by at least one of the three main political parties since the 1990s (Arzaluz 2002; Guarneros-Meza 2006; Porras 2005). It is difficult to assess what needs to be built up first, the institutions promoting citizen participation or the capacity for sustaining these institutions. Chávez and Goldfrank argue that those Latin American municipal governments that have promoted new direct forms of citizen participation have been able to improve the quality of public services (Chávez and Goldfrank 2004). It is also possible to argue, however, that managerialist practices need to be implemented and developed in order to guarantee the effectiveness and efficiency of those participatory forms (Arzaluz 2002).

The three discourses can be understood and applied by stakeholders for different policy purposes based on their own interests and subject to national and local specificities, including historical traditions and cultural norms. In clarifying how local PRD bodies could take into account citizen and grassroots views within local decision-making processes, the party could begin to differentiate itself from the neoliberal participatory forms promoted by the PRI and PAN. In failing to clarify the rules of local participation, deliberation and decision-making, the PRD has linked itself to the hegemonic model of neoliberal participation. Furthermore, while the PRD has been an innovative stakeholder at the local level, its national leadership has failed to integrate these practices into the party's national agenda.

Conclusions

The importance of local governance cannot be ignored when studying Mexican politics. This is partly because of national policies that have combined decentralization and democratization discourses. Both processes have tended not only to consolidate local institutions of representative democracy, but also to promote inter-sectoral collaboration and new routes for participatory democracy to influence the policy-making process. The institutionalized left in Mexico dominated by the PRD has run the risk of interpreting governance in the same way as that adopted by the centre-right-wing political parties. Both the PAN and the PRI understand governance as a procedure to facilitate efficient administration rather than a way of strengthening the contribution of grassroots movements and community organizations to policy-making. The reason why the PRD adopted the same interpretation was because it emerged at a time when perspectives on democracy were shaped by the dominance of the neoliberal economic model and the reforms it implemented (Stolowicz 2004).

The PRD needs to re-evaluate its approach towards its municipal government achievements and integrate them into its national agenda. This would in itself not solve the PRD's problems as defined by commentators such as Denise Dresser, who argues that López Obrador and the PRD must consider how to introduce legislation rather than just blocking that of other parties, how to surmount the right's intransigence and how to become protagonist rather than victim (Dresser 2007). Nevertheless, this chapter's purpose has been to suggest a way in which the PRD can become more distinctive by accentuating its accomplishments in the implementation and evaluation of local policy-making. Other governments, such as those of Brazil and Venezuela, have recognized the importance of local governance, as is demonstrated by their embrace of participatory budgeting and the Barrio Adentro programme. Recognizing the significance of their municipal initiatives and replicating them at a national level has greatly assisted in defining the identity of these governing parties. The PRD is aware of these programmes, but has not yet managed to follow their example.

It is important for the PRD to define its identity as a political force and to resolve the ideological differences that have led to its fragmentation. The PRD's factions disagree on whether the priority should be to consolidate the party's institutional capacity or its electability, or to strengthen its relationship with the popular movement. This internal crisis has been interpreted by the centre-right as a forerunner of the eventual disintegration of the institutionalized left. This might be an exaggeration, but nevertheless the PRD needs to be cautious and make strenuous efforts to reconcile its warring factions. Certainly, it has made great progress, becoming the second-most important political force in the country following the 2006 elections. This has enabled it to highlight the fact that Mexico is a society divided between rich and poor, a condition that neoliberal reform has done nothing to ameliorate and one that continues to preoccupy the popular movement. Moreover, the PRD's electoral appeals have stimulated debate on the need to reform the electoral system.

Democracy and decentralization have brought greater political diversity to Mexico and the PRD should recognize this and adopt a stance of acceptance, dialogue and tolerance to others on the left who do not support it. In contrast to other countries discussed in this book, Mexico has not yet elected a left-wing government. A left does exist but it is divided. Apart from the factionalism that besets the PRD, there are other groups such as the EZLN which prefer not to engage with electoral politics and which prize their political autonomy (EZLN 2005; Hérnandez-Navarro

2006). The *Caracoles* (literally, snails) and Juntas de Buen Gobierno (Good Government Councils) run by the Zapatistas are examples of local political autonomy in that they develop local policy-making based on the communities' customary law. On the one hand, these councils have brought issues such as human rights and environmental conservation into the national arena and have introduced new governance structures that challenge traditional approaches to participation and state structures within the Mexican federal system. On the other hand, however, the political autonomy that the Zapatistas claim to have has also been shaped by the political and social changes the country has experienced. The promotion of the rights of women and children is a challenge for these groups as indigenous customary laws privilege community values, which in many cases undermine the rights of minorities. It is important that the PRD supports the development of these autonomous communities and regains their trust.

Looking forward to the 2012 elections, it is likely that the PRD will try to form alliances with others on the left. This will be a difficult task, made harder by the fact that the differences between Izquierda Unida and Nueva Izquierda have intensified since the 2006 elections. If the PRD decides to become a distinctive and trustworthy party, it will need to design a strategy that facilitates reconciliation between the need to ensure the distinctive identities of social movement identities and the need to have institutionalized political activity. A step towards this may have been the PRD and FAP's joint opposition to President Calderón's oil privatization plans in May 2008. Their protest postponed the Congress's ordinary sessions, thus giving all political parties more time to reconsider an initiative that had not been fully worked out. The PRD organized conferences and seminars with the participation of professional and expert groups with the aim of justifying maintaining oil nationalization at the same time as developing technology to support it. These activities provided the PRD with the means to combat the privatization proposals, which were supported by the PAN and PRI. This collaboration is just an initial step, however, and it remains to be seen whether the PRD can move closer to the grassroots as well as expanding its influence within a democratic political culture characterized by negotiation and debate. A PRD victory in 2012 would be of enormous political significance. It would bring the most populous Spanish-speaking country in the world, a country in NAFTA, into the orbit of the new Latin American politics and could raise expectations of social justice to new levels of intensity.

9 | Brazil: has the dream ended?

SUE BRANFORD

Luiz Inácio Lula da Silva, a former industrial worker, was elected president of Brazil on 27 October 2002. Not only was he Brazil's first working-class president, he was also one of the founders of a new-style political party, the Partido dos Trabalhadores (PT, Workers' Party), which promised both far-reaching structural reforms and an end to Brazil's corrupt, clientelist politics. Brazil has long been one of the most unjust societies in the world, with land and income concentrated in the hands of a small elite. Finally, it seemed, these deep-seated problems would be tackled.

Not surprisingly, a wave of excitement swept through the country. 'São Paulo's Avenida Paulista is a monument to money: the wide avenue is lined with the solid concrete and glass towers of giant banking corporations,' wrote one journalist.

> But on election night, a sea of red flags lapped at the doors of the banks as thousands of supporters of the victorious PT waited for their hero, chanting campaign slogans. When he appeared on a giant screen making his acceptance speech, men and women wept with joy – and disbelief. Was this really happening? After thirteen years and three failed attempts at the presidency, was Luiz Inácio Lula da Silva really President of Brazil? Had the left-wing finally come to power after 500 years of rule by the elite, the military, the landowners, the bankers? (Rocha 2002: 9)

> The celebrations occurred all over the country.

> About 3,000 kilometres to the north, in the poverty-stricken rural hamlet of Caetés in the interior of the state of Pernambuco, people poured out into the streets as soon as the election result was announced on television. Old people hugged each other. Young people danced around the *trio elétrico* (a procession float), decked out in the Workers' Party's distinctive red flags, as it made its way through the streets, blaring Carnival music. Fireworks went off. Here in the so-called 'Republic of the Silvas' nearly everyone carries the surname and is – or claims to be – a relative of the new President. 'We never thought it would happen,' said a cousin, fifty-three-year-old José Ricardo Silva. 'We just dreamed it would, like we dream each year for rain.' (Rocha 2002)

The election of the PT government was widely seen as the most exciting political development in Latin America since the election of the Marxist Salvador Allende in Chile in 1970. Lula's victory came at a time when the region, which for more than two decades had been dutifully and painfully implementing the IMF's neoliberal reforms, was coming alive with protest again. In Venezuela, Hugo Chávez had somewhat unexpectedly been elected to power in December 1998, because of widespread disillusion with the old, corrupt political parties. In Bolivia, Evo Morales, who had gained national prominence by organizing the coca growers, came close to winning the presidential elections in 2002 on a strongly anti-neoliberal programme (and was eventually elected in 2005). In Argentina the spectacular collapse of the neoliberal project in December 2001 had led to the emergence of exciting new forms of local participatory democracy such as the *asambleas populares* (popular assemblies) and factory takeovers by workers. Against this background of simmering discontent, the PT's victory in Brazil's presidential election was clearly the most important gain for the left until then. There were real hopes that the PT would lead a continent-wide search for a genuine alternative to neoliberalism. This chapter analyses the reasons for PT's subsequent economic orthodoxy in office; assesses its achievements and limitations in the areas of social, agrarian and environmental policy; and notes the continuation of Brazilian ambition to be the region's dominant state.

Reality check

The euphoria was short-lived. The first two years of Lula's first administration were marked by severe budget cuts and highly recessionary monetary policies, in strict obedience to the IMF (Branford and Kucinski 2003). The original PT manifesto had promised 8 million new jobs in four years. Instead, the government's policies led to the loss of more than half a million jobs in just five months. PT militants were bitterly disappointed. They were particularly astonished by Lula's decision to hand control of the Central Bank and some other key areas of the economy, such as exports and agricultural production, to prominent bankers and other representatives of the *ancien régime*. The centre–left alliance envisaged in the original manifesto was replaced by an alliance with conservative forces. There were widespread complaints from PT grassroots supporters that Lula had betrayed his promises.

Two factors largely account for Lula's decision to adopt highly orthodox policies. One stems from the transformation that the PT had undergone. The PT emerged from the 'new' trade unionism of the late 1970s. In 1975, when Lula was elected president of the metalworkers' union of

São Bernardo and Diadema, the heart of Brazil's booming car industry on the outskirts of São Paulo, unions were largely apolitical. Workers turned to them for subsidized health treatment and other social benefits, not for higher wages or better working conditions. Lula and the other young union leaders changed this, developing a union movement that, through a series of strikes in 1978, mounted the first serious challenge to the military government. Other strikes soon erupted, and that year over half a million workers were involved, many winning pay rises above those authorized by the government. The government's wage policy came under serious threat for the first time. But the strikes did not deliver the benefits that the union leaders had hoped for: wage increases were eroded, and companies reneged on their promise not to carry out reprisal sackings.

The experience convinced Lula and other union leaders of the need to create their own political party, the first party created and run outside the control of professional politicians. By then, the military government, in power since 1964, was faltering. Intellectuals, and Catholic radicals influenced by 'liberation theology' priests, were also pressing for the restoration of democracy. In 1980 these forces came together and formed the PT. A new phase in Brazilian history began. The PT grew rapidly and restoration of civilian government in 1985 approached. The PT began to win elections, first for municipal governments and then at state level. In the early 1990s, however, Brazil belatedly adopted the neoliberal reforms being imposed on much of Latin America at the time. Trade barriers were slashed and the market flooded with cheap imported manufactured goods. One-third of manufacturing jobs were lost. State companies were privatized, and thousands of public sector jobs were wiped out. The social base of the PT was shattered. The party responded by moving to the centre and focusing on becoming an efficient, professional political machine. In what many see as a betrayal of the PT's original vision, power became concentrated in the hands of professional politicians, and the earlier practice of consulting the base on important decisions was weakened and eventually abandoned. Although the PT constantly reiterated its commitment to ethical government – a message popular with the middle classes – it lost its original commitment to absolute honesty and transparency. Desperate to raise campaign funds, it secretly began to involve itself in the corrupt practices it had so strongly criticized in the past. Activists were profoundly shaken when, in 2005, evidence was uncovered of systemic political corruption by elements within the PT.

In spite of municipal and state-level victories, the big prize of the national presidency eluded the PT. In 1998, shortly after his third presidential defeat, Lula made it clear to the PT leadership that he would run for a fourth time only if he were given a free hand to form alliances across the political spectrum. The new strategy, devised with the PT's president, José Dirceu, was rigorously enforced. The PT ran an all-inclusive presidential campaign in which, with the support of some sugary and politically dubious TV commercials built around the slogan 'Lula, Peace and Love', it sought to win over traditionally hostile sectors of society, particularly the business community. It selected Senator José Alencar from the small, right-of-centre Liberal Party as Lula's running-mate. Alencar, who owned Brazil's largest textile company, Coteminas, and had a personal fortune of about US$500 million, was progressive to the extent that he paid his workers a decent wage – at least by Brazilian standards – and allowed them to form independent unions. And he was a nationalist. Even so, he was still clearly part of the business establishment. Many of the PT's oldest supporters, above all left-wing intellectuals, were horrified, particularly because the Liberal Party was closely linked to the socially conservative, evangelical Universal Church of the Kingdom of God. But Lula's strategy worked, and he won the second round of the 2002 elections with a large majority. Afterwards he commented that he had won just as he had always dreamed of winning: in a clean contest without personal abuse or dirty tricks. It soon became clear, however, that Lula had toned down the PT's strategy in order to cement the new alliances.

The second factor behind the Lula government's unexpected decision to adopt highly orthodox economic policies was external. Four months before the 2002 election, the Hungarian-born US financial speculator George Soros said that Brazil would face economic meltdown if it elected Lula. Foreign newspapers described Lula as a 'left-wing populist', close to Hugo Chávez and Fidel Castro, and some right-wing Miami papers even included him as part of the 'axis of evil', alongside Iraq, Iran and North Korea. José Serra, the other leading presidential candidate, added to the climate of panic by warning that Brazil, under Lula, could become another Argentina – a reference to the crisis that hit the Argentine economy and political system in 2002 after the government defaulted on its foreign debt. Opinion polls showed that the fear of an Argentine-style crisis was widespread, particularly among the poor and the lower middle class. Lula and his aides became convinced that they must take pre-emptive action, to forestall a speculative attack on the currency which could wreck his administration even before it started. Two months before polling day, Lula issued a 'Letter to the Brazilian People' which reiterated his promise to change the country's economic policies, but also undertaking to respect existing contracts and commitments, a coded message that his government would not default on the foreign debt or, for that matter, on the even larger domestic debt.

Even so, by January 2003, when Lula was sworn into office, the national currency, the real, had lost 30 per cent of its value against the dollar, and some rating agencies were putting 'Brazil risk' at over 1,300 points, one of the highest rates in the world. This meant that Brazil's foreign debt certificates (the so-called C bonds) were traded on the speculative secondary market at an interest rate thirteen percentage points above that of US Treasury bills. More than US$6 billion in hot money left the country in three months. George Soros's prediction was becoming a self-fulfilling prophecy. Luiz Dulci, Lula's closest aide, says that the new government was facing meltdown:

> We reckoned that the chronic financial instability, now reaching a new peak, had disorganized the Brazilian economy to such an extent that it was having an impact on social behaviour and public morality. The country had lost not only international credibility, but also confidence in itself. It was becoming a plaything in the hands of world speculators. (Interviewed in Branford and Kucinski 2003: 8)

This was the background against which Lula and his advisers decided to hand over the running of the Central Bank to the bankers themselves – although under the direction of a high-ranking and long-standing PT cadre, Antônio Palocci, who became finance minister. The agreement with the IMF was quickly reaffirmed, and the target for the public sector surplus, required to service the internal debt, was set higher, at 4.25 per cent of GDP, than even the IMF demanded. This was designed to produce a 'credibility shock' among foreign investors and to appease speculators and banks.

A month later, Lula also introduced a 45 per cent budget cut, which affected most programmes, including social ones. The 'credibility shock' worked on the foreign front, reversing the outflow of capital, drawing praise from conservative quarters. But a parallel 'loss of credibility shock' rocked left-wing intellectuals and economists, and many PT supporters. Lula himself went through an initial period of anguish in which he could barely sleep, visibly tormented. As time passed, conservative figures in the Central Bank gained enough political autonomy to confront the government itself. The Central Bank not only kept interest rates high, but even increased them to 26.5 per cent, the highest in the world. By May 2003, unemployment in São Paulo, the country's largest conurbation, reached a record 20.6 per cent. Inflation was forced down, but at the cost of wiping out economic growth during the first year of Lula's term. Many PT stalwarts believed that the party could still deliver far-reaching structural change and economic growth, once external creditors had been reassured. But was this what the government was planning?

Growth at any cost

By the end of the first PT administration in 2006, it was clear that this was not Lula's strategy. Indeed, it was later revealed that Lula had decided very early in his administration that he had to accept the central tenets of the neoliberal agenda. According to a report in *Valor Econômico*, in May 2008 (reported in *Folha de S. Paulo*, 11 May), confidential documents from the US State Department revealed that Lula had promised the Bush administration not to produce 'surprises' in economic policy. Any hopes nurtured by PT activists that Lula would slowly construct an alternative to neoliberalism were a pipe dream. Lula's overriding priority was more modest and more achievable: to get the economy growing strongly again. This did not mean that Lula abandoned his earlier desire to improve the lot of the very poor, but it was no longer to be achieved through structural change, rather through a much bigger outlay on social welfare.

During the Lula administrations, Brazil's global integration has been strengthened. The government's big investment project, called Projeto de Acceleração do Crescimento (PAC, Acclerated Growth Project), envisages a total investment of R$504 billion (£153 billion) by the end of 2010. PAC forms part of a much bigger South American project, Iniciativa para a Integração Regional da Infraestrutura Sul-Americana (IIRSA, Initiative for the Regional Integration of South American Infrastructure). It consists of 350 projects, some involving very heavy investment, in the fields of transport, energy and communication. The objective is to provide an adequate infrastructure for the transformation of Latin America into a huge export platform for raw materials and partially processed agricultural goods. What worries many left-wing activists, such as the Brazilian economist Marcos Arruda, is that IIRSA does not stem from a coherent alternative vision for the genuine, autonomous socio-economic development of Latin America (Arruda 2008a). He fears that, on the contrary, IIRSA, which has been elaborated in conjunction with transnational corporations, will strengthen neoliberalism, with a further concentration of capital and power, and a deepening of profound social inequalities. The very name PAC, he says, is indicative of the conceptual error: the goal is growth, rather than sustainability.

Moreover, the government has not developed a coherent plan for economic growth, in which incentives are given to priority sectors. Time and again respected economists right across the political spectrum have complained of the government's failure to elaborate a strategy for industrial growth (Mendonça de Barros 2008). After surviving the first scary months in 2003, the government appears to have settled for growth of almost any kind. And, indeed, the economy gradually recovered, growing by 3.2 per cent in 2005 and 3.7 per cent in 2006. This was undoubtedly a success in that orthodox economists had warned that a good rate of growth demanded even tougher reforms in the areas of welfare, tax and labour law. But what has worried many observers is that, far from becoming a world leader in technology, Brazil is reverting to its earlier role as a basic industrial producer. The share of sophisticated products in industrial output declined from 36 per cent in 1996 to 30 per cent in 2006 (IBGE 2007).

Multinational corporations have also strengthened their presence. Indeed, several Brazilian economists believe that transnational capital now dominates both the industrial and banking sectors, even though it has only a minority share of total investment (Arruda 2008b). It is not difficult to see the hand of the multinationals at work. To the bitter disappointment of a small group of environmentalists and consumer activists, who had successfully fought for more than six years to keep out GMOs (genetically modified organisms), at least until proper safeguards were in place, the Lula government lifted the ban, saying that so many GMO seeds had been smuggled across the Argentine border that it was impractical to maintain the prohibition. The decision was taken after intense lobbying by Monsanto, the US biotechnology company, which was determined to get Brazil to accept its Roundup Ready (RR) soya. Brazil was the last bulwark to fall. Now the world's three leading soya producers – the USA, Brazil and Argentina – are all cultivating GM soya. Non-GM soya will become a niche market for consumers prepared to pay a premium.

Capital, and foreign capital in particular, enjoys all kinds of privileges. Brazil is the only country in the world that allows big, capitalized companies to consider as tax-deductible the interest payments they would have paid on their capital if they had borrowed that capital from banks. It has been estimated that this concession costs Brazil R\$3.2 billion (£900 million) a year (FBO 2005). Since 1996, the owners of companies, whether Brazilian or foreign, pay no income tax on dividends or profits, so profit remittances sent abroad are tax-free. The cost of this privilege is estimated at R\$6.4 billion (£1.8 billion) a year (FBO 2005). PT supporters had expected Lula to abolish such benefits when he took office, but such action has never even been seriously discussed.

It has, therefore, been the willingness of Lula's government to continue the very neoliberal practices implemented by President Fernando Henrique Cardoso (1995–2002) which has most irritated his erstwhile supporters. Lula's handling of the foreign and domestic debts is a case in point. In February 2008 the Central Bank announced that, 'for the first time in our economic history', Brazil's international reserves and other foreign assets were greater than the country's net foreign debt (Batista 2008). The Central Bank said that, in January 2008, the country's foreign assets were worth US$7 billion more than its debts. This was announced as a great achievement for a country that in the mid-1980s would have defaulted on its enormous foreign debt, had it not been bailed out by the International Monetary Fund in a deal conditional on a ferocious programme of structural adjustment that, to some extent, marked the arrival of neoliberalism in Brazil.

There is no doubt that a milestone had been reached and that, despite mounting difficulties on the world financial market, Brazil was now enjoying much greater financial stability. But, unfortunately, the Central Bank figures told only half the story. The government had omitted intercompany loans, the debts that subsidiaries of foreign companies held with their head companies. These debts had doubled in 2007, from US$20 billion to US$42 billion. Why had these loans risen so heavily? The explanation is simple: foreign companies had brought money into Brazil to buy government bonds, which were paying the highest interest rates in the world. And Brazilian companies also take out loans abroad, on which they pay a relatively low rate of interest, and bring the money in to purchase government bonds. Because it has adopted wholesale the neoliberal belief in the primacy of the market, the government has not imposed any limit on the influx of dollars, issuing bonds to soak them up. As a result, Brazil's internal debt exploded: it had grown by 40 per cent in two years, reaching R$1.4 trillion (£426.5 billion) by December 2007 (de Ávila 2008).

The whole process produces a host of problems. First of all, it means that the government has to pay out more in interest payments and amortization on this large internal debt, much of it unnecessary. Second, the influx of dollars leads to an appreciation of the real. This creates problems for exporters, who find their goods priced out of the world market, but provides an extra bonus for foreign investors, who, at the end of their investment period, usually less than a year, can buy more dollars for their reais after they cash in their bonds. And third, the Central Bank has little option but to invest the US dollars it holds in US Treasury bonds, which pay a third of the interest that Brazil pays on its own bonds (helping the Bush administration to finance its foreign operations, such as the war in Iraq). The Central Bank is estimated to have spent R$58.5 billion on this costly scheme between January and October 2007. For many Brazilian analysts it is not just the wasted money which is painful: it is the realization that a PT government has not had the courage to end the plundering of the Brazilian economy. In many ways, the internal debt is just a new mechanism for carrying on with the age-old pillaging of Brazilian resources by a small elite of rich foreigners and Brazilians.

Social welfare

Yet it would be wrong to see the Lula administration as a mere continuation of the neoliberalism implemented by Fernando Henrique Cardoso. The first Lula government brought real advances for the poor. The first achievement was to halt the general decline in the purchasing power of the average wage, which had been falling since 1996. This was achieved in 2004, when the purchasing power of the average income remained stable, with the real income of the poorest half of workers increasing by 3.2 per cent while that of the wealthier half of the population declined (*Folha de S. Paulo* 2005a). At last, it seemed, income inequalities were decreasing in Brazil. This certainly was the interpretation that the government gave to the statistics. There are, however, important qualifications. First, the government's statistics, based on declared incomes, almost certainly failed to capture the huge profits that an elite was making on the financial market. Second, a closer examination of the figures revealed that the income of the poorest sector of the population had increased only because of a rise in the value of government handouts. Indeed, a huge 89 per cent of the income of the poorest 10 per cent of the population came from social welfare payments, compared with only 48 per cent in 1995 (Folha de S. Paulo 2005b). This is not to deny that real advances occurred. The value of the minimum wage, which is such an important yardstick for measuring poverty in Brazil, rose by 42.8 per cent in real terms during the period of the first Lula government (Rands 2008). More than eleven million families benefited from the *Bolsa Família*, the government's welfare scheme, through which very poor families are paid half a minimum wage per month for each child of theirs who attends school. The advances are modest, but they were an important factor in Lula's re-election in October 2006.

Throughout the preceding year the country had been rocked by an apparently never-ending series of exposures of rampant corruption within the Lula government. It was revealed that the PT was paying a monthly stipend, the so-called *mensalão*, to members of smaller parties in Congress so that they would vote with the government. A PT leader was caught with a large quantity of dollars hidden in his pants. Several ministers in his government were forced to resign after being found guilty of 'forming a gang'. And just before the election, members of the PT were jailed for trying to buy a dossier that allegedly would have incriminated the opposition candidate in the election for the governorship of São Paulo.

Despite this flurry of revelations, Lula won the second round of the presidential election, gaining a comfortable 60 per cent of the vote. Several factors seem to have contributed to his impressive ability to distance himself from the scandals and retain the trust of the majority of the population. The right-wing politicians probably blundered. They almost certainly could have started impeachment proceedings against Lula in the second half of 2005, but they decided against it. They thought that, given Lula's demoralization, they would easily win the election and that impeachment proceedings might have backfired and provoked a reaction among the poorer section of the population, where Lula had his strongest supporters. Although the criticism of Lula in some newspapers was vitriolic, the vast majority of Brazilians do not read the printed press. The main television network, TV *Globo*, which often has an audience of nearly eighty million for its daily news programme, *Jornal Nacional*, did not carry out a systematic attack on Lula. Indeed, many Brazilian businessmen had no reason to lobby hard for a change in government.

Even so, the most important factor accounting for Lula's success was almost certainly the massive support he received from voters in Brazil's poorest states in the north-east: he obtained 84 per cent of the vote in Maranhão, 82 per cent in Ceará, almost 78 per cent in Bahia and Pernambuco, and 77 per cent in Piauí. Brasília seems a distant place to most poor families in the north-east. What mattered for them was that their lives had improved and that Lula was the first president ever who came from a poor family and spoke a language that they could understand. In contrast, Lula lost in Brazil's wealthier states, such as Rio Grande do Sul, Santa Catarina, Paraná and São Paulo.

In 2007 the second Lula government pushed ahead with its growth strategy. The economy expanded by 5.3 per cent. Unemployment fell. By early 2008 some 200,000 new jobs were being created each month. There is no doubt that the economic recovery was being achieved within the tight constraints of the neoliberal model. For instance, while in 2007 the government spent R$237 billion (£74 billion) on the payment of interest and amortization of the foreign and internal debts, its expenditure on health was only R$40 billion (£12.5 billion), and even less – R$20 billion (£6.25 billion) – on education. But the modest improvements in the economy were enough to restore Lula's personal rating in the opinion polls to close to 70 per cent. There was even talk of the government pushing through an amendment to the constitution so that Lula could run for a third term in the elections in October 2009.

Agrarian reform

Perhaps no area reveals with greater clarity the contradictions within Lula's policy-making than the vexed question of agrarian reform. Since its foundation in the early 1980s, the PT had repeatedly promised that, in power, it would carry out far-reaching agrarian reform. In its origins the PT was undoubtedly an urban party, yet from the outset it strongly identified with the rural poor, particularly Brazil's 4 million landless families. In the run-up to the 2002 election, Lula travelled all over the country, reaching isolated rural areas. Everywhere he spoke with passion and conviction, promising land to the landless. On one occasion he said: 'With one flourish of my pen I'm going to give you so much land that you won't be able to occupy it all' (quoted in *Folha de S. Paulo*, 7 March 2004).

When Lula was elected president in October 2002, landless peasants believed that finally their hour had come. Thousands of families spontaneously moved into provisional camps that Brazil's powerful landless movement, the Movimento dos Trabalhadores Rurais Sem Terra (MST, Movement of the Landless), and other landless organizations had hurriedly erected at roadsides all across the country. These families hoped that they would be among the first to benefit when the massive programme of agrarian reform was enacted. Many took the initiative, occupying big unproductive estates, confident that the Lula government would legalize their occupation. According to the Catholic Church's Pastoral Land Commission, a record number of people – 124,634 families – took part in land occupations or moved into roadside camps in 2003. At the same time, about half a million people across the country took part in demonstrations for agrarian reform (CPT 2004: 7). On 2 July 2003 an MST delegation met Lula in the presidential palace. Before the TV cameras Lula donned a red MST cap, saying that he regarded agrarian reform as a 'historic commitment'.

Change did not come as quickly as the thousands of families hoped, however. For months, the government prevaricated, saying that it had to put its house in order before it could implement reform. Finally, it called in Plínio de Arruda Sampaio, one of the country's foremost agrarian experts, a founding member of the PT. Sampaio set to with a will. He signed up a team of eight university lecturers, all experts in agrarian matters, and got authorization for fifty employees from the Instituto Nacional de Colonização e Reforma Agrária (INCRA, National Institute of Colonization and Agrarian Reform) to work with him. Sampaio said that, in drawing up the plan, he considered two aspects to be fundamental – the quantitative and the qualitative:

> Quantitatively, we had to draw up a programme of agrarian reform that would expropriate enough land from the *latifúndio* to make a real rupture with the old system of land tenure. We needed to change the economic, social and political structures. Agrarian reform means strengthening the peasantry.

He calculated that they would need to settle 1 million families over a three-year period (2004–06) to achieve this rupture. This was clearly an ambitious target, given INCRA's depleted resources, but it was feasible, in that Brazil had enough underused land and families desperate for a plot. Moreover, Sampaio did not set out to disrupt Brazil's neoliberal economic system, which is dependent on exports from the large, modern farms in the hands of the agribusiness elite. 'The idea was, in the beginning at least, to create two poles – the peasantry and agribusiness. In time, the peasantry would grow stronger and perhaps challenge agribusiness, but this would be another phase.'

In October 2003 Sampaio presented his plan to the minister. He argued that it would provide 3 million jobs, directly and indirectly, and would thus help to solve Brazil's serious social crisis. Sampaio's research suggested that it would have been perfectly possible for Lula to have adopted his plan, despite the PT's lack of a majority in Congress. 'We didn't need to change the constitution or even to get congressional approval,' he said. 'The president could have implemented the plan with presidential decrees. The process would have been made easier with changes in one or two laws, but this wasn't necessary' (Plínio de Arruda Sampaio, personal communication). What was required, however, was political will. 'The government needed to give agrarian reform great priority and to mobilize the population around the programme.' According to Sampaio, the cost was high but not exorbitant. 'We calculated that it would have cost R\$24 billion [£7 billion] over the three years. For a country that spends R\$170 billion [£49 billion] on debt servicing every year, this is affordable.' Even before he officially presented his plan, Sampaio became aware of the resistance he faced. 'I thought our programme was very reasonable but it frightened a lot of people.' The minister of agrarian reform, Miguel Rossetto, called him in on several occasions. 'We don't have the money, Plínio, to carry out the kind of programme you want and we haven't the technical expertise to carry out a programme like this. You've got to be realistic.' Sampaio replied to the minister, 'No one says it'll be easy, but you can't carry out agrarian reform like any other programme. You've got to mobilize people. That's the only way to do it. We must put the country on a war footing and tackle problems as they arise.' But this response, said Sampaio, just alarmed people more, particularly in INCRA. In the end, the minister congratulated Sampaio and his team for their contribution, and sent them away.

This did not mean, however, that the PT abandoned completely the idea of agrarian reform. In the run-up to the 2006 elections, the government claimed to have achieved a 'record for agrarian reform: 381,000 rural workers without land were settled during Lula's first presidential term (2003–6)' (*Folha de S. Paulo*, 19 February 2007). The MST later claimed, however, that the figures had been artificially inflated by including families that had been settled under previous governments or were living in forest reserves. Almost half of the families, they said, were not genuinely new beneficiaries (Osava 2007). At the same time, the government provided better support for small family farmers. Time and again Rossetto stressed the importance of small-scale family agriculture to the national economy. 'Family agriculture is responsible for most of the food that arrives each day on the tables of Brazilian families,' he wrote in a Brazilian newspaper. 'Seven out of every ten rural workers are engaged in family agriculture. Almost 40 per cent of Brazil's gross agricultural output comes from family agriculture' (*Jornal do Brasil*, 13 July 2004). Rossetto increased the volume of resources available to family farmers through the Programa Nacional de Apoio à Agricultura Familiar (PRONAF, National Programme for the Support of Family Agriculture), which is the main programme of subsidized credit for family farmers. The volume increased fourfold during the Lula government to R$10 billion (£3.1 billion) in 2006/07.

Lula and the environment

Probably the policies for which the Lula government has received the harshest criticism concern the environment, particularly with respect to the Amazon basin. Lula has never been very environmentally aware. He spent his formative years in São Paulo at a time when the city was growing very fast and becoming the country's industrial heartland. Coming from a poor family, which, like hundreds of thousands of others, had migrated to São Paulo from the impoverished north-east, Lula realized the dream of most young men from poor families at that time: he got a job in one of the booming car factories in the city's industrial suburbs.

And, as was discussed earlier, he gained national prominence through his work as a trade unionist.

As a result, environmentalists had low expectations of the Lula government. They were pleasantly surprised when he appointed one of the country's most passionate environmentalists – Marina Silva – as his environment minister. She grew up in a family of rubber-tappers in a remote area of the Amazon basin, and was brought into politics by Chico Mendes, a rubber-tapper leader assassinated in 1988. She helped to found the PT in the Amazon and forged a close friendship with Lula. She had a meteoric career: at the age of thirty-six, she was elected senator for the PT, the youngest person in Brazilian history to have been elected to that office.

Marina Silva brought into office with her some highly respected environmentalists, including João Paulo Capobianco, who became Secretary for Biodiversity and Forests. Together, they tried to reshape completely the government's environmental policies. Arguing that Brazil would achieve lasting social and economic development only if it worked with the environment, not against it, they tried to implement a policy of 'tranversality', by which they meant building environmental considerations into every stage of policy-making. But they failed. Although Lula felt great personal warmth and respect for his minister, he never took her views very seriously. In his zeal to boost economic growth, he allied himself closely to big landowners because of their capacity to boost farm exports, particularly beef, soya and sugar. On more than one occasion he referred to Marina's environmental concerns as 'a bureaucratic obstacle'.

The ministry of the environment lost many battles, the most serious of which was its failure to persuade the government to place environmental concerns at the heart of policy-making. But it also had some successes. The most important came after satellite images had shown that a huge swathe of Amazon forest had been felled in 2003/04: 27,429 square kilometres, the second-largest area cleared in a single year. Then, shortly after these figures were announced, a landowner killed an American nun, Dorothy Stang. He had been enraged by her repeated denunciations to the authorities of his violent attempts to force forest dwellers off their land. The murder was widely reported in the foreign press. An embarrassed Lula agreed not only to send in the federal police to stop further illegal jungle clearance but also to create the conservation unit that Dorothy Stang had been campaigning for. Rates of forest clearance fell for three consecutive years. It seemed that the relentless front of loggers, cattle rearers and soya farmers pushing its way into the Amazon basin was finally being halted, or at least slowed down. Building on this success, the ministry created a series of different kinds of conservation units which together covered more than 230,000 square kilometres, an area almost as large as the state of São Paulo, in the very centre of the forest. Many of these reserves can be inhabited by small traditional communities of fisherfolk and peasant families, who have shown over decades that they can earn their livelihoods from the forest without destroying it. Taken with older conservation units and indigenous reserves, they covered one-third of Amazonia.

Real progress was occurring, it seemed; but then came the backlash. The ministry had enacted its plans at a time when commodity prices were low on the world market. Brazilian farmers had had no financial incentive to bring further land under cultivation. But in 2007 came the commodity boom. Soya prices rocketed. Biofuel fever infected the world. Lula got excited at the prospect of Brazil becoming the world's leading exporter of ethanol, made from sugar cane. While it is not common for tropical forest to be felled and then planted directly with soya or sugar cane, a commodity boom leads to a rise in land prices and tends to displace cattle rearers. Satellite images began to detect an alarming increase in forest clearance. Marina Silva responded with a clampdown on illegal forest clearance. In February 2008 she pushed through the national monetary council a resolution that made it impossible for private or public banks to make loans to farmers in the 550 *municípios* (local districts) in the Amazon basin unless they had obtained a certificate showing that they were respecting the government's tough environmental legislation. No one expected the new resolution to end illegal logging and forest clearance, because farmers can often buy certificates from corrupt officials, but the measure was an indication of the government's seriousness.

At the same time, it was becoming clear that Lula's flagship project – PAC – would do immense damage to the environment unless the government imposed very strict controls. Environmentalists warned that no fewer than 322 areas of great importance for biodiversity would be threatened by the roads, hydroelectric power stations, ports and gas pipelines planned under PAC (*Folha de S. Paulo* 2008b). Marina Silva called for the creation of further conservation units to protect vulnerable ecosystems and drafted a special plan – PAS (Plano Amazônia Sustentável, Sustainable Amazonia Plan) – with this in mind. It was a step too far. Reportedly in response to pressure from Blairo Maggi, the governor of Mato Grosso state and one of the world's biggest soya farmers, Lula snubbed Marina Silva. Without even informing her beforehand, he announced at a public meeting that Roberto Mangabeira Unger, the Harvard-educated minister for long-term planning, would be in charge of PAS. Mangabeira had been ridiculed by environmentalists earlier in the year for proposing to transfer water from the Amazon basin to the drought-ridden north-east of Brazil. Completely ignoring the dependence of fish, plants and people on the annual flooding of the river, he baldly stated that it made sense to link 'a region where there is a useless abundance of water with another where there is a calamitous lack of water' (*Folha de S. Paulo* 2008a). The message could not have been clearer: Marina Silva, for long an isolated voice within a pro-development cabinet, felt in May 2008 that she had finally lost the battle over the environment, and had little option but to leave the government.

Brazil and Latin America

Over the last decade the geopolitical landscape has shifted in Latin America. The traditional regional rivalry between Brazil and Mexico has subsided. After the signing of NAFTA (North America Free Trade Agreement) in 1994, Mexico has become ever more firmly subsumed within the US sphere of dominance. For a while, George Bush (senior) attempted to extend NAFTA to the whole region, with his goal of creating by 2005 a giant Free Trade Area of the Americas (FTAA) from Alaska in the north to Magellan Strait in the south. This strategy failed, largely because of stiff resistance from Brazil. Since then, a different power struggle has ensued. Brazil has sought to establish itself firmly as the regional power in South America, challenging US hegemony. The regional trade bloc Mercosur, with Brazil at its heart, was founded in 1991 and by 2008 had five full members: Brazil, Argentina, Paraguay, Uruguay and Venezuela; and five associate members, Bolivia, Chile, Colombia, Ecuador and Peru. Despite tensions, Mercosur has survived and advanced, and in May 2008 UNASUL (União de Nações Sul-Americanas, the Union of South American Nations) was formed, bringing together the ten Mercosur states with Guyana and Surinam.

UNASUL forms part of Brazil's long-term plans to dominate a regional power bloc, one of a handful of such blocs throughout the world. At the heart of Brazil's ambition lies its desire to extend the reach of its home-grown multinationals: corporations such as the oil giant Petrobrás; the construction companies Odebrecht and Camargo Corrêa; the aircraft manufacturer Embraer; and the banks Itaú and Bradesco. This strategy is being elaborated in collaboration with US multinationals, many of which are working with Brazilian companies in the giant IIRSA infrastructure projects referred to above. Brazil has ambitious goals for UNASUL, hoping that eventually it will create its own central bank, have its own currency and set up its own regional defence council.

Despite this cooperation at an economic level, the US authorities are reacting with dismay and some anger at a geopolitical level. The USA has been pressing ahead with the strategy of incorporating Latin American countries into its power bloc through bilateral trade agreements. For the USA the key ally is Colombia, with which it has created strong economic, political and military links. By 2008, Colombia had 210,000 troops on the ground, even more than Brazil's 190,000 soldiers, despite Brazil's much larger size. This news was, in turn, greeted with some alarm in Brasília. This dynamic as the two largest nations in the Americas, the USA and Brazil, fight a turf battle is likely to be the key source of tension within the region for the next decade.

Conclusion

At the time this book went to press, Lula had not completed his second term, yet the characteristics of his government were firmly established and seemed unlikely to change. It seems probable that Lula will be remembered as Brazil's first working-class president, who got the economy growing again and put food in the mouths of millions of the poorest Brazilians. At the same time, he is the president who put Brazil firmly on the route to becoming the hegemonic power within South America. These are perhaps modest achievements, especially in the area of social reform, for a man in whom so many hopes were deposited, but Lula himself may well be happy with such an epitaph.

10 | Brazil: third ways in the Third World

GUY BURTON

During Latin America's 2005/06 election cycle, Jorge Castañeda observed two distinctive lefts: one, led by Venezuela and Bolivia, was characterized as turbulent and uncertain; the other, associated with Brazil and Chile, was seen as a more secure social democratic alternative (Castañeda 2006). More recently Sandbrook et al. have suggested that while the governments of both the Workers' Party (PT) and its predecessor the Brazilian Social Democratic Party (PSDB) were social democratic, Brazil itself was not a social democracy (Sandbrook et al. 2007: 238–42). Both suggestions seemed odd in the light of the PT's supposed political and fiscal irresponsibility prior to its first presidential victory in 2002, and of the PSDB's association with neoliberal policies. Indeed, both parties appear to share an identity that is centre-left, and increasingly middle-class, and have advocated social policies and programmes that would enhance the opportunities of the poor, including cheap AIDS drugs, and the *Bolsa Escola*, a grant paid to families to put their children in school (for this process, see Cunningham 1999 on the PSDB; Branford and Kucinski 2003 on the PT).

While these two parties currently dominate Brazil's political system, however, their origins, and their vision of social democracy, differ. This can be seen very clearly at the sub-national level. Taking education policy as a case study, this chapter examines the main differences between the PT in Rio Grande do Sul state between 1999 and 2002, and the PSDB in the relatively poorer north-eastern state of Ceará since the 1980s. Making a comparison of education policy is particularly appropriate: not only has national concern about the country's educational situation risen since the 1990s, but Brazil's federal structure means that states are key educational actors, being jointly responsible for both primary and secondary education and spending proportionally more than either the federal government or municipalities (Schwartzmann 2003). To examine the features of Brazilian social democracy by focusing on the PT and PSDB and their approaches to education, this chapter is divided into the following sections. The first considers the Latin American left and the diversity that characterizes the origins of social democracy, a diversity present in Brazilian party politics and illustrated by the emergence of two distinct types of social democratic politics in Ceará and Rio Grande do Sul. The second section outlines the main policy directions taken by each of these distinct social democratic parties in education, while the third highlights the continuing challenges faced by each.[1]

Distinguishing the left in Brazil

During the 1990s, Castañeda's earlier and influential model of the left (see above) was refined by Kirby into three broad currents: conservatives, reformers and radicals (Castañeda 1994: 4; Kirby 2003: 200). For Kirby the conservative left was represented by two historic groupings: communist parties and guerrilla groups inspired by the Cuban revolution; and national-populist governments such as those under Perón and Vargas. Both regime types pursued a top-down, state-led model of development through 'import substitution industrialization', supported by sections of the working class. The reforming left included those who saw conventional socialism as declining in relevance, who favoured a less class-based and more catch-all support for their parties, and who were criticized as technocratic, elitist and opportunistically aligned with the centre of the electorate (Bresser Perreira 2001; Schmidtke 2002: 6–7). While this delivered electoral success, they failed to deal with the inequalities and disadvantages associated with their accommodation with neoliberalism. This may be seen in the politics of the FREPASO–Radical, Socialist–Christian Democrat and PSDB–PFL coalitions in Argentina, Chile and Brazil respectively (see Ellner 2004).

Against the reformers and conservative lefts, an alternative, radical strain emerged that challenged the prevailing political and socioeconomic status quo. It consisted of new parties and coalitions, such as the PT in Brazil, the Frente Amplio (Broad Front) in Uruguay and Causa Radical (Radical Cause) in Venezuela, with support from new social movements based on demands for democracy and human rights (see Castañeda 2006; Baiocchi 2003: 10). The return to democracy throughout the region offered these parties their first experience of government and political reality, but primarily at the local level. Since the 1990s falling union memberships, union bureaucratization, growing informal labour markets and electoral pressures have all weakened the anti-establishment rhetoric and policy stance of such parties (Petras 1999: 6). Consequently, the radical left approach has become similar to the reformers', while retaining their links to social movements. Nevertheless, in spite of this trend, a second generation of radicalism can be identified, at least in rhetorical terms. This is most apparent in Bolivia and Venezuela, yet whether this second generation will be able to transcend the challenges faced by the first-generation radicals remains to be seen. In terms of these distinctions, Brazilian social democracy consists of the reformist and first-generation radical tendencies, represented by the PSDB and PT respectively. Their origins differ, as shown by their formation at the local level. While Ceará's social democrat movement emerged from within the economic elite during the 1980s, in Rio Grande do Sul the left was based on decades of active social mobilization.

Reformism in Ceará and radicalism in Rio Grande do Sul

Ceará's political and economic elite consisted of a conservative oligarchy for most of the twentieth century. By 1985 this elite was under threat, enabling the PT to gain an unexpected victory in the mayoral election in the state capital, Fortaleza. The administration suffered, however, from low levels of voter identification and gaining a reputation for nepotism, divisiveness and radicalism, all of which contributed to the mayor's eventual expulsion from the PT (Baiocchi 2003: 17–18). In the absence of the PT's radical alternative, the modernizing impetus fell to an emerging class within the elite, led by a group of young businessmen under Tasso Jereissati, the son of a prominent Ceará senator. Jereissati led a campaign for state reform, poverty reduction and an end to old clientelistic practices. Affiliated to the main national opposition party, the PMDB, he won the state governor election in 1987.

The new administration introduced spending cuts, reduced the state's personnel and sought greater bureaucratic efficiency (de Sousa interview). These policies divided the Ceará PMDB, prompting Jereissati and his allies to join the newly founded PSDB. Thus began the PSDB's domination of Ceará politics throughout the 1990s, controlling both the executive and the state legislature. Although the emphasis of successive PSDB administrations has been on state reform and industrial issues, after 1995 greater attention was paid to the social agenda (Vieira and de Farias 2002). This approach was constrained, however, by the PSDB's relatively weak roots in civil society. In addition, in the absence of strong external opposition, the PSDB was increasingly subject to growing internal differences, resulting in it losing the control of the state in 2006.

Unlike in Ceará, the emergence of social democracy in Rio Grande do Sul owed more to the role of grassroots activism and its opposition to neoliberalism (Marques 1998). Trade unions, including the teachers' union, played a key role against the military regime (de Oliveira 1995). The teachers' union, the CPERS, would subsequently be involved in the formation and the development of the PT itself. Lúcia Camini, a former teachers' union president, became the *petista* (PT) state education secretary in

1999. This relationship between social mobilization and party activity in Rio Grande do Sul benefited parties like the PT. Mettenheim shows that whereas the PT had almost no support in the north-east during the 1982 elections, highlighting the unexpected nature of the party's 1985 electoral success in Fortaleza, in the south its standing among the public was far more favourable (Mettenheim 1995: 144).

In 1989, the former bank workers' union leader and PT member Olivio Dutra won the mayoral election in the state capital, Porto Alegre. But the *gaúcho* (Rio Grande do Sul resident) PT was notably different from the party as a whole. While the centrist Articulação (Articulation) group dominated the national party leadership, in Rio Grande do Sul and Porto Alegre it was members from the Trotskyist Democracia Socialista (Socialist Democracy) who occupied the executive (Goldfrank and Schneider 2003: 160–61). The new administration pursued a series of innovative policies, the most notable being the participatory budget, which sought to weaken the power of political and economic elites by giving the poor and excluded more of a say in how the municipal budget was spent. During the 1990s the PT built up its position across the state at the expense of its main rival on the radical left, the PDT. Although party polarization was high, this disguised a largely stable set of electoral coalitions and voter preferences (Grohmann 2001). Finally, in 1998 the PT won the gubernatorial election under Dutra. The new *petista* administration faced a number of problems from 1999 on. These included a state debt of around R$1.4 billion, the relocation of a Ford motor plant after its contract was renegotiated, tension between pro-GM soybean producers and environmentalists, land occupations by the MST, and teacher strikes. In addition, following strong opposition in the legislature, the administration was unable to scale up the participatory budget to state level (Löwy 2000: 16). By 2002 the party appeared tired, losing the gubernatorial and state elections of that year. This decline appears to have continued, with the party losing control of Porto Alegre in 2004, and failing in the 2006 gubernatorial election.

The different versions of social democracy represented in Ceará and Rio Grande do Sul are reflected not just in their political complexions but also in the social policies they have undertaken, including education. This is evident in the contrasting approaches of the PSDB and the PT to the aspects of educational policy analysed here: state planning and popular participation; finance; literacy campaigns; decentralization and the role of the state; democracy within schools; party–union relations; and methods of student and school evaluation.

State planning, participation and finance

The PSDB's technocratic approach to education is most evident after 1995, when the government introduced its education plan (Naspolini interview; Borges 2008). The details were defined through an executive-led consultation of the educational community by the state's educational bureaucracy, SEDUC, involving university educators, teachers, unions and the state legislature's education committee (Naspolini interview). One of the state's two teachers' unions, Sindiute, however, challenged the notion of an equal engagement, claiming that certain NGOs and the third (or private) sector gained a more privileged position in the debate than other groups (Baima interview). Furthermore, the relative lack of internal institutional life, other than at election time, may have limited the involvement of ordinary party members (de Sousa interview).

By contrast the PT sought a more participatory approach. In 1999 it launched the Constituente Escolar, School Constituency, which encouraged debate between education actors from school level to a state-wide conference (Hatcher 2002). Rather than developing a single model, the aim was to address local needs. The Constituente was, however, subjected to opposition. The CPERS wanted to discuss teachers' salaries prior to public debate, and the union leadership officially withdrew from the Constituente when the PT refused (Rodrigues, Camini, Farenzena interviews). The parents' association saw the Constituente as a talking shop and was concerned its activities would supersede those of individual school councils (Souza interview). Finally, opposition came from within the PT itself. The former Porto Alegre education secretary, Esther Grossi, claimed that the process only delayed action, since most of the problems facing Rio Grande do Sul's education system were already known (Grossi interview).

After 1995, the federal government under recently elected PSDB candidate Fernando Henrique Cardoso began reforming Brazilian education. A 1996 constitutional amendment required that 15 per cent of state and municipal tax revenues be spent specifically on primary education. This was formalized in a new federal fund, FUNDEF (Elementary School Maintenance and Development Fund and Professorship Valorization), which increased spending for primary education and teachers' salaries; set a minimum amount of spending per student; and reduced regional funding inequalities by increasing spending in the poorer north-east (Araújo and Oliveira 2004: 54–5). Formally, municipalities were primarily responsible for nursery schools and states for secondary education; both would be accountable for primary education (Farenzena interview). FUNDEF did not completely solve the funding crisis, however: there was insufficient funding for the smallest and poorest cities, while only marginal improvements in educational quality occurred. In addition the emphasis was on primary education, thereby overlooking pre-school and secondary levels, while teachers complained about the continuing deterioration of their work conditions (Levačić and Downes 2004; Vieira 2005).

FUNDEF received support from the Ceará administration, owing to its political alignment with the new federal government. By contrast, the PT highlighted its position as the main national opposition party through the involvement of the Rio Grande do Sul administration in a nationwide campaign against the narrowness of FUNDEF's goals, conducted by the party and social movements associated with education, including the national teachers' union, the CNTE. In particular, it claimed the system did not provide enough resources, with spending being both too low and unconcerned with teaching beyond the primary stage (Rodrigues interview). The PT and its allies wanted to see FUNDEF replaced with a FUNDEB fund that would cover pre-school and secondary education alongside the primary level. This, it was argued, would be achieved through higher taxes and a crackdown on tax evasion. In 2006, the PT government's FUNDEB bill was passed by Congress.

Literacy campaigns and decentralization

In Ceará tackling illiteracy was achieved by increasing formal school admissions, thereby reducing illiteracy at a faster rate than the rest of the north-east of Brazil between 1991 and 2001. The total population that was illiterate fell in the state, from just over a third to nearly a quarter, although 1.26 million people aged over fifteen remained illiterate, and functional illiteracy persists.

In Rio Grande do Sul the PT sought a more popular, non-school-based form of literacy education through the MOVA-RS campaign. The administration claimed it reached 140,000 young people and adults outside of the classroom between 1999 and 2002 (Camini 2001). The campaign was seen as an alternative to traditional ways of teaching, and involved popular educators who did not have conventional teaching qualifications (Farenzena interview). Despite the party's general support for this approach, dissident elements within the PT were critical of the apparent lack of a coherent methodology and an emphasis on political education over that of basic literacy (Grossi interview).

Decentralization or municipalization in education was a process that had been occurring since the 1980s but was formalized by the 1996 constitutional amendments and the establishment of FUNDEF (Naspolini interview; Draibe 2004: 397). This formal approach was reflected in the

Ceará 1995 education programme, which stressed 'partnership' between state, municipality and school. Schools would be provided with technical support, financial resources and democratic school councils. Municipalities would be responsible for delivering primary education, and the state would help coordinate policy implementation and provide technical and financial support and evaluation of schools and municipalities through twenty-one Educational Development Regional Centres (CREDEs) (Naspolini 2001; Naspolini interview). Critics claimed the system was much too bureaucratic, however, with the state-level SEDUC willing neither to negotiate with the school community nor to tackle local financial mismanagement of FUNDEF funds. Furthermore, it was argued that decentralization had 'hollowed out' the state by passing on responsibility to municipalities without providing sufficient financial resources or development of structural capacity (Baima interview).

Similar fears were reflected in the *gaúcho* PT's approach to educational municipalization. The Education Secretariat's first task was to halt the previous administration's decentralization agenda, winning support from the teachers' union (Rodrigues and Farenzena interviews). *Petistas* were also worried that not only was funding insufficient for municipalities to successfully supply high-quality education, but decentralization would adversely divide responsibility for pre-school, primary and secondary education between the state and municipalities (Vasconcelos interview). Municipalization would increase the powers of individual mayors over education, reduce efficiency and transparency, and increase the likelihood of school privatization. These concerns were backed up by an apparent correlation between high levels of municipalized education and poverty, and a belief that decentralization increased regional disparities (Farenzena interview).

The *petista* response was to focus on the *Constituente* and the involvement of the school community within the process to address educational challenges. Coordination between the state and its regions and schools was still necessary, however, prompting the establishment of twenty-nine regional agencies which would oversee the government's educational objectives throughout the state (Cattelan interview). There were difficulties, though, over how these *coordinarias* would be used. For some within the PT the *coordinarias'* main purpose was to implement the government's policies within the regions; others felt that they should limit themselves to overseeing educational initiatives at the municipal level (Camini interview). This tension reflected internal differences within the PT, between those who felt the state government should have the main role in policy development, and those who believed that it should emerge bottom-up.

School democracy and party–union relations

The development of democracy within schools occurred at varying speeds across the country during the 1990s (Grindle 2004: 9, 74). This occurred, however, against a general backdrop of limited community and associational involvement in the management of schools (Draibe 2004: 385). In 1995 and 1998 the first direct elections for school principals were held in Ceará schools, with subsequent elections held every four years thereafter. Candidates had to fulfil certain criteria, including possession of a higher qualification and completion of a training course, tests and a selection process (Naspolini interview). These direct elections were complemented through elected school councils consisting of parents, students, teachers, school workers, management and civil society representatives, chosen to represent the school community (Naspolini 2001). SEDUC claims the number of individuals involved in the election process has risen (Gonçalves interview). Analysis of the 1995 and 1998 elections indicates that democratization within schools is yielding some results, including both public support and a reported greater legitimacy for principals (Maia et al. 2001). Several concerns have been raised, however, including the risk of elections causing divisions within schools, and how to manage public expectations given schools' limited control over state-provided funds. In addition, parental awareness of their role and function on school councils remains poor, while there is a high dependence on key individuals such as school principals to ensure measures are carried through. Many school community members do not feel they have ownership of these changes. Finally, the directors of the state's regional CREDEs do not face election. They are selected from a field of 606 following a series of evaluations by SEDUC (Naspolini interview). The Sindiute union has criticized this approach and outcome, claiming that it has encouraged a trend towards bureaucracy and an unwillingness to negotiate (Baima interview).

In Rio Grande do Sul there was less division between the PT administration and the teachers' union over the issue of school democracy. Since the 1980s both had supported election of school principals with less restrictive criteria and pre-selection tests (Bulhões and Abreu 1992). Alongside this, the PT administration also considered allowing non-teaching staff in schools to run for election as well. Nevertheless, other factors did limit *pet-ista* efforts to develop democracy, most notably what the relationship was between the *Constituente* and school councils; the relationship between government officials and school councils; parents' limited knowledge of financial matters; and the dependence of school councils on principals and their decisions (Souza interview; Levačić and Downes 2004: 76–8).

Trade unions can either support or obstruct education reformers. To a great extent their position depends on their strength and stance relative to key actors. The circumstances in both states meant that the influence of civil society, and hence trade unions, differed. In Ceará not only was civil society weak, but the teachers were also divided between two unions, APEOC and Sindiute. In Rio Grande do Sul, 85,000 teachers and other school workers were united in one of the largest unions in the state, the CPERS. Further, despite claiming organizational autonomy, in Brazil unions tend to align more closely with those political parties, such as the PT, that have stronger roots in social movements. Nevertheless, despite its historical links with the unions, the *gaúcho* PT administration faced difficulties with the CPERS. Although the CPERS had actively campaigned for PT candidate Dutra in 1998, and its spokespeople proclaimed the resulting benefits in 1999–2002, the relationship remained tense. Early frustration was felt when the new *petista* education secretary and former CPERS president Lúcia Camini failed to increase teachers' salaries immediately (Rodrigues interview). This led to teacher strikes in 2000 and 2001, prompting pay rises of 14.9 and 14 per cent respectively (Goldfrank and Schneider 2003: 162). Additional concessions also included the introduction of public competitions for teaching positions, and career plans for both teaching and non-teaching staff (Rodrigues interview).

While PT–CPERS relations were difficult, in Ceará the PSDB faced negligible opposition. Although teachers publicly opposed the first Jereissati administration and campaigned for higher pay and democratic school councils, these objectives were not met (Vieira and de Farias 2002). This was complicated by the presence of two teaching unions, APEOC and Sindiute. Of the two, APEOC was the larger, but also both weaker and more bureaucratic. Compared to the more confrontational Sindiute, APEOC had closer personal links with the government and was generally more supportive of its initiatives and proposals (Baima, Naspolini interviews; Borges 2008). The teaching profession's division encouraged *cambebistas* (Ceará state personnel) to engage in a process of divide and rule between the two teaching unions.

Student performance, evaluation and continuing challenges

National assessment of students' performance is carried out on a sample basis at primary level through biannual SAEB tests in Portuguese and maths. On average, scores are generally higher in the south than in the north. But despite *gaúcho* students' scores generally being higher than both *cearense* students (of Ceará) and the national average, there has been little noticeable improvement between 1995 and 2003: exam results have remained broadly the same within each state throughout (INEP 2004: 49–52). The PSDB and PT administrations held differing perspectives on evaluative mechanisms. The *tucanos* (PSDB) publish the results in SEDUC's official publications and acknowledge the use of SAEB results as a means to develop education policies at all levels (Vidal and de Farias 2005). In addition the *cambebistas* have developed their own state-level form of evaluation, SPAECE, which has operated since 1992 and assesses the quality of schools and teaching (Naspolini 2001).

By contrast, the PT opposed evaluation by SAEB at both national and state level in the 1990s, questioning its methodology and its use as a ranking system (Camini 2001). But because SAEB is a national system, the *gaúcho* PT could not block its use in schools. Its solution was to withhold active support for the programme. This was reflected in official *gaúcho* educational documents that make no reference to the results under the PT. *Petistas* searched for alternatives, including teacher and student self-evaluation alongside ongoing assessments (Vasconcelos and Camini interviews). Not all supported the PT's position, however. For the parents' association, the alternative forms of evaluation pioneered under the PT in Porto Alegre were not deemed successful (Souza interview). Furthermore, Esther Grossi, a former PT education secretary in Porto Alegre, was opposed to the scrapping of uniform evaluation, as she believed it necessary to maintain a certain degree of homogeneity in learning (Grossi interview).

Although achievements have been made in both Ceará and Rio Grande do Sul in terms of education progress, there still remain considerable, and broadly similar, challenges that current and future administrations will both need to address. Despite increased enrolments in Ceará's schools, performance is poor, judging by continually low SAEB results. This has been explained as being due to the expansion of primary education with insufficient resources, poor infrastructure, a lack of teaching equipment, distortions between students' ages and grades, low levels of training and financial security among teachers and limited parental assistance or capacity (Comissão de Educação, Cultura e Desporto 2001). Some observers cite financial constraints imposed by the federal government on states and municipalities as a reason for the lack of resources (Baima interview). Others believe the lack of basic operating standards, limited civil society involvement and a lack of incentives in the state's education strategy have contributed to the current situation (World Bank 2003: 57). Finally, as enrolments and retention in predominantly municipal-based primary schools improve, so pressure will build on the states to increase the number of secondary-school places.

Notwithstanding PT policy innovations, such as the literacy programme and participatory processes like the *Constituente*, several years after the *petistas* left office many of the problems faced in 1999 persisted (Farenzena interview). These included truancy, repetition, low teachers' salaries, limited funds, irregular and infrequent public examinations for teachers and poor building maintenance (Souza interview; Comissão de Educação, Cultura, Desporto, Ciência e Tecnologia 2003). Some believe that many of these problems cannot be resolved without a systematic reform of taxation (Farenzena interview). Others bewail the loss of democracy in state schools since 2003 (Rodrigues interview). PT supporters claim that given the party's one four-year term, it was impossible to reverse all these problems. By contrast, at the municipal level in Porto Alegre a series of more long-standing educational reforms were attempted between 1989 and 2004, including 'cycles of learning' that downplayed the hierarchical grade system, and an emphasis on class struggle in the curriculum. Yet it is still unclear whether the 'cycles' might be contributing towards a new form of hierarchy, and a concentration on class risks overlooking other struggles, including gender and race. Finally, the *petistas*' commitment to grassroots democracy presents its own difficulties, not least when participation clashes with other commitments, including schooling or work (Gandin and Apple 2002).

Conclusion

The experience of the PSDB and the PT in education policy in Ceará and Rio Grande do Sul presents contrasting examples of social democracy, and of the sub-national processes that have frequently prefigured national breakthroughs for left-of-centre parties in the so-called 'pink tide'. Coming from different branches of the left, the social origins and contexts of the PDSB and the PT offered contrasting solutions to common educational problems and challenges. The *gaúcho* PT arguably represents a more conventional notion of social democracy, being based on a strong labour movement of teachers. By contrast, the *cearense* PSDB has much weaker links with civil society, being more closely associated with a reformist clique within the state's elite. The differences between these two parties were reflected in their approach to policy-making: whereas the PT adopted a more participatory approach, the PSDB's was more top-down. Despite these differences, both administrations sought to improve educational opportunities for the least advantaged groups, either through popular literacy programmes or increasing formal school enrolments. In achieving this, the *cearense* PSDB was helped by the changes instigated by the national government, including constitutional changes and greater financial investment, especially in the north-east. By contrast the PT's *gaúcho* experience must be understood in the context of the party's national opposition to the PSDB Cardoso government. This explains the party's concern with evaluation and FUNDEF, and the use of the *gaúcho* administration for campaigning purposes. Furthermore, given the stronger relationship between the party and organized labour, the PT faced particular challenges and demands, most notably from the teachers, that the 'weaker' social democratic experience in Ceará did not face.

Notwithstanding the contrasting approaches, the educational results in each case remain largely uncertain, owing to the limited time that has elapsed since the adoption of these policies. Furthermore, the emphasis on these two case studies at state level overlooks the influence of other important actors in Brazilian education, namely the federal government and the municipalities, and the key factor of teacher–student interaction within the classroom. In addition, the immediate prospects for further PT or PSDB policy initiatives in these states remain similarly unclear. Despite the two parties' national importance, in 2006 both failed to gain control of the respective states discussed in this chapter.

More generally, the experience and fate of the PT in Rio Grande do Sul and the PSDB in Ceará offer an insight into the way that social democracy has emerged and worked in Latin America. While both parties may have distinct roots and different approaches to policy-making, their educational goals and policies show a commitment to change and action within clearly defined institutional boundaries. Indeed, since 2003 the two have become much more closely identified as the national PT government has largely followed and broadened the educational policies initiated under its predecessor. This has included the expansion of finance from primary education to all pre-university levels, and the deepening of evaluation mechanisms and effective subsidies to private higher education. At the same time the PT government's approach has been distinguished by a more consensual relationship with the educational community compared to the Cardoso administration's more fractious and confrontational one.

Whether at federal or state level, the PT and PSDB governments demonstrate the importance that social democrats place on working within constitutionally set parameters. In the Ceará and Rio Grande do Sul cases, this meant the governments either using the existing state infrastructure (e.g. the formal school system and federal government finance) or reforming them (e.g. the creation of the *Constituente* and elections for school principals) accordingly to achieve their policy objectives. In contrast to the institutionally oriented PT and PSDB, in Venezuela and

Bolivia (and recently Ecuador) governing elites have adopted a more combative approach that seeks not to work with but to challenge the state. At the macro-level this involved changing the rules of the game by rewriting the constitution while in education it took the form of creating new institutions that parallel the state's functions, most notably in the *misiones* (missions) running social programmes. Essentially, the differences between these two lefts may be characterized as those between a reformist social democratic path and a more revolutionary alternative. While the former with its incremental emphasis may appear less glamorous than the latter – having arguably received less international attention during the recent 2005/06 election cycle – it has also been less prone to generating social polarization. In the medium and long term this may make social democracy the true Cinderella of the story: initially overlooked and underrated, but whose shoe may ultimately best fit the various competing demands; and this in a region where radical dreams have had an unfortunate tendency to either collapse or be defeated. For that reason, social democracy in Latin America should be worthy of greater attention and study. This applies at both the national level and, as illustrated here in the case of Brazil, at the sub-national level, where Latin American federal systems give greater scope for local political initiative, and for pursuing the sort of reforms associated with the 'pink tide' of left-wing presidencies.

Note

1 I would like to thank both the individuals who kindly gave up time to allow themselves to be interviewed and all those others in Brazil and Britain who do not appear in the following pages but deserve as much recognition for the time and effort they gave to help. I would also like to thank the Convocation Trust at the University of London for their financial support, which enabled me to undertake fieldwork in Brazil during June 2005. The following interviews were conducted. In Fortaleza, Ceará: Gardênia Pereira Baima, Sindiute co-ordinating committee, 16 June 2005; Zirlánea da Silva Gonçalves, Planning and Program Department, SEDUC, 15 June 2005; Naspolini Naspolini, SEDUC Secretary (1995–2002), 20 June 2005; Marcondes Rosa de Sousa, UFC and UEC Professor, 14 June 2005. Porto Alegre, Rio Grande do Sul: Lúcia Camini, State Education Secretary (1999–2002), 27 June 2005; Fani Maria Cattelan, Research, Evaluation and Institutional Evaluation Division, Education Secretariat, 24 June 2005; Nalú Farenzena, Political Studies and Education Management Department, UFRGS, 29 June 2005; Esther Grossi, former Porto Alegre Education Secretary, 29 June 2005; Selene Barbosa Michelin Rodrigues, General Secretary, CPERS/Sindicato, 30 June 2005; Indiara Souza, President, Parents–Teachers Association (ACPM-Federação), 30 June 2005; Maria José Vasconcelos, Education Editor, *Correio do Povo*, 27 June 2005.

11 | Chile: swimming against the tide?

PATRICIO SILVA

It has become commonplace to see the names of Ricardo Lagos and Michelle Bachelet linked to those of Evo Morales, Hugo Chávez and Lula da Silva in studies examining the expansion of moderate left-wing governments in Latin America, the inference being that the political ascendancy of these Chilean leaders should be seen as part of the 'pink tide'. According to most analysts, the recent proliferation of such governments in the region has been mainly the result of the failure of the neoliberal reforms of the 1980s and 1990s. This led to widespread poverty, the crisis of most political institutions, and the emergence of (neo-)populism and anti-Americanism in the region (Panizza 2005, 2006). These factors were certainly the basis for the generalized anti-neoliberal mood existing in Latin America and paved the way for the election of moderate left-wing leaders. In the Chilean case, however, these factors have been almost totally absent. Hence, they cannot provide a convincing explanation for the presence of political figures such as Lagos and Bachelet at the head of Concertación governments (based on an alliance between the Chilean Socialist and Christian Democratic parties).

Neoliberal reforms in Chile were introduced by the Pinochet regime from 1975 onwards, thus preceding Thatcherism and Reaganomics as well as the emergence of the Washington Consensus. Although Pinochet's 'Chicago Boys' based their model on economic postulates formulated by Hayek, Friedman and other neoliberal thinkers, they applied these principles to concrete policies and institutional arrangements (Valdés 1995). In contrast to the situation in other Latin American countries, Chilean reforms were not imposed by international financial institutions. Furthermore, the profound transformation of the economy along neoliberal lines has generally been regarded by Chileans and international observers as having been successful. Following democratic restoration in 1990, the centre-left Concertación governments continued applying the neoliberal model and, over time, Chile has become one of the most prosperous countries in the region. There has been a dramatic reduction in the level of poverty, which has fallen from almost 40 per cent in 1990 to 13 per cent today (Mideplan 2008). The process of democratic transition and consolidation in Chile took place in a relatively orderly manner and within a solid and stable institutional framework. Political parties from both government and opposition reached general agreements (the so-called *política de acuerdos*) on fundamental policy areas, thus facilitating high levels of governability (Moreno 2006). Political parties have also successfully avoided embracing populist postures or adopting confrontational attitudes towards political adversaries. Chilean voters strongly disapprove of the use of such tactics. Additionally, since 1990, Chile has followed a diplomatic and commercial strategy that has been consciously oriented to maintaining excellent relations with the United States and the western European and Asian countries that constitute its major trade partners. It has adopted a proactive approach in seeking free trade agreements with the largest world economies and in attracting foreign investment. This strategy has no place for the anti-imperialistic or anti-globalization rhetoric that can frequently be heard in other Latin American countries.

In this chapter, I explore some factors that have been critical in shaping Chile's social democratic developmental model. These factors are almost exclusively connected to the country's own political development and hence can barely be linked to the conditions that generated the 'pink tide' elsewhere in Latin America. In order to understand the unique social democratic path adopted by the Concertación since the restoration of democracy, I focus on the following four main features of Chilean political reality. First, the profound impact of the experience of both the Unidad Popular government (1970–73; UP, Popular Unity) and the military regime (1973–90) on Chile's political culture in general and that of the left in particular. Second, the deep penetration neoliberalism has achieved in all spheres of Chilean society and the support market-oriented policies still generate among the majority of the Chilean population. Third, the strong political and institutional constraints the moderate left has had to deal with as a result of both the coalition nature of the Concertación government and the existence of a huge right-wing opposition. And last but not least, the marked technocratic nature of policy-making in Chile, in which most national problems are treated as technical issues, as a way of avoiding populism and the consequent politicization of national debate.

Allende, Pinochet and the social democratization of the Chilean left

When present-day Chileans listen to the very combative rhetoric used by 'pink tide' leaders such as Chávez and Morales, many among them cannot avoid the sensation of déjà vu. Their memories return to the early 1970s, a time when the Chilean left gained power and made use of similar revolutionary rhetoric in support of the UP government and in order to attack its many internal and international enemies. For most Chileans, the use of a passionate leftist discourse is strongly connected with the past and is not seen as a possible component of any political project for the foreseeable future. Any attempt to connect Chile to the current 'pink tide' cannot ignore the important fact that Chile, in contrast to many other countries in the region, has already had the experience of having a paradigmatic left-wing government which ended under dramatic circumstances. Needless to say, the bloody military coup of 11 September 1973 and its aftermath represent an extremely traumatic experience for the entire Chilean left. For former UP supporters, that was the day when all certainties about the irreversibility of the socialist process were mercilessly destroyed in one fell swoop.

During the first years after the coup, Chilean leftist parties referred to the military takeover as a *derrota* (defeat), thus stressing the militaristic nature of Salvador Allende's downfall (Altamirano 1977). In this manner, the actions of the armed forces were presented as a kind of extragalactic meteorite, which unexpectedly hit the surface of the country and interrupted the consolidation of socialism. With the passing of time, however, a process of demystification and secularization of the UP experience took place within the Chilean left, in which the Allende government's own errors and deficiencies were placed at the centre of analysis (De Vylder 1976; Sigmund 1977; Valenzuela, A. 1978). An increasing number of political leaders began to talk about the *fracaso* (failure) of the UP experiment, stressing by this the coalition's own responsibility for the debacle (Garretón 1987). They were particularly critical of its economic policies, which were, if not the sole factor, certainly the main cause of the widespread crisis (expressed in hyperinflation, serious food and consumer goods shortages and a huge fiscal deficit) which affected the country in 1972–73. The recognition that the UP's economic policies had failed would have important consequences for the traditional economic thinking of the Chilean left. People learned that the adoption of a state-based economic strategy, the nationalization of enterprises and banks, the expropriation of farms, and price controls did not per se constitute the answer to Chile's social and economic problems, as many had implicitly believed in 1970. They accepted the point that economic policies did not have to be correct according to some ideological criterion, but they had to work, and that this had not been the case in Chile (Bitar 1986). So by the early 1980s, the moderate sector of the Chilean left had begun to accept the continuation of free market policies after the expected replacement of the military government. This was not the consequence of abandoning an ideal *in abstracto*, but rather the outcome of a serious evaluation of both the UP experience and the growing evidence that the neoliberal reforms were producing results.

The second major self-criticism was related to the UP's inability to retain the support of the middle classes and to forge a political alliance with the Partido Demócrata Cristiano (PDC, Christian Democrat Party). In retrospect, it was accepted that in order to implement such radical social and economic reforms as the UP government had attempted, you needed a clear majority of the population behind you, and this had not been the case. This represented an implicit acceptance of the idea of majority rule, a central element of liberal democracy (Hite 2000). The a posteriori recognition that left-wing parties had made a serious mistake when they did not resolutely support Allende's attempts to find a negotiated solution to the crisis with the Christian Democrats had important political implications for the position later adopted by the moderate left towards the latter. Many Partido Socialista (PS, Socialist Party) leaders began to see that the creation of a centre–left alliance that enjoyed the support of the majority of the population was the only way to form a strong and stable government in the post-Pinochet era. They also realized that such an alliance could be possible only if its political objectives were limited to the restoration of democratic rule (the main common goal uniting the socialist movement and the PDC), and did not include socialist demands.

A third major factor in producing the social democratization of a significant part of the Chilean left was the phenomenon of exile. This factor has been deeply underestimated in most analyses of the genesis of the Concertación. The critical debate concerning the UP experience took place between 1973 and 1985 in the countries of western and eastern Europe, where most of the UP leaders lived as political exiles (Kay, D. 1987). It is estimated that, at the very least, 200,000 Chileans left the country after the military coup (Angell and Carstairs 1987: 159). The European exile would prove to be decisive for the initiation in the mid-1970s of the so-called *proceso de renovación* (process of renovation), which led to a definitive break with Leninism and an explicit reappreciation of democracy (Angell and Carstairs 1987). The personal experience of many Chilean political leaders who lived for years in eastern European countries resulted in their repudiation of these regimes as they were directly confronted with the dark side of 'really existing socialism'. In meetings held in western European cities, they began openly to express their discontent with state repression, the lack of political freedom and the bad shape of the economy, which characterized Eastern Bloc countries. Many eventually relocated to western European countries. This is for instance the case of Jorge Arrate, who moved to Rotterdam after difficult years in East Berlin and initiated a profound theoretical and programmatic discussion within the Chilean socialist movement (Arrate 1983, 1985).

What has not been sufficiently stressed up to now is the fact that the influence of western Europe on Chilean socialist leaders was not limited to ideological discussions within the left. What perhaps had the greatest impact on them were western European societies as a whole – their people, their social and political customs and institutions, and their ability to solve problems in a consensual manner. No less important were the many daily personal experiences they had in all aspects of their lives, the new friends they made and, last but not least, the *cariño* (affection) they felt for those countries. Many admired the way in which governments and oppositions in western Europe have been able to achieve political agreement and recognized that it was possible to be a loyal opposition to a government. They also realized that there was such a thing as the general interest of 'the nation', an idea that in the past had been labelled as a manipulative weapon of the bourgeoisie to distract the working class from defence of its real interests. Another important side effect of long exile was the emergence of a new kind of identification with their home country as a result of their deep nostalgia for Chile, the land and its people. They began to look at Chile in its totality, from Arica to Punta Arenas, and from a genuine world perspective, abandoning their previous, narrow, Santiago-based vision of the country. They now viewed Chilean society as a whole, as a single nation rather than a group of conflicting classes. In today's Chile, most politicians who have lived in exile talk almost exclusively about 'Chile', 'our nation' and 'the Chileans', and avoid referring to specific segments of society (Silva 1993).

Over time, the Chilean left was also forced to reformulate its initial assessments about the nature and viability of the military regime. To begin with, the latter was simply analysed in ahistorical terms as representing the temporary triumph of an ill-defined fascism; many were convinced that the Pinochet regime was politically and economically unviable and expected it to collapse within a matter of months or, in the worst scenario, a few years. It was felt that the military would prove unable to establish a stable and workable coalition in order to obtain broad support for its authoritarian project, and that the orthodox neoliberal policies introduced by the 'Chicago Boys' would quickly lead to the total collapse of the Chilean economy and hence of the regime. It soon became clear to everyone, however, that the regime had consolidated itself and that its neoliberal policies had started to deliver the goods. The Chilean left also had to accept the indisputable fact that the military regime received considerable support from broad sections of the population and, as a consequence, the road towards democratic restoration in Chile would be a long and difficult one. From this perspective, accommodation with the Christian Democrats and even the military regime itself would be necessary to find a peaceful way out of authoritarian rule.

Neoliberalism and the consolidation of market economics in Chile

Some 'pink tide' Latin American leaders are highly critical of neoliberalism, which is seen as responsible for most of the serious economic and social problems affecting the region. Although Chile is often presented as one of the main bastions of neoliberalism in Latin America, little effort has been made to attempt to explain how these policies have achieved significant socio-economic results. Contemporary Chile represents an exception within Latin America in terms of its socio-economic development and political stability. While for the last two decades the levels of poverty have increased in practically the entire region, they have dramatically decreased in Chile, and there are all kinds of safety nets and social programmes in place for those who still need state assistance (Pizarro et al. 1995). The country possesses one of the most dynamic economies in the region with increasing levels of productivity, steady expansion of exports, and high levels of foreign investment. Furthermore, Chile has one of the most stable political systems in Latin America, as demonstrated by high levels of political consensus within the political class, and the absence of the phenomena of populism and open ideological confrontation. Democratic governments maintain high levels of authority and legitimacy and government–opposition relations are institutionalized.

In order to understand the exceptional evolution of Chilean politics and economy, and the ways neoliberalism has been able to deeply penetrate Chilean society, the following factors have to be taken into consideration. First, neoliberal reforms were implemented by a cohesive team of technocrats who possessed, rightly or wrongly, a strong conviction that their reforms were the solution to the country's most urgent problems. These reforms were strongly supported by the Pinochet government, the political right, the entrepreneurial class and the army. Nowhere in Latin America had political and economic elites felt so threatened as they had in Chile in the early 1970s, where they were simultaneously confronted with a threat 'from above' (the Allende government) and one 'from below' (the radicalized masses asking for expropriation and socialism). This particular scenario explains the high degree of cooperation and support provided by these elites to the military government in its efforts to reform the economy. From this perspective, neoliberalism was seen not just as a means of reactivating the Chilean economy but also represented a conscious attempt to eradicate all the social, political and economic factors that had in the past facilitated the emergence of a combative labour movement and strong left-wing political parties. This was the reason why the economic elite supported the application of neoliberalism, despite the fact that it often had a negative short-term impact upon its interests (in terms of foreign competition and the elimination of subsidies and state support). This constitutes one of the most important differences with other Latin American states where neoliberal reforms have been implemented, as other governments have seldom offered such decisive and cohesive support for them and economic elites have had serious doubts about the need for these changes and in many cases have openly resisted them.

A second and directly related point is that, in Chile, neoliberal policies were applied, in a radical and relatively consistent way, in all spheres of society, from the financial to the health and education sectors. The existence of a cohesive group of economists in charge of these reforms facilitated their systematic formulation and application, whereas in other countries they were implemented more erratically as opposition and pressure groups forced governments to withdraw certain measures and reformulate others. This led to contradictory measures which adversely affected the public's trust in the economy. Third, the relative success of the reforms has facilitated the acceptance of neoliberalism by broad sectors of the population, despite the fact they were originally implemented by an authoritarian regime. In the rest of Latin America, most neoliberal reforms introduced during the 1980s did not produce visible improvement and, indeed, some ended in total failure and the fall of governments. Today in Chile, the existence of an open market and a privatized economy is not up for discussion, and there is a sense that the country has finally found the way to achieve development and prosperity. In the rest of the region, the failure of economic reforms, together with the emergence of populist leaders, has engendered a political climate in which the adoption of an anti-neoliberal stance provides instant political and electoral benefits. This is not the case in Chile, where populism is deeply mistrusted by the majority of people and where political parties, although they are less strong than in the past, still possess the capacity to maintain a consensus on economic policy.

Finally, the consolidation of neoliberalism in Chile has been facilitated by a growing awareness by Chileans that their country is exceptional within Latin America. Every day, they see media reports about the many conflicts and crises affecting neighbouring countries and the entire Latin American region, with presidents being ousted by angry demonstrators and poverty levels reaching explosive levels. Chileans have learned to value the existence of democratic stability, institutional strength and growing economic prosperity, and they wish to protect these achievements in order to avoid suffering the same fate as the rest of Latin America. As a result, most Chileans strongly distrust those 'pink tide' Latin American leaders who condemn neoliberalism and adopt populist measures in order to win the support of their people.

Checks and balances under the Concertación governments

Many 'pink tide' governments do not have to contend with opposition forces that are able to check the actions of the executive and compel it to negotiate on proposed policy changes. As a result, presidents such as Hugo Chávez, Néstor Kirchner and Rafael Correa have had almost unlimited room to manoeuvre. The Chilean experience is vastly different in that the political process is shaped by the existence of checks and balances that have reduced the ability of the moderate left to decisively influence the pace and nature of the policies implemented by governments since 1990. It must be remembered that the Chilean transition process was shaped by the 1980 constitution introduced by Pinochet. That document determined that a plebiscite should take place in 1988, in which Chileans would decide whether they wanted to extend Pinochet's rule for another eight years (the 'yes' option) or to have free general elections within fourteen months (the 'no' option). In August 1983, the Christian Democrats, the Socialists and other smaller political parties formed the Alianza Democrática (AD, the Democratic Alliance) with the aim of forming a future government. In 1985, the 'National Accord for the Transition to a Full Democracy' was signed by the majority of opposition forces, including some on the right (this was facilitated by the mediation of the Catholic Church). As the date of the plebiscite approached, democratic forces mobilized for this historical trial of strength between the military government and the opposition. Paradoxically, the fact that there was just one candidate (Pinochet) and that people could say only 'yes' or 'no' on 5 October 1988 helped to facilitate the unification of the democratic opposition forces around a single common denominator: saying 'no' to Pinochet. The *Comando por el No*, formed in February 1988, included almost all the opposition with the exception of the communists, who refused to participate in a plebiscite organized by the military. The triumph of the 'no' option demonstrated that an important part of the Chilean population had got over its anxiety about a restoration of democracy. The opposition parties obtained the people's confidence because they made it clear that they did not want a return to the past. After the plebiscite, the eleven parties constituting the *Comando por el No* decided to establish the Concertación de Partidos por la Democracia, an electoral coalition which would contest the general elections scheduled for December 1989. The fact that no chaos or violence followed the plebiscite, and that the opposition was magnanimous in victory, convinced many Chileans that the Concertación coalition was trustworthy and that December 1989 could be the beginning of a peaceful transition to democracy.

From the very beginning, the Concertación governments had to operate within the restrictions imposed by the 1980 constitution. These included the permanence of Pinochet as chief of the army, the introduction of a group of senators for life (all pro-Pinochet), the supervision of the government by a Council for National Security, and the existence of electoral laws that clearly benefited the right. The right-wing forces, organized in the Unión Democrática Independiente (UDI, the Independent Democratic Union) and Renovación Nacional (RN, National Renovation), obtained significant representation in parliament, which has meant that Concertación governments have had to negotiate with them over much in their legislative programme.

The power of the moderate left, represented by the PS and the Partido por la Democracia (PPD), has also been restricted by the fact that the Concertación is a coalition and they, thus, have to seek consensus with their Christian Democratic partners. This has meant that the so-called *temas valóricos* such as abortion, divorce and homosexuality were left off the policy agenda. The moderate left, which wanted to avoid any suspicion that it might try to implement radical policies reminiscent of the Allende government, was also willing to allow the Christian Democrats to provide the first two presidents, Patricio Aylwin and Eduardo Frei. During the first decade of democracy, the idea of having a socialist presidential candidate for the Concertación was clearly taboo. One of the most remarkable aspects of the new Chilean democracy has been the strong readiness shown by both government and opposition to compromise on economic, political and social matters. As Tulchin and Varas observed:

> after seventeen years of military dictatorship, Chilean political leaders all across the political spectrum began to put an end to a long tradition of bitter confrontations, and slowly to value more and more democratic stability through compromise. An important modernization of political

life occurred under the authoritarian regime. It consisted of a more pragmatic, non-ideological approach to political issues and a consensual commitment to the maintenance of democratic rules of the game. The trauma of the military coup and its long and bloody aftermath were powerful incentives for all political sectors not to recreate the same conditions that produced the breakdown of democracy. (Tulchin and Varas 1991: 4)

Alejandro Foxley, former minister of finance in the Allende government and latterly minister of foreign affairs under Bachelet, echoed these sentiments when he noted that 'we are living in a new situation of social peace, constructive intentions and optimism. These circumstances came about as a means of surviving a long period of profound social divisions and instability. We must make good use of this opportunity and ensure it continues into the future' (Foxley 1993: 42).

The first Concertación government, and particularly President Patricio Aylwin himself, was extremely cautious in each step it took in order not to jeopardize the still-delicate political stability the country had achieved following his installation in March 1990. In contrast to other countries in the region, democratic rule was inaugurated under quite auspicious circumstances given that the country's economy had enjoyed steady growth for many years. Moreover, as O'Donnell and Schmitter argue, countries that have previously had a long experience of democracy have a significant advantage in transitions to democratic rule over those who are shaping a democratic order for the first time (O'Donnell et al. 1986: 23–4). It was evident that both Chilean politicians and citizens felt very comfortable with the re-establishment of democratic rituals, seeing this as a re-encounter with their national roots. It was also the case that bad memories about the period leading up to the 1973 coup came into play. As Valenzuela indicates:

> such cases of reconsolidation of democracy are ... hampered by returning images of the crisis that led to their breakdown, which opponents of the democratic process will usually attempt to emphasize. Successful redemocratizations therefore require a deliberate effort on the part of the democratizing elites to avoid resurrecting symbols, images, conducts, and political programs associated with the conflicts leading to prior breakdown. (Valenzuela 1992: 79)

One of the most painful memories of the pre-coup period was of the effects of economic crisis and, therefore, one of the main fears in the new democratic period was whether the Aylwin government would be able to maintain the economic and financial stability it had inherited from Pinochet. A particular concern was how the trade unions would deal with the government and entrepreneurs, now they were free to use their rights (including strikes) to demand improvements in their wages and working conditions. The Concertación wanted to destroy the myth that authoritarian governments are better than democratic ones in procuring economic growth and development. If the Aylwin government succeeded in showing its ability to provide even higher levels of social and economic development, this would not only legitimize democratic rule but also reduce fears among Chileans about a return to the past. In the light of these fears, the new finance minister, Alejandro Foxley, and his team were determined to maintain and increase economic prosperity. As Oppenheim Hecht indicates:

> Chileans remembered well the turbulent and chaotic days that had preceded the fall of Salvador Allende, along with the violence that ensued. The country had suffered a collective trauma. As a result, Chileans were extremely sensitive to situations that they thought might recreate previous crises. For example, many Chileans associated inflation and economic dislocation with the Allende government; consequently, the Aylwin government made the day-to-day management and stability of the economy a major priority. (Oppenheim Hecht 1993: 207)

The Aylwin government introduced the practice of regular consultations with opposition parties, entrepreneurial organizations and trade unions in order to obtain broad political and social support for its economic policy. This practice, which was continued by Eduardo Frei, helped to reduce the traditionally high levels of distrust in Chilean politics. This *política de acuerdos* permitted, among other things, raising taxes to finance social programmes, an increase in the minimum wage, and improvement of labour legislation (Foxley 1993; Cortázar 1993). The relatively good relations between government, opposition and entrepreneurs concerning economic policy were undoubtedly rooted in the fact that the governments continued to apply neoliberal policies (Petras and Leiva 1994). The Aylwin and Frei governments embraced the views of the 'Chicago Boys' on the subsidiary role of the state in economic activities; the revaluation of the role played by foreign and local private sector capital in achieving economic development; the adoption of market mechanisms and efficiency criteria as the main instruments for the allocation of fiscal financial resources; and the need to keep public finances healthy and to consolidate macroeconomic stability. In this manner, right-wing parties and entrepreneurial circles were, in general, satisfied by the economic path followed by the new authorities. Furthermore, they were also very reluctant to adopt a more oppositional stance as this might lead to a strengthening of the more radical sectors within the Concertación, resulting in a partial or complete abandonment of neoliberalism.

The Concertación government realized that political stability would not be achieved just by simply guaranteeing macroeconomic and financial equilibrium. Something had to be done to improve the living conditions of the millions of Chileans who had been excluded from the fruits of economic growth. The poverty issue, however, had to be dealt with very cautiously as any governmental initiative to combat poverty could be interpreted in right-wing circles as a disguised attempt to pursue populist or even socialist objectives. The governments consciously depoliticized the social question to prevent confrontation on this matter. In contrast to the pre-coup period, contemporary social inequalities are not approached in extreme ideological terms, but from the perspective of modernization. Government and opposition share the view that in a country such as Chile, which is experiencing a fast process of modernization and reaching satisfactory standards of development, it is simply not possible to have large segments of your population living in a situation of extreme poverty. The latter is seen as not only ethically deplorable but also technically unacceptable in a soon-to-be-modern developed nation. Social justice is presented as the efficient elimination of poverty and, in this way, it can be reconciled with the goals of economic efficiency and political stability. An important step forward in the attempt to reduce the levels of poverty and social insecurity among the most vulnerable sectors was the introduction of a substantive pension reform in March 2008. This has led to the creation of the Pensión Básica Solidaria (PBS) by which all low-income Chileans who were previously not members of a scheme will receive a state pension. In addition, the new legislation will reduce the existing gap in the value of pensions between men and women (the latter presently receive substantially less than men). This new legislation has been the result of a two-year study by a special commission appointed by President Bachelet in which groups from civil society also participated.

The technocratization of decision-making

One very visible difference between most 'pink tide' leaders and Chilean presidents is the use of language. While the former often utter eloquent proclamations and constant accusations against some individual, country or economic power, the latter have adopted a technocratic vocabulary when referring to social targets and economic goals. The manifestly technocratic nature of governmental decision-making in the economic, financial and administrative fields has been a constant feature of the Concertación governments of Aylwin (1990–94), Frei (1994–2000), Lagos (2000–06) and Bachelet (2006–10), and they all appointed powerful technocratic teams to take charge of their economic policies. Their aim was to send a strong message to local entrepreneurs and the international business community that the Chilean economy was being managed efficiently. The governments also adopted, to varying degrees, a technocratic discourse based on the modernization of the economy and the public sector, the search for efficiency, and a government 'of the best'. The objective of accomplishing economic growth and financial stability on the one hand, and reducing social inequality in the country on the other (exemplified by the slogan 'growth with equity'), has, however, created tensions between technocrats and politicians. These have been increasingly evident since the Frei presidency and reached intense levels under Michelle Bachelet as politicians attacked the technocratic inner circle which she, initially, created.

Political developments in Chile since 1990 provide an excellent example of how democracy can coexist with technocratic groups occupying key positions in government. The vital role played by technocrats has been facilitated by the existence of a kind of *empate político*, a political tie between the centre-left forces in power and the strong right-wing opposition, including the business community and the military. The presence of competent technocrats in charge of the government's economic and financial decisions acted as a guarantee that the Concertación would not introduce fundamental changes to the economic model. This understanding is not, however, the only factor that explains the adoption of technocratic formulas. What was even more important was the long and painful process of political learning which Concertación leaders went through after the breakdown of democratic rule in 1973. After years of retrospective analysis, many came to the conclusion that a vital factor in the fall of Allende and the subsequent destruction of democracy was the politicization of state agencies, which had hindered the application of coherent policies.

Concertación governments have been constantly challenged by the tension between their aim of maintaining high rates of economic growth and efficient administration of the state on the one hand, and the need to facilitate spaces for popular participation on the other. What the Chilean example shows is that achieving notable success in the social and economic fields (a sharp reduction of poverty and high levels of economic growth and prosperity) does not necessarily legitimize the technocratic structures that have, in part, made them possible. The growing demands for participation, made manifest during the Bachelet government, have forced it to search for arrangements that can combine the technocratic rationale with opening spaces for civil society representation. Despite the marked socio-economic and political achievements experienced in Chile in the last decade, a certain sense of disenchantment with the accomplishments of the new democracy can be perceived. Some people, for instance, are disappointed by the inability of governments to reduce the income gap between the richest and the poorest segments of the population. The restoration of democracy has brought a clear improvement in human rights and in the general macroeconomic situation, but huge inequalities in the distribution of the fruits of modernization and economic growth remain. This is partly inherent in the nature of neoliberal policies, as their emphasis lies in generating economic growth and not in producing a more equitable income distribution. The Concertación governments have not played an active role in the area of income distribution, as that would have been regarded as a return to the old interventionist state and would certainly not have obtained parliamentary support from the right.

In recent years, a number of social actors have forcefully demanded more rapid improvement in their socio-economic situation and full recognition of their cultural rights. Thus, for example, since May 2006 Santiago secondary-school students have been regularly protesting on the streets, demanding real improvements in the quality of education in public schools. Additionally, copper miners have staged several strikes to demand a greater share in the enormous profits earned by the Chilean state as a result of the huge increase in international copper prices. Finally, the Mapuche Indians in southern Chile have mobilized and undertaken land seizures to demand that the Chilean state return their ancestral territory and recognize their cultural rights. The government has been castigated for failing to deliver full citizenship to the Mapuche and for imprisoning community leaders under anti-terrorism legislation. For some (particularly those in right-wing circles) the increasing climate of social unrest is due to President Bachelet's inability to impose her authority and that of the rule of law on those who violate it. For others, however, this new scenario simply reflects the fact that the Chilean transition is finally over and citizens are no longer afraid to exercise their civil rights in the knowledge that democratic rule is now firmly consolidated. Nevertheless, democracy has experienced a loss of prestige as a result of cases of public corruption among politicians and public officials. Although Chile has one of the lowest levels of corruption among developing countries and a long tradition of probity, these cases have been sufficient to reduce citizens' respect for politicians and politics in general. Paradoxically, political apathy has become general in Chile despite (and perhaps because of) the manifest improvements in the general socio-economic and political conditions of the population. Although the Chilean political class is alarmed by increased political indifference, there are observers who explain this phenomenon as just being the consequence of the high levels of political and economic stability existing in the country, as is the case in most Western democracies.

The future of Chile's social democratic model

'There is nothing more successful than success itself.' This seems to be the secret for the consolidation of neoliberalism in Chile and for the broad political support it enjoys. Irrespective of who will become the next president after the 2009 presidential elections (a politician of the Concertación or from the right), there are unlikely to be major changes to Chile's new social democratic model and the *política de acuerdos*, and huge investment in social policies will remain fundamental to this. Chilean presidents will also continue to maintain a safe distance from 'pink tide' populist leaders who reject everything that Chile represents: neoliberalism; the provision of a friendly environment for multinational corporations; good relations with the United States; and a positive engagement with globalization. Chile is also unhappy with the support, both explicit and implicit, given by some 'pink tide' leaders to Bolivia's historic claim for access to the Pacific. Hugo Chávez has openly supported it, declaring that he dreamed of swimming from a Bolivian beach during the November 2003 Ibero-American summit at Santa Cruz. The fact that he made similar remarks at the 2007 summit in Santiago did not endear him to President Bachelet. Additionally, relations with the Kirchner and Fernández administrations have been seriously damaged owing to Argentina's approach to the delivery of gas to Chile. This has revived tensions that seemed to have disappeared following the restoration of democracy. On the other hand, relations between the Concertación governments and the Toledo and García administrations in Peru have also been difficult owing to the latter's attempts to reconfigure the maritime border between the two countries. This has led to a legal battle at the International Court of Justice in The Hague and will mean that tensions continue in the future. In addition to these geo-political questions, the growing disparity between Chilean prosperity and social and political tensions in and between neighbouring countries (including the conflict between Colombia and Ecuador over the former's military incursions over the border in pursuit of guerrillas) have led many Chileans to adopt an increasingly isolationist stance with the aim of protecting Chile from such turmoil. They have also convinced them that Chile is following the right path.

Since the restoration of democratic rule in Chile the concept of democracy has lost its participatory implications with respect to the decision-making process. Instead, the Schumpeterian view of democracy has been tacitly accepted. From this perspective, democracy is conceived as a method of reaching political decisions in which various elites compete for votes and citizens decide by whom they will be governed. Today, the use of traditional methods of civil pressure and protest (such as property seizures, unauthorized street protests and politically motivated strikes) are generally considered illegitimate by political elites and are portrayed as old-fashioned in the media. Negative collective memories about the populist past and profound changes in the political culture of most of the left, together with the relative success of the neoliberal model, have facilitated the almost unchallenged rise of technocrats in governmental circles. It is probable that a further depoliticization of Chilean society will take place in coming years, but this does not mean that the country will be spared social mobilization and political tensions. The goal of modernizing society must involve a massive effort to reduce large income disparities as well as expanding access to education, health and housing for those social groups that still do not enjoy the fruits of economic prosperity.

12 | Argentina: reforming neoliberal capitalism

ERNESTO VIVARES, LEONARDO DIAZ ECHENIQUE
AND JAVIER OZORIO

In March 2002, a few months after Argentina's financial meltdown, two eminent economists advanced a plan to the International Monetary Fund (IMF), the international financial institutions (IFIs) and the G7 countries: to boost its external financial credibility, the Argentine government should 'solicit a foreign stabilization commission that runs the central bank, in exchange for the disbursement of an important stabilization loan and control of budget implementation' (Caballero and Dornbusch 2002). Despite the consensus of economists in favour of this proposal, the country rejected it, and five years later had made a startling comeback from economic chaos by adopting unorthodox prescriptions that prioritized social, domestic and regional commitments. In June 2006, Argentina cancelled its US$9.8 billion IMF debt facility and began the renationalization of its privatized social security system, and was exhibiting an outstanding average of 8.8 per cent annual growth in GDP. Nevertheless, different factors have been undermining the model. The international rise in food and other commodity prices is accentuating clashes between the agricultural and export sectors and the government. This chapter explores the development strategy followed by Argentina since the IMF-sponsored 'convertibility regime', and its construction of more substantive forms of democracy and social justice.

The strategy of the administrations of Peronists Néstor Kirchner (2003–07) and Cristina Fernández de Kirchner, who succeeded her husband after a first-round victory in the presidential election of December 2007, must be understood within the framework of two Argentine phenomena, constraints that illustrate Marx's famous proposition that people cannot make history as they please, since 'they do not make it under circumstances chosen by themselves but under circumstances directly encountered, given and transmitted from the past' (Marx 1962: 252). The first of these phenomena is Peronism as a national and popular movement, the major historical force since the 1940s, and the political force driving the government today. The second phenomenon is the conservative–neoliberal economic project of the 'convertibility regime' of the 1990s. A critical analysis of these elements will help make sense of the political-economic nature of the development strategy of Argentina since 2003, within the framework of strategies elsewhere in Latin America. Argentina is a regional case that needs to be considered beyond the limited and elitist cold war, Anglo-Saxon understanding of populism and developmentalism. This chapter assumes the existence of indissoluble links between the regional and domestic, and the centrality of the political sphere after two decades of neoliberal reforms, with development influenced by new regional models as well as the neoliberal world order.

Latin America, Argentina and Peronism

Peronism takes its name from Juan Domingo Perón, who was president from 1946 to 1955, when he was ousted in a military coup, and, upon returning from exile, from 1973 until his death in 1974. Combining nationalist economic policy with pro-labour social policy, Perón became Latin America's most celebrated so-called 'populist'. Historically, Peronism was essentially a counter-hegemonic movement that allied sectors which had been historically excluded by the classic Argentine economic model based on agricultural exports, and by a conservative social base aligned first with British and then with US hegemonic interests. Peronism refounded the country; contested the role of the 'granary of the world' that produced social and political exclusion; and sought autonomy from the USA, and competed with it for trade leadership (Rapoport 2002; Franco 2002; Bulmer-Thomas 2003).

The basic element of the current Peronist strategy of development is a national, popular and regionally oriented movement with bourgeois characteristics, aiming not only to produce a domestic and social revolution, but also national autonomy and market coordination to increase consumption, social justice and human rights (the last because of its painful history). Peronism pursues development based on rebuilding a regional and autonomous capitalism. From this are derived two central components in the current Peronist strategy of development. The first is its belief in the primacy of politics, not least to produce the capital–labour relations needed to achieve sustainable development. The second element is its belief in the region as a central framework of development.

With the military coup of 1955, Peronist administration came to an end, and its political expression was proscribed for decades. Given its social bases in popular forces, however, and key elements of capital and labour, Peronism resisted all attempts to eradicate it. In 1972, Perón returned from exile, in the midst of armed conflict between left-wing and right-wing Peronist groups over the political future of the movement. In the 1980s, after almost a decade of persecution, kidnapping, torture and murder of its militants, against the odds and the predictions of intellectuals, Peronism reappeared, but now transformed into an electoral machine dominated by its right-wing sectors. By the 1990s, under Carlos Saúl Menem, the Peronist Partido Justicialista (PJ, Justicialist Party) led the conservative neoliberal transformation of the country. With the movement having been the central actor in Argentina's deepest economic crisis, today Peronism's progressive sectors are, paradoxically, leading the national recovery.

The 'convertibility regime' and Argentina's *transformismo*

The 'convertibility regime' launched in 1991 'hard-pegged' the US dollar–Argentine peso exchange rate at one-to-one. It was the outcome of almost twenty years of conservative and neoliberal strategies of development, and its impact can be traced in the balance of forces between capital and labour (Basualdo 2001; Rapoport 2002). Capital enjoyed an unprecedented privatization of strategic state assets, producing an increasing financialization of these sectors, and the dominance of financial over industrial capital. The whole period of the 'convertibility regime' (1991–2001) is marked by a deep regionalization and/or internationalization of the Argentine economy, which ended with a division of interests within the hegemonic bloc, a division reflected in the changing of IFI attitudes towards the Argentine government. Briefly, the process was marked, first, by the transfer of assets from the state to partnerships of domestic and international capital; and second, by a transfer of these assets from domestic to international capital, notably Spanish, US, Chilean, French, Italian, German and Canadian (Kosacoff 1999; Kulfas 2001; Basualdo 2001; Azpiazu 2002).

The structural changes of the period 1989–2001, in what some scholars have named Argentine *transformismo* (transformation), set the scene for the administration of Néstor Kirchner, against the background of the consolidation and then decline of the conservative neoliberal hegemony that had evolved since the mid-1970s (Basualdo 2001). The *transformismo* represented a domestic–international bloc of alliances between the leading actors in economic development. It was characterized by a capacity to repackage international neoliberal guidelines as domestic prescriptions, by depoliticizing them and presenting them as universal technical solutions, as in the cases of privatization, welfare policy, free trade and an independent central bank.

The Argentine *transformismo* was also characterized by its capacity to absorb and co-opt opposition political forces through processes of political compensation or exclusion based on the use of state resources

Argentina

(Basualdo 2001; Etchemendy 2005). The country's history since 1975 shows the adaptability of the conservative–neoliberal hegemony and Argentina's dominant groups. The economic actors that emerged during the dictatorship, the main beneficiaries of the democratic openness, were the neoliberal apostles of the Menem administration and of the regional alliance Mercosur, and have been the central actors of the current regional reindustrialization process (Etchemendy 2005).

In terms of labour, the conservative–neoliberal period brought about profound social change, with very negative results for the labour sector, characterized by falling salaries and rising unemployment. Taking 1976 as the base year indexed at 100, salaries fell from around 150 in 1975 to around 75 in 1977, rose again to around 115 by 1985 but then fell steadily to about 65 in 2000, the lowest value in forty years. Unemployment rose from a low point of about 5 per cent in 1979 to peak at about 33 per cent in 1996, before recovering to about 30 per cent at the end of the century (Basualdo 2001: 76).

As the system worked like the old gold standard adhered to by conservative governments before 1930, the Menem administration believed that the 'convertibility regime' of dollar–peso parity would necessarily attract capital flows, creating a sound credit system. As the dollar appreciated, however, so Argentine exports became less competitive. With the US decision to raise interest rates in February 1994, followed by the crises in Mexico, Thailand and Russia, the Argentine balance of payments and of trade worsened. The rate of interest on debts grew, and unemployment increased, magnifying the increasingly deflationary and exclusionary character of the neoliberal strategy (Weisbrot and Baker 2002). Given the country's scarcity of capital, international movements of private capital generated a deep vulnerability to external financial shocks. The Menem administration recognized this in 1995, and accelerated structural reform of social security to reduce external vulnerability, maintain investor confidence and widen the base of its political coalition. The reform of the system, implemented in alliance with the IFIs, aggravated the problem it was supposed to solve (Lousteau 2003; Mesa-Lago 2004). Privatizing social security required financial resources to be transferred to the private industrial sector, pending an economic recovery. Rather than sustaining the cohesion of the bloc, it increased division between the financial and industrial sectors, and accentuated the social deterioration of a country already in a great depression (Weisbrot and Baker 2002; Lousteau 2003). Once the model of transferring state and social resources to the private sector was exhausted, the end of the 'convertibility regime' became inevitable.

The end of convertibility split the pro-market coalition. One grouping, associated with the interests of a foreign coalition – foreign banks, subsidiaries of foreign companies, foreign companies in control of public services – sought to deepen convertibility through full dollarization of the economy. This would ensure that revenues kept their US dollar value, and enable foreign investors to retain their strategic export platform inside the Mercosur market. The second grouping was formed by domestic and foreign interests that wanted to abandon the 'convertibility regime' through a sharp devaluation of the peso. This proposal had huge support among traditional domestic exporters of commodities, since it implied a massive transference of resources to them (Basualdo 2003).

Both coalitions sought to maintain the hegemonic order via a political system that absorbed popular demands, and defused growing social discontent. As their differences intensified, accompanied by a worsening in the social situation with serious limitations on welfare provision, the contradictions of the 'convertibility regime' and of the conservative order began to be reflected in national debate. Since democratic institutions were limited in terms of social representation, global integration was producing poverty and social exclusion, international partnership was not leading to growth, and local governments were weak and unable to contain social discontent. The growing debate came to focus on the search for a long-term, balanced reconstruction of a regional and autonomous capitalist development.

The conservative–neoliberal legacy and national popular change

The process that culminated in 2001 with the collapse of the 'convertibility regime', and the split in the conservative–neoliberal coalition, had regional and domestic elements. At the regional level, the neoliberal project had paradoxically failed as a result of its major achievement: the advance of capital against labour, and the generalized social decline that it generated. The degree of conflict and protest varied locally, but shared a common feature. State workers, the unemployed, the informal sector, small and medium enterprises and farmers played a central role in the conflict, and participated actively in the construction of alternative models of development.

In Argentina the conflict united workers, the middle class and the unemployed in a common demand, *'que se vayan todos'* ('out with all of them'), but with important features that had been missing in previous periods of history, central to understanding the limitations of the anti-neoliberal turn of the Kirchner administration. Immersed in a major historical crisis, social chaos and economic depression, in 2003 the

Kirchner administration seemed to face the dilemma of either recovering the historical line of development – the regional, national and popular project – or reverting to neoliberalism, which seemed the logical option for a broken state that was lacking internal and external credibility. The coalition behind the new administration included, however, some central components of the Argentine *transformismo*. The names of companies like Perez Companc, Techint, Astra (Reposol), CEI Citicorp Holdings, Loma Negra, Macri and Soldati are prominent throughout. These had emerged as state suppliers, and major debtors, in the late 1970s and 1980s. They were the local partners of the domestic–international community of business in the 1990s. They then became the strategic allies of the Kirchner administration, controlling the powerful Unión Industrial Argentina (Argentine Industrial Union) (Basualdo 2002; Etchemendy 2005; Katz 2004). These actors had supported the model of industrialization and export orientation promoted by the Peronist Eduardo Alberto Duhalde's administration (2002–03), against the model demanded by the IFIs, and were now supporting the Kirchner administration. On the other hand, the new administration came into power with weak electoral support: Kirchner won 22 per cent in an election featuring three competing Peronist candidates (whose combined vote was 67 per cent). Furthermore, there was continued pressure from the IMF to avoid any unorthodox programme that might hurt international investor interests.

The IMF, social security, agribusiness and financing of development

Following the installation of the neoliberal model in the 1990s, IFIs and the transnational neoliberal network became central to Argentine development, and key allies of the administration. The state had become an agency for adjusting national economic practices and policies to the demands of global financial governance. In this respect, the Kirchner administration has produced three major structural changes: first, relations with the IFIs; second, reducing the power of international financial actors over state finances; and third, regulating the powerful agro-export sector to maintain the exchange rate, national reserves and domestic mass consumption.

Arguably, the IFIs, and in particular the IMF, enjoyed more power and influence in Argentina than in any other developing country. This grew with the consolidation of the international–domestic alliance under Menem, and began to decline with the division, after the crisis of 2001, between international financial actors who favoured dollarization, and domestic industrial actors who favoured devaluation of the peso. In 2003, the Kirchner administration confronted the major obstacle to implementing any strategy of development in Argentina: defaulting on external debts and facing the harsh reaction of the IFIs. To resolve the problem, the administration rescheduled the whole debt. It adopted different strategies for the $150 billion of official debt to the IMF and the Paris Club, and for private foreign debt to international investors, hedge funds and pension funds. The idea was simple: to segment international creditors, confronting them and negotiating with them on an individual basis.

There was plenty at stake. Politically, Kirchner's promise to stand up to the IFIs had won considerable public support, creating legitimacy that the government could not risk. Without rescheduling the external debt on a more flexible basis, there was no way out economically, let alone any chance of following an unorthodox economic policy. The influence of the IFIs and the IMF seemed insuperable. The IMF had publicly insisted that no reschedule would be possible until Argentina accepted its prescription and abandoned unorthodox economic measures. The choice was between neoliberal austerity and growth. The IMF demanded very high interest rates and budget cuts, which were guaranteed to deflate the economy and place the burden of 'adjustment' on the poor (Weisbrot 2001). The Argentine position was that devaluation would not generate inflation, since it would make exports cheaper and imports more expensive, thus improving the trade balance and stimulating growth. To follow its own policy, the Kirchner administration had to define its relation with the IMF through the only means possible, that is by playing politics: to gain either support or silence from the G7 states, or to pay back official debt in order to reduce IMF pressure.

The issue of cancellation of external debt with the IMF displays contrasting aspects of the administration's strategy. The Argentine government, with the backing of the Brazilian administration, cancelled the entire Argentine external debt with the Fund. This was only a small proportion of total external debt, but its cancellation had clear and direct beneficiaries. It favoured exporters, industrial producers and domestic bankers, against the interests of foreign debtors and privatized companies (Katz 2004). The IMF had acted for the latter against the former. In this way, the Kirchner administration mediated in favour of the industrial domestic sector against the internationalized sector. Without this move there would have been no room for unorthodox policies. In short, independence from the IMF was as much a question of political management as of political economy (Grugel and Riggirozzi 2007). This option was crucial, if Argentina was to move away from a model defined by financial interests, and adopt policies focused on industrialization.

The government, therefore, rejected the classical IMF prescription of high interest rates and cuts in fiscal spending, which were intended to honour the external debt and restore international investor confidence. Instead, the government favoured the industrial and export sectors by maintaining a favourable exchange rate, controlling the cost of public services, and promoting domestic consumption through wage increases in the public and private sectors (Katz 2004). This approach enabled the administration to promote agricultural exports in order to finance industrialization and increase the purchasing power of salaries. The fiscal surplus became a strategic political economic tool to reduce dependence on capital markets and IFIs, and agro-exports made possible a reduction in interest rates, in order to control speculative capital and promote domestic credit.

The second major change involved key reforms to the mixed system of social security. The market-oriented transformation of the social security system initiated in 1994 had been inspired by the reforms enforced by the Chilean dictatorship in 1981, and promoted by the IMF, the World Bank and the International Development Bank. In the belief that it would attract major foreign direct investment and reduce fiscal deficit, it was made compulsory for Argentinians to join the private pension sector (Weisbrot and Baker 2002). The reform redefined the political-economic landscape of the country, putting the control of state debt in the hands of alliances and actors who later became a central target of the Kirchner administration. In 2007, the government reformed this pension system. It was no longer compulsory to join a private pension scheme, pension funds would be invested in production (e.g. energy and infrastructure), and the state would regulate and guarantee the funds on the basis of inter-generational solidarity. The measure was simple, and it permitted people to join a state scheme. Within a few months, the bank-owned pension schemes had lost nearly a million members, and the state gained more finance to foster domestic development. Moreover, the re-establishment of the state system of social security represented a structural reform of the neoliberal model, since it weakened the international banks and financial institutions that had controlled state financing and debt.

A third area of change has been agriculture. Argentina is the world's third-largest soybean producer, just behind the USA and Brazil. In 2003, the production of soya used 10 million hectares of land, and by 2008 it used 15 million. The Argentine agro-export model was consolidated during these years, favoured by internal and external factors. Internally, the sector received indirect subsidies through the exchange rate policy, as well as through direct subsidies for oil and gas. Internationally, the rise in prices of food, along with the promotion of grains as biofuel substitutes for carbon-based oil, strengthened agro-exports, and accelerated the 'soyization' of the countryside. This model is regulated by the transnational companies that control the production of transgenic seeds. And this domination of agricultural land by the monoculture of soy production for export reduced domestic food supplies, raising food prices beyond the resources of the population. In March 2008 the new government of President Cristina Fernández introduced, by presidential decree, a sliding scale of taxes on agricultural exports. The system aimed to contain domestic inflation, limit the expansion of grain monoculture, protect domestic food supplies and prices, and redistribute some of the windfall wealth arising from world food price inflation. The measure was fiercely opposed by farmers in the interior, by landowners and by agricultural entrepreneurs. A farmers' 'strike' took the form of refusing to market their products, and was accompanied by roadblocks and mass protests. The first major political crisis since 2002, accompanied by sometimes violent demonstrations and counter-demonstrations, engulfed the government. In July 2008, the measure was sent back to the Congress for ratification. The Chamber of Deputies ratified it, but the Senate rejected it on the casting vote of the Argentine vice-president. Fernández's Head of Cabinet resigned, and the measure was revoked. The conflict had put the government's redistributive strategy at the centre of national debate, and, following the revocation of her tax, Fernández pledged to maintain her battle for redistribution.

From a variety of viewpoints the government's general strategy is seen as some kind of neo-developmentalist return to import-substitution industrialization (Gerchunoff and Aguirre 2004; Godio 2004; Ricupero 2004). This theme is prominent in debates in the region, as mainstream scholars attempt to explain the post-2003 Argentine administration within the conceptual framework dominated by a particular blend of Keynesianism and cold war ideology, notably in the notion of developmentalism (e.g. Gerchunoff and Aguirre 2004). Argentina's recovery and the Kirchners' strategy have, however, owed little, in recent years, to exports or to favourable prices on world markets (Weisbrot and Sandoval 2007; Frenkel and Rapetti 2007). Table 12.1 is central for understanding this debate and summarizes the contributions to GDP growth of the major variables for the period 2002–07. What is striking is that the major variables at the centre of Argentina's recovery are domestic consumption, accounting for 63.0 per cent of growth over the five years, and investment, accounting for 45.2 per cent. The important sectors were construction, transport, storage, communications, manufacturing, retail trade and repair services.

Significantly, domestic growth emerges as positively correlated to the decline of unemployment and poverty: unemployment fell from 21.5 per cent in 2002 to 9.6 per cent in 2007, and household poverty fell during the same period from 41.4 per cent to 16.3 per cent (Weisbrot and Sandoval 2007: 7).

The region as a framework of development

One of the most important changes since 2003 has been the political relocation of the country within its original roots, Latin America, turning away from the elitist and conservative ideological paradigm based on aligning Argentina with its European immigrant tradition and culture. Indeed, there is a strong link between the positive achievements of the post-2003 administration and the new regional approach towards development. This correlation is without precedent in the history of Argentina, but it is consistent with the Peronist approach, which has always placed regional political integration and economic cooperation at the heart of its strategy. The return to Latin American roots is not simply the work of the Kirchner and Fernández administrations, but is part of a new material and cultural reality that the government has succeeded in converting into a strategy for development (Kulfas 2001; Basualdo 2001). By the beginning of the new century, the country was signalling a new development strategy oriented towards the renegotiation of external debt, the promotion of the domestic industrial sector, and the recovery of the state's role in dealing with critical social conditions. This unorthodox strategy did, though, affect the interests of countries that had benefited under the Menem administration. Japan, Germany, Italy and France were the first in the queue lobbying for orthodox policies and subordination to the IMF recipe.

In a context of international isolation, Argentina rediscovered the vital importance of the region, notably by securing the support of Brazil in terms of relations with the IFIs, and in the Venezuelan financial backing that fended off the IMF and enabled external debt to be rescheduled. Cultural and social changes had preceded this regional realignment. During the past six decades, urban, rural and labour identities in the country had been reshaped by regional tendencies, and the crisis in 2001 made Argentinians appreciate their regional roots. After six decades of the contributions of Bolivians, Paraguayans, Chileans, Uruguayans and Peruvians to the country's development, many of them suffering discrimination, the Argentine cultural landscape was regionalized. The post-2003 administration has sought to highlight this social change, extending citizens' rights to these people, stimulating their political participation and thereby widening the popular base of the general strategy.

The administration has not yet developed, however, a substantial state policy towards two key allies, Bolivia and Paraguay. This redefinition of the socio-political landscape can be observed in different protests. For instance, after the failed attempt to align the country with the First World, Argentinians blamed all their ills on the 'convertibility regime', Menem, the USA, the IMF and neoliberalism.

Further, renewed support for regionalization was manifested in the massive repudiation, on the occasion of George W. Bush's visit to the country in 2005, of integration into the proposed ALCA (Área de Libre Comercio de las Américas, or Free Trade Area of the Americas). In 2003 one of the central election debates was whether or not to revive the strategic alliance with the USA. The neoliberal sectors and conservative Peronism stood for the integration into ALCA, as a model compatible with the dollarization of the economy. The alternative, supported by Peronist groups around Kirchner, was to align the country with Latin American partners. By then three options were open: the US-aligned model of Chile and Colombia; the socialist path of Venezuela and Cuba; or the regional leadership of Brazil. By 2004, the choice was evident: good relations with Chile and Colombia, particularly military cooperation with Chile, but not as political-economic models. It was soon clear that Brazil, Venezuela and Bolivia would be Argentina's preferred regional development partners. An indicator of this Latin Americanization is the volume of international agreements signed between May 2003 and December 2007. In this period, the country signed 398 bilateral agreements of which 61 per cent were with Latin American and the Caribbean countries, 22 per cent with Europe and Central Asia, and 6 per cent with the USA and Canada (López 2007). Unsurprisingly, the variety and scope of agreements with Venezuela, Brazil, Bolivia, Chile and Ecuador stand out.

In the steady process of economic recovery promoted by unorthodox policies, the increasing demand for energy, for industrial and social consumption, came to the fore. Here regional alliances again proved crucial, with Venezuela and Bolivia supplying the energy needs of Argentina's rapid industrial recovery. The main reasons for this support were political, but economic relations benefited too as Argentina has become a net 'regional trader' and supplier for these countries (Bouzas 2007). The positive acknowledgement of Brazilian regional leadership in Argentine foreign policy has modified a historical relationship characterized by mutual mistrust and disputes over regional supremacy. This has consolidated an alliance channelled through Mercosur, the regional customs union that is projected to move towards a greater political union, and through UNASUR, the wider alliance created in 2008, based on Mercosur and Andean Pact states. Another strategic regional change has been the regional impact of Venezuela and the Chávez administration. The Venezuelan government is indisputably a central ally of the Kirchner and Fernández administrations, through strategic support in the energy crisis, but mainly through its role in regional integration. The inclusion of Venezuela into Mercosur is redefining the latter's internal power structure, opening the door for a greater participation of small countries such as Paraguay and Uruguay, and the probable inclusion of others such as Bolivia and Ecuador. Notably, Argentina has been the key partner of Venezuela in this process. Similarly, Venezuela and Argentina have been leading the creation of the regional development bank, Banco del Sur (the Bank of the South), in order to foster regional integration without subordination to Washington.

The other model of regional integration, represented by the Venezuela–Cuba axis of the Bolivarian Alternative for the Peoples of the Americas (ALBA, Alternativa Bolivariana para los Pueblos de Nuestra América), offers different formulas of integration, but ones compatible with Argentina's regional strategy of development. ALBA is basically a system of exchanges, not unlike the Comecon of the former socialist countries: privileging the political criteria of social development and economic sustainability over sectional economic interests. In this regard, it complements Argentine policy in strategic areas – for example, in agreements between Argentina and Venezuela such as TeleSur, a regional TV system, the exchange of food technology for oil, the participation of Venezuela in one of the major agricultural Argentine cooperatives, Sancor, and the participation of Venezuela's state oil company PDVSA in the Argentine northern pipeline. Argentina's participation in oil exploitation in the Orinoco region demonstrates the strategic significance of the partnership.

State strengthening and new alliances

On 25 May 2003, in his first presidential speech, Kirchner set out the central guidelines of his government. He focused on reconstructing a viable capitalism in Argentina, a capitalism in which the state plays an intelligent role, regulating, controlling and mitigating where necessary problems that the market does not solve. The second major mission was that the state should act to combat social inequalities, to secure the implementation of the constitution and, above all, to strengthen the democratic state through an uncompromising defence of human rights. Many criticisms can be made about Peronist control of the central government and of the party, but more academic attention should be paid to the undeniable capacity that it has demonstrated to dismantle the Menemist order, rebuild the political capacity of the state and region-alize the country.

At the core of the post-2003 administrations, alongside other centre-left groups, are members of 1970s Peronist youth groups that were vio-lently excluded from the movement by conservative Peronist factions, and later persecuted by the dictatorship. In the 1970s they had attempted to build a new national and popular force out of the ashes of the historical Peronism. Marked by their urban, Catholic, professional and middle-class origins, after two painful decades they have come into power. The strategy of the Kirchner and Fernández administrations, their successes and failures, reflects the experience of these politically skilful groups and their regionalism and critical pragmatism. Their victory followed their displacement of Menemist and other Peronist fractions as they reconstructed the Partido Justicialista. They have gathered support for major projects through a mixture of policies that have shaped a new constellation of social forces, in what remains a quite fragmented national political landscape. Initially, the declaration of principles was marked by a Keynesian and anti-neoliberal rhetoric, but soon turned instead towards a mix of policies linked to Argentine national and popular discourse, a mix that can be labelled as either neo-developmentalism or neo-populism, two old elitist and economistic categories used by mainstream academics during the cold war to explain historical trends in Latin American politics that they disapproved of.

The trademark of post-2003 policy has been the reclaiming of politics as the master tool for changing social reality, a particular form of Latin American critical realism, and a pragmatism that contrasts with the strat-egies of economization and depoliticization of neoliberalism and develop-mentalism. The new policies mix orthodox and unorthodox measures, such as strict fiscal discipline, accumulation of reserves, control of tax evasion, active intervention in the economy, a pro-export exchange rate, recovering the value of salaries, major spending on infrastructure, increas-ing social welfare, and increases in pensions. On the other hand, the state has brought back into the public sector privatized companies, domestic- and foreign-owned, such as the national postal service, water, railways, electrical energy, the national airline, air traffic control, maritime control, and military factories. The Peronist sectors running the government and the party place the role of the state within a regional capitalist framework. They are critical but pragmatic about the extent to which changes can be made in a highly internationalized and regionalized economy that is marked by unprecedented inequality and social conflict as a result of rising commodity prices, particularly for food, oil and gas. Within this scenario, the Kirchner and Fernández administrations have moved both to promote development where they can generate results effectively, and to recast the political power and popular legitimacy of the state for the new model of development. Prominent in terms of state power have been the reform of the national army high command and the replacement of conservative members of the High Court.

In the area of social policy, the government has reduced unemployment and poverty, although after nearly three decades of neoliberalism, the Argentine social landscape still mirrors the conservative vision of a rich country with poor people. Argentina's economy has been growing at an average annual rate of 8.5 per cent since 2003, but it will need at least another two decades of such growth, and a battle to institutionalize a model of income redistribution: to deal with the worsened social conditions in massive sectors of the population and in the provinces; to reduce social inequality; to integrate the informal economy; and to reduce unemployment. The new Peronist administrations recognize the need to revitalize relations between capital and labour through sectoral agreements. Reflecting one of the major weaknesses of the model, however, this state-led process has been largely confined to the industrial and labour sectors, leaving unresolved the agricultural and export sectors and the poorest regions. It is not entirely clear why the government has had serious difficulties with the latter, sometimes leaving them out of major projects, and without a clear policy on the highly monopolistic and conservative agricultural sector. One reason may be the historical identification in Peronist political culture of the link between these sectors and the dictatorships.

The government's relationship with other social actors has been characterized by coalition-building through incorporating sectional demands into policies and agreements based on its political objectives. This Peronist strategy has built a popular and massive coalition, but one as fragmented as the structure of the country. It has built a new configuration of social forces, but one geographically concentrated on the interests of the provinces of greater Buenos Aires, the Litoral and Patagonia. These regions remain the beneficiaries while the north-east and central areas of the country still depend significantly on trickle-down economics and welfare. At the political level, the weakening and fragmentation of the conservative political opposition, and the shift from the neoliberal and international project towards a national and regional capitalism, have produced new social realignments and raised the role of the media in the political struggle between the conservative and the national popular projects. Important sectors of the media and journalists (e.g. Mario

Grondona and Joaquín Morales Solá), and reactionary political leaders (e.g. Elisa Carrio and López Murphy), have given voice to the conservative forces that have lost political power. The government's underestimation of the power of these forces, and the lack of state policies for specific sectors, has created conflict within society, aligning the white middle and upper classes with the agro-export and finance sectors. Through the media, conservative sectors have politicized social conflict, characterizing the new administrations and popular social forces as a fascist regime with a neo-populist face permeated by clientelism and corruption.

The Kirchner and Fernández administrations are far from leading a revolutionary process, and their capacity to institutionalize a model of redistribution remains much discussed, but it certainly does not represent a new kind of social–fascist coalition based on neo-populist clientelism (Feinman 2008). Peronism aims to build a Latin American welfare state and bring about conciliation between social classes, centralizing power in the distributional state. Historically, it has never had a good relationship with the First World-oriented middle and upper classes. In this sense, the Argentine social structure is no different from its Latin American neighbours. The middle and upper classes also resent Peronism's accumulation of power. The clashes and contradictions in Argentina reflect its changing nature and regional reorientation, and the fact that greater social justice cannot be pursued without conflict. Human rights, the new role of labour unions, the absence of repression of social protest, regaining control of social security, investment in public work, and agro-export taxes, all necessarily affect specific interests. In a letter sent to the major national newspapers in 2008, as a result of the government's decision to reopen the legal case against him for his participation in the detention and disappearance of people, Martínez de Hoz, the former minister of economy in the dictatorship, stated,

> [This is] a personal persecution … commanded by … President Kirchner … in reference to the economic programme of 1976 … imputing me for industrial genocide … [M]ost of the members of this government had close links and/or were members of the terrorist organizations of the 1970s and … attempted to murder me and my most important collaborators … Today from their official positions they seem to be continuing the struggles of the past. (Martínez de Hoz 2008; authors' translation)

Conclusion

The new administrations have sent out decisive signals in favour of: human rights, independent justice, regional commitments, independence from Washington, the European Union and the IFIs, distance from the Iraq and Afghan invasions, and international support for Cuba and Venezuela. At the domestic level, they have rebuilt domestic industry, public works and public services, inflation has been kept down, unemployment has fallen, the state has been strengthened, and the purchasing power of salaries has recovered. Nevertheless, there are important structural and agential factors that cast doubts on the sustainability of the strategy. Argentina is not an exception compared with its Latin American neighbours, but a country pursuing the construction of regional capitalism on the basis of a reformist strategy, institutionalized in part in its regional alliances in Mercosur and, since 2008, in the more widely based UNASUR. It is constrained by its own 'successes', its origins and its power, to construct a substantive democracy within and beyond the boundaries of its once Europeanized greater Buenos Aires, and the provinces of the Litoral and Patagonia. The new path of Argentina emerges conditioned by its past, by a heritage of decades of social repression and neoliberal reforms, by its geographically concentrated wealth, but also by its present.

Today, domestic and international constraints plus the orientation of the political–economic alliance at the core of its government cast doubts upon the sustainability of the strategy and upon hopes for the reconstruction of its identity. Now as never before, the country has the historical chance to refound itself in realistic terms, regionally framing its political economy and identity, reconstructing and democratizing the state and, above all, institutionalizing a redistributive and social welfare model. The Peronist strategy still has a long way to go, however. The domestic line of conflict is today fostered by the international rise in food prices, enhancing the power of the conservative agro-export sector, and of the north-oriented middle and upper classes. Today the situation in Argentina reflects the clash at the very base of its political economy, between a north-oriented country and a regional-integrated country, between a poor country with rich people and a rich country with poor people.

13 | Conclusion: *Nuestra América* – the spectre haunting Washington

GERALDINE LIEVESLEY AND STEVE LUDLAM

There have been various allusions in this book to supranational relations between Latin American states and between them, both individually and collectively, and the United States. The latter's promotion of neoliberalism and free trade agreements has been challenged by ALBA, the network of countries and organizations which aims to replace conditionality and unilateralism with reciprocity and collaboration. Reference has been made in the introductory chapter, and elsewhere in this volume, to the range of state-level economic and social programmes already under way under the banner of ALBA. This level of agreements is only one dimension of what, in ALBA, is a very flexible conception of development and collaboration. ALBA also hopes to incorporate into regional development strategy dimensions built 'from the bottom up by the transnational interplay between state and society actors' (Muhr 2008: 148). Thomas Muhr's research in Nicaragua, before the election victory of Ortega, demonstrates how ALBA can encourage linkages within and between countries, involving town councils, social movements, squatters' organizations, peasant leagues and many others. This may sound utopian, but it offers a way to open new political avenues and new forms and types of political engagement, as well as offering support to the left in states where activists are still building a presence at sub-national level, a trajectory apparent in states where the left has won office, as several chapters here have illustrated. Imagine, for example, an alliance between ALBA and the current mayor of Mexico City, Marcelo Ebrard of the PRD (Partido de la Revolución Democrática, Party of the Democratic Revolution). Ebrard, whose PRD mayoral predecessor, López Obrador, narrowly lost the controversial 2006 presidential election, launched a 'backyard' urban agriculture programme in 2007 with the aim of creating food security for the capital's population. People are offered technical support to form a cooperative and grow their own crops by utilizing available space. Modelled on Cuba's sustainable, organic model, the programme enables the PRD to mount a practical challenge to the neoliberal Mexican state's inability to protect its people, almost half of whose 106 million population live below the poverty line of $5 a day (Thomson 2008). Networking such schemes across the region, with ALBA facilitating the sharing of knowledge, collaboration across borders and access to ALBA banking services, could thus contribute to a realistic alternative development paradigm, and also to political change where conservative national governments continue in power.

Some would argue that the ALBA states have been able to 'get away' with an increasing assertiveness, with the formation of what has been termed the building of the new regionalism or continentalism because the USA's attention has been focused upon others areas of the world. A 2008 Council on Foreign Affairs report stated: 'The era of the United States as the dominant influence in Latin America is over ... [the Monroe Doctrine] is obsolete' (Grandin 2008: 5). This could not be farther from the truth. US policy towards Latin and Central America during the presidency of George W. Bush was as interventionist and imperial as ever: in his administration's elaborate transition programme for a post-socialist, post-Castro Cuba; in the encouragement of the activities of the political opposition to Chávez and Morales in Venezuela and Bolivia; in the pursuit of bilateral trade agreements with the aim of breaking the unity of Mercosur and ALBA; in its complicity with the repression unleashed by the Colombian government and its paramilitary allies upon the Colombian people in the name of drug eradication and counter-insurgency. Washington justifies its activities as promoting democracy and castigates radicals such as Chávez for destabilizing the region. For General James Hill, former commander of US Southern Command, addressing Congress in March 2004, the major security threat was 'radical populism'; he maintained that 'some leaders ... are tapping into deep-seated frustrations ... to reinforce their radical positions by inflaming anti-US sentiment' (Barry 2005: 12). This is similar in sentiment to the conclusions of the report of the US-funded Foundation for Analysis and Social Studies, which is chaired by the right-wing former Spanish prime minister José María Aznar. Published in March 2007, the document identified as 'enemies of the West' the '*altermundialistas* ["another-world-is-possibilists"], indigenous movements and populists' and stated that its aim was to 'dramatically defeat the project of "twenty-first-century socialism"' (Zibechi 2008: 13).

Optimists speculated during the US presidential primary contest in 2008 that the era of neoconservatism might be coming to an end. Bush's foreign policy was predicated upon the necessity for the USA to achieve global hegemonic power. The neoconservatives argued that global domination was the best form of world government in that it allowed the USA to ensure there was stability and security, thus making the world safe for democracy. The disastrous results of their Project for the New American Century can be seen around the world. If the Republicans won in November 2008, commentators believed that John McCain would introduce a more pragmatic and less combative approach, but the real fascination was what would happen if Barack Obama found himself in the White House. At the start of the primary campaign, Obama provoked the ire of right-wing commentators by suggesting he might talk to pariah countries such as Cuba and Iran; by the end of it, he was promising the Cuban American National Foundation (the spiritual home of the enemies of socialist Cuba) that he would maintain the embargo, almost accused Bush of 'losing Latin America' and attacked Iran for its 'influence' over Venezuela. With respect to Colombia, he supported the Bush administration's policy and committed himself to supporting 'Colombia's right to strike terrorists who seek safe-havens across its borders', a stance that put him totally out of step with most of Latin America, which condemned the Colombian army's incursion into Ecuador. Finally, he endorsed the *Merida* anti-drugs initiative, which was denounced by Amnesty International as applying the 'Colombia solution' to Mexico and Central America. An Obama government would provide vast financing to combat drugs and gangs (and, we might infer from Colombian experience, proponents of social justice) and indeed would seek to 'press further south as well' (Grandin 2008: 8). Democratic presidents are known for their pursuit of illiberal foreign policies, whether it be Kennedy's Alliance for Progress, which for all the 'development speak' was really an all-out effort to prevent structural change and also empowered the military to unleash massive repression in the dark years of dictatorship; or the Bay of Pigs invasion of Cuba in April 1961; or Jimmy Carter's refusal to even acknowledge Archbishop Oscar Romero's plea for the USA to stop selling arms to the Salvadorean military in 1979. So Obama's window on the world is not an original one, and may perpetuate the historical antagonism between the USA and much of Latin America. On the other hand, an Obama presidency might break with tradition and attempt to institute a new relationship with Latin America, one based on partnership and multilateralism (an aim announced by Bill Clinton at the start of his administration but one which he failed to fulfil). It would be likely that a Democratic president would try to separate centre-left governments such as those of Brazil and Argentina from the more radical bloc around Venezuela.

Latin America has developed strong links with other Global South states and is increasingly vocal in international institutions, and these initiatives may help to balance, although never neutralize, the threat of US intervention. Brazil lobbies for more equitable trading arrangements at the World Trade Organization and, together with India and South Africa, coordinates lobbying on behalf of the world's poorest nations. It also has strong links with many African countries, while Venezuela has extensive trading, cultural and diplomatic relations with countries as diverse as China, India and Iran. The strengthening of South-to-South networks is imperative if the dominant global structures of power – represented by the USA and institutions such as the IMF and the WTO – are to be challenged.

If Latin America is asserting itself, it is doing so in the full knowledge that although its attention may sometimes wander, Washington is always watching. In this context, Rafael Correa's announcement that he would not renew the soon-to-expire US lease on the Manta airfield in Ecuador, the most important airbase in Latin America, and Chávez's call for the creation of a Latin American army and navy are courageous but also realistic. Washington's reactivation of the US Navy's South America 4th Fleet, created in 1943 for anti-Nazi operations and disbanded in 1950, was widely interpreted as implying a military threat to Venezuela and other ALBA states, and prompted adverse reactions by key Mercosur governments, including Brazil and Argentina (Chirinos 2008). Regular US armed intervention in Latin America states is not that far in the past (Pearce 1982). US militarization of Colombia, and similar 'national security' plans for Mexico and Central America, demonstrates the possibility of more 'full spectrum domination' in the continent.

Different perspectives, different expectations

As both the introductory chapter and the remarks that follow later in this conclusion maintain, it is impossible to compartmentalize the experience of radical social democracy in contemporary Latin America. One can detect parallel developments and trajectories at the same time as recognizing profound differences, some of them to the point of conflict. When the idea of this book was first mooted, it was in a spirit of enquiry and discovery rather than in a deterministic fashion. We hoped to understand better the fascinating process which has been unfolding, and to see whether we could draw it together in terms of a broader perspective. What has resulted is an interesting microcosm of the larger picture. Individual chapters vary greatly in their focus and conclusions. Motta, Burton, Guarneros-Meza and Lievesley are concerned with the sub-national building blocks of popular, participatory democracy and how the political engagement of the people is intrinsic to the deepening of radical social democracy into a more revolutionary project. Crabtree signals the equal necessity of the inclusion of indigenous communities in the reconfiguration of constitutions and state structures.

Others are preoccupied by the national dimension of politics. Here, however, there are also contrasting approaches. Buxton rightly recognizes that Venezuela is farthest to the left on the radical democratic continuum, but wonders whether Chávez will translate his own centrality to the process into a more institutionalized but bottom-up form of Bolivarianism. Close is preoccupied with Daniel Ortega's customization of the Nicaraguan state in order to perpetuate his personal power and sees this as engendering future political problems, while both Guarneros-Meza and Burton are concerned to identify routes into government for left-leaning parties and, when they are there, how they are able to create strong and distinct political identities. Silva analyses the depoliticization of Chilean politics as a necessary consequence of the dictatorship's legacy, of the need to ensure that consensus stays at the heart of the body politic. This makes the integration of popular movements into Chilean social democratic politics problematic. Both Silva's chapter and that on Argentina by Vivares, Diaz Echenique and Ozorio testify to the importance of context, in its historical and cultural manifestations, in shaping the way that political systems respond to changing circumstances and decide what kinds of government they will undertake. The Argentinian case study also demonstrates how important it is that governments stand up to the might of the IMF and carve out their own political economies (something that has not occurred in, say, either Brazil or Chile), but elsewhere in this book Lievesley discusses how their Peronist antecedents permeated the authoritarian governing style of both Kirchner and Fernández and brought into question their legitimacy.

Along with the chapter on Argentina, Branford's on Brazil contends that the dominant global financial powers and institutions are still extraordinarily powerful and unwilling to let Latin American states plough their own furrows. In discussing the threat of secession by gas-rich provinces in Bolivia, Crabtree illuminates the fact that political and economic elites react strongly to any attempt to reduce their power and that they will always be supported in this by Washington. This, of course, has always been the case, as Dominguez reveals in his stirring survey of the bloody struggles of Martí's *Nuestra América* (Our America) against oppression. Cuba's recent evolution, in spite of its unique characteristics, also illustrates some core themes in this book. In analytical terms, it presents warnings against typecasting and oversimplification. Cuba, Ludlam suggests, displays powerful social democratic and socialist impulses and its authentic radical tradition cautions against easy typecasting. The complexity of Cuba's 'exceptionalism' also warns against simplification. In the new politics of *Nuestra América*, Cuba is now less exceptional, less isolated. In the United Nations, no Latin American state votes for the US blockade. Many Latin American states are now led by politicians for whom Cuba has been an inspiration, rather than a threat, and a source of internationalist support in their welfare reforms. In its domestic sphere, however, above all in its state-managed economy and its political institutions, Cuba remains resolutely different, and is likely to remain so.

The vexed issue of populism

The different preoccupations of our contributors, which reflect their own experiences and political views, thus mirror a central concern of this book to help readers, when making their own judgements, to take into account some of the normative content of some old terms used to analyse the new politics of Latin America, whose radicalism is often portrayed as a threat to democracy requiring a 'battle for Latin America's soul', as in the title of one recent study (Reid 2007). As noted in the introductory chapter, the word 'populism' has often been applied to political movements in an extremely disparaging fashion, particularly by North American and European commentators. Its use in Latin America, while long-standing and widespread, is controversial and contested, but not always negative. Ernesto Laclau argued that all use of the term has one point of departure – 'the people' – but that this is a category that has no conceptual precision. His concept of 'the empty signifier' is of great relevance to how we try to define both populism and socialism in the early twenty-first century. An empty signifier is one which you can define as you wish; it can incorporate as much or as little as you want it to. This has led Venezuelan intellectual Margarita López Maya, who has been a trenchant albeit not unsupportive critic of Hugo Chávez, to suggest that '"Socialism of the twenty-first century" is an empty signifier. It's a program that represents a large number of unsatisfied demands, all of which have been linked – chained to one another – in Chávez's populist discourse' (interviewed in Rosen 2007: 5). For Laclau, the dominant contradiction in any state is that between 'the people' and the power bloc, the latter not just representing relations of production but a whole complex of political and ideological forms of domination (Laclau 1977). One of the most important early Latin American debates between socialists and populists involved, in the 1920s, José Carlos Mariátegui (of the Peruvian Socialist Party) and Victor Raúl Haya de la Torre (of APRA, the American Popular Revolutionary Alliance). They disagreed on the nature of the revolution and who would constitute the revolutionary class. Haya stressed the American nature of the political problem and its solution. He called for a continental multi-class alliance against imperialism, which he identified as the principal enemy, not capitalism. The 'nation' became the 'people'. The middle class must lead this struggle because the working class was neither organized nor politically conscious. For Mariátegui, it was axiomatic that the middle class would always betray the working class; what was needed was an anti-capitalist alliance between workers and peasants. The 'poor' would become the 'people' and the 'nation' (Haya de la Torre 1970; Mariátegui 1974).

As the left evolved through its Stalinist, Trotskyite, Maoist and New Left identities, notions of 'the people' became entangled with ideas about *vanguardismo* (vanguardism). The political elite would represent the working class and peasants and lead them to socialism; popular movements became subjects to be acted upon. This didactic and artificial approach resulted in many left parties becoming centralized, sectarian and isolated from the popular movement. Now that we are in the era of 'pink tide' governments that have effectively become part of Laclau's power bloc (some more than others), how then do we define who the 'people' are and determine how much influence they are able to exercise? Furthermore, given that many popular movements seek to reorganize civil society rather than to take state power, and view citizenship as a collective undertaking rather than as the individualist condition of formal liberal democracy, how can their aspirations be integrated into or reconciled with 'pink tide' agendas? Can national, even sometimes elitist, left politics sustain a mass movement for change? In Latin America populism emerged when the inter-war world economy collapsed and, lest we forget, most of Europe also turned to military and often fascist leaders to save the 'nation' from the left. It is this Latin American history, notably the regimes of Perón in Argentina and Vargas in Brazil, which leads Crabtree to insist that the key feature of populism is control of the masses from above when a threat from below is perceived (Crabtree 2000). In her recent analysis Raby seeks to resituate the concept, or at any rate the social dynamic it represents. Noting the failures of vanguardism on the Latin American left, she also warns against the new social movements' lack of a strategy to win state power; she acknowledges the presence of populist orientations on both the right and the left. But Raby refuses to condemn the dynamic process of progressive mobilization that populism can represent, drawing on Laclau's analysis and Cammack's emphasis on the historical conjuncture of political economy, ideology and social institutions, in their analyses of populism (Cammack 2000). Raby concludes that if, as Cammack argues, populism can resolve the social and economic crises that produce it only by creating a new 'foundational project', then that project has to be socialism (Raby 2006a: 253–7). She portrays the Cuban revolution as having moved from progressive populism to socialist revo-lution, and identifies *Chavismo* in Venezuela as having the potential to make the same transformation. On this view, the key relationship now for the left is that between popular movements and charismatic leaders. The new spectre haunting the world, from this perspective, is the spectre of populism (Raby 2006a: 255; and see Robinson 2007).

If, for the sake of argument, we call Chávez a populist because of his direct appeal to the people, then we can also see that, as Cammack sug-gests, his chances of surviving the initial crisis that opened the door to Bolivarianism may depend on reconstituting Venezuelan politics, exactly what Chávez has sought to do in promoting participatory democracy, constitutional reform and launching a new mass party (Harnecker 2007b). It remains to be seen whether the narrow defeat of his 2007 constitutional reforms, which included many measures aimed towards Twenty-first-century Socialism', is a permanent setback.

A social democratic continuum?

If populism is best seen as a method of rule, which can be right- or left-wing in terms of programmatic content, Janus-faced, like nationalism more generally, then this suggests that some populism can be placed on a left spectrum, and raises further issues that need to be addressed. Given the cautions issued about characterizing the 'pink tide' and interpreting typologies, where does this leave us conceptually? In the histories of social democracy and socialism there are many parallel and overlapping debates: on the limits of private ownership; on the role of markets; on the relative importance of material and moral incentives; on the relationship between equality of opportunity and distribution of wealth. These debates have often been bitter, but the end of the cold war should now enable students of politics to consider a variety of social justice programmes free of the prejudice and polemic that characterized left debate in the second half of the twentieth century. In particular, we should turn on its head the insistence of cold war social democrats that the pursuit of particular ends, notably equality, should be liberated from a dogmatic attachment to particular means, notably state ownership. The rejection of state ownership as obsolete since the Keynesian era needs to be evaluated with an open mind when considering the prospects for social justice in states hobbled by legacies of colonial and neocolonial economic exploita-tion and obscene inequality. Even during the cold war social democrats found it possible to support insurrection against tyrannies in countries like South Africa and Nicaragua, but often criticized associated threats to free markets, as if the European social democratic model had settled for ever the argument about the appropriate economic foundations of social justice. A quarter of a century of rampant neoliberalism should have now buried such prejudice, and induced a little modesty in critiques of social justice strategies in the developing world.

The need for unprejudiced analysis is especially strong now that in Latin America political movements are shaking off the twin horrors of military tyranny and unrestricted neoliberal exploitation. Social democrats in the developed states should at least be willing to consider the validity, as means to social democratic ends, of the policies of nationalization and regulation being introduced by, for example, the governments of Venezuela and Bolivia in the face of such hostility from the US government. As the editors of one influential collection on European social democracy put it, regarding strategic methods, 'The only real test is whether there is a plausible and intelligent connection between means and ends' (Gamble and Wright 1999: 4). So, for the sake of the argument here, two definitional assertions are made, both challengeable but both defendable. In the first place, an assertion is offered about what is distinctive about social democracy. Leaving aside the nineteenth-century use of the term as synonymous with socialism and indeed Marxism, social democracy is not an ideology or a class movement, but became a series of national political programmes of social amelioration within liberal capitalist societies, programmes varying in different countries and at different times. So what could be said to be distinctive about social democracy? Many competing political traditions claim to be committed to social amelioration, not to mention other broadly progressive reforms across a range of policy areas such as civil rights, constitutional structures, educational and social policy, internationalist foreign policy and so on. The view taken here is that the distinctiveness of social democracy lies in the commitment to greater equality, not only of meritocratic opportunity, but also of distribution of resources to make opportunity real, and because unequal opportunity-taking, intelligence or ambition do not justify unequal happiness. This is crucial because it implies that the key distinctive commitment of social democracy is not reducing absolute poverty, but reducing relative poverty, compressing income and wealth differentials. By contrast, the view asserted is that the distinctive feature of socialism in the twentieth century, beyond the egalitarian ambition shared with modern social democrats, is the extension of democracy from the political into the economic sphere. This requires the subordination of individual to collective property interests through some form of social ownership and control. It is this democratic, political domination of markets which matters, rather than, as often assumed, the creation of the

225

monopolistic political institutions of the 'previously existing socialism' of the mid-twentieth century.

Conventionally, social democracy has been seen as a political movement that can only emerge in industrialized societies with a labour movement strong enough to underpin an electoral strategy of social reform, and with an economy wealthy enough to permit a dividend of growth to be redistributed without undermining capital accumulation, or driving the bulk of taxpayers to the right. The developing states figure mainly as a market and a source of cheap labour chipping away at the industrial bases of social democracy in the 'North', although Sandbrook et al. (2007) have demonstrated that social democratic egalitarianism, in any of the forms they identify, can be pursued in the Global South. If social democratic practice has been contingent upon historic economic and electoral circumstances, we should apply the label with care. Consider a comparison. Few would today argue with the description of post-war British Labour prime minister Clement Attlee as a modest social democrat. Yet, within three years of taking office, he had nationalized more strategic industries and utilities, including the Bank of England, and universalized public services and social insurance more inclusively, than has Chávez after ten years. Attlee faced virulent opposition from free market fundamentalists, and Winston Churchill threatened that this mild-mannered reformer would need a British Gestapo to implement his programme, an astonishing attack at the time. So if Chávez is tail-ending Attlee, why is he demonized as a populist threat to social democracy?

The answer is context. For all the desire to create a Twenty-first-century Socialism, the record so far, on the basis of the definitions asserted here, can be portrayed as delayed twentieth-century social democracy. In other words, it is a policy to reduce inequality that requires greater national political control of national economic resources, pursued constitutionally through electoral politics in a mixed economy. Confronting social democratic egalitarianism in Venezuela (as elsewhere in Latin America) stand those, within and without the country, who have held power and wealth for generations through their exploitation of the country's people and natural resources. Their neo-Churchillian hostility reflects the fact that radical reforms are needed to redistribute that wealth and power, just as they were in Britain in 1945. Instead of crouching behind crumbling ideological Berlin Walls and seeing every act of state intervention as a threat to liberty, liberals and social democrats in the developed world should judge whether Chávez, Morales and others, in their twenty-first-century context, are sincerely trying to make their societies more equal, as Attlee did in his context. It is worth asking who benefits from damning

Chávez, Morales or other *albaïstas* as enemies of social democracy. The answer of course is that those who benefit are those who despise Chávez, like those who once despised Attlee, Erlander in Sweden and indeed all of Europe's pioneering social democrats, precisely because of their intention to redistribute wealth and power.

In Latin America today, the organizational forms of struggle for social democratic egalitarianism are complex, involving a variety of political alliances of parties, social, labour, rural, women's and indigenous movements. Further, Latin America political systems are presidential, use a variety of electoral systems, and involve different degrees of federalism and other sub-national divisions of power. If we acknowledge such complexity, and step aside from European models, some of Latin America's populist movements can be seen as particular vehicles of social democracy. After all, as Dunkerley has noted, the economic policies pursued by social democrats in post-war Europe were pursued in Latin American by populists (Dunkerley 1994). The same regimes, he points out, later managed the turn to neoliberalism, as indeed did some social democrats in Europe (Callaghan 2000; Pierson 2001).

A further question prompted here is how elastic the concept of socialism as fundamentally a programme for economic democracy on principle can be? The rigid distinctions made in the past between socialism and other left-wing programmes have lost much purchase since the demise of Soviet 'Marxism-Leninism', and the conversion of China to market economics. Socialism, as revolutionary Cuba's history has demonstrated, is not exactly a simple staging post between capitalism and communism. But we can argue that what has emerged in the redder currents of Latin America's 'pink tide' is precisely the kind of democratic, reformist socialism that was displaced in twentieth-century Europe by social democrats (Przeworski 1985; Sassoon 1996). In other words we may be witnessing in Latin America the revival of the socialism that rejected the revolutionary method in favour of reforming capitalism into socialism by winning elections and wielding state power. Twenty-first-century Socialism as pursued by ALBA leaders looks a lot like the democratic reformist socialism of mid-twentieth-century Europe. One key distinction is the attitude to constitutional reform. Several ALBA states have moved to insert institutions of popular democracy into their constitutions. ALBA leaders may be carrying out reforms within liberal democracies of a sort, but there is no reason why they should make the European assumption that the states they manage are neutral machines that can be steered in any direction. No one aware of the history of Latin America in the twentieth century can trust in such neutrality, especially not since the Chilean coup in 1973. Popular democracy may not be a conspiracy to demolish the 'bourgeois state' from within, but it could help inhibit unconstitutional resistance from the right, and help ensure that social welfare reforms whose delivery is placed partly in the hands of the new popular institutions have a better chance of surviving the restoration of neoliberal governments. Another key distinction lies in the degree of internationalism. While social democrats and democratic socialists in Europe were frequently unable to break with their states' imperialism, a strong current in the 'pink tide', drawing on a long history of anti-colonialism and anti-neocolonialism, has been a left-wing internationalism, or at least a popular continentalism, and a defiance, in many words and some deeds, of *el imperio* in the North and its assumption of economic and political domination. Both of these distinct elements of radical social democracy in Latin America, on constitutional reform and anti-imperialism, are easily portrayed in the media war as threatening 'populist' instability. Understood in their context, they are no more threatening than the abolition of the hereditary principle by European social democrats.

So, finally, to make sense of the 'pink tide', there should be a focus on the core objectives respectively of social democrats and socialists, of reducing relative poverty and of installing economic democracy, and left-wing politics should be seen as a continuum along which progress will be determined by many factors, internal and external. If aims, not methods and agencies, are defining characteristics, then that continuum can include some of the so-called 'populist' governments and movements that have acted to reduce inequality. It might also exclude some parties that describe themselves as social democratic but have not acted to reduce inequality, although the rise of a few super-rich may be making it harder than previously to make simple statistical judgements about reducing relative poverty. Similarly, social democratic might better define some who describe themselves as socialist but who have not acted to impose democratic political control over private markets. What matters above all is the substance of political actions in these core policy areas, not the self-labelling of parties or movements or their polemical labelling by others. A key question confronting analysts of Venezuela today, for example, is where exactly might social democratic egalitarianism, which clearly is being pursued, turn into Twenty-first-century Socialism, which is the stated aim? What degree of economic democracy would trigger a shift of terminology? Old distinctions between minimalist and maximalist programmes are being drawn again, old debates about the limits and risks of reformism are being reworked in a continent where, in the not very distant past, they have been life-and-death issues. But what the 'pink tide' signifies above all, for all of the complexity that the term conceals, is that across Latin America millions of people are once again engaged in struggle, often bitter and still dangerous, to transform some of the most unequal and oppressive societies on the planet. An honest analysis of the political, social and economic conditions and inheritances that confront this struggle is required, before making too many simple assumptions, dismissive or triumphalist, about the participants' aims, strategies and prospects of success.

Notes on contributors

Sue Branford is a freelance journalist and writer and a visiting lecturer in the Department of Journalism at City University in London. Her recent publications include *Politics Transformed – Lula and the Workers' Party in Brazil* (2003, with Bernardo Kucinski); and *Cutting the Wire – The Story of the Landless Movement in Brazil* (2002, with Jan Rocha).

Guy Burton is a PhD candidate in the Government Department at the London School of Economics. His main research interests include social democracy, political parties and education policy.

Julia Buxton is senior research fellow in the Centre for International Cooperation and Security, University of Bradford. Her research is focused on Latin America. Recent publications include *The Political Economy of Narcotic Drugs* (2006); and *The Failure of Political Reform in Venezuela* (2001).

David Close is professor of political science at Memorial University, St John's, Newfoundland and Labrador, Canada. He has specialized in Latin American politics, with a particular emphasis on Nicaragua, for over twenty-five years. Among his publications are *Undoing Democracy: The Politics of Electoral Caudillismo* (2005, edited with K. Deonandan), and several books on Nicaraguan politics, including *Nicaragua: The Chamorro Years* (1999).

John Crabtree is a research associate at the Latin American Centre, Oxford University. He has published widely on the politics of the Andean countries, specifically Peru and Bolivia. His recent books include *Unresolved Conflict: Bolivia Past and Present* (2008, co-edited with Laurence Whitehead); *Making Institutions Work in Peru: Democracy, Development and Inequality since 1980* (2006); and *Patterns of Protest: Politics and Social Movements in Bolivia* (2005).

Leonardo Díaz Echenique is associate professor at the Department of Political Sciences at the Universidad Autónoma de Barcelona and researcher at the Institute of Government and Public Policies. He researches and teaches political science, public policy and social movements in Latin America.

Francisco Dominguez is head of the Centre for Latin American Studies at Middlesex University. He specializes in the political economy of Latin America. He has recently edited *Mercosur: Between Integration and Democracy* (2003), and he is the author of 'Violence, the left and the creation of un nuevo Chile', in W. Fowler and P. Lambert (eds), *Political Violence and Identity in Latin America* (2008), and 'The rise of the private sector in Cuba', in A. I. Gray and A. Kapcia (eds), *The Changing Dynamic of Cuban Civil Society* (2008).

Valeria Guarneros-Meza researches comparative local governance. Her doctoral research (awarded 2006) was on partnership and participation in Mexican urban governance. She has published articles in *Urban Studies* and the *International Journal of Urban and Regional Research*. She was a Research Fellow at the Local Governance Research Unit in De Montfort University and is now at the Centre for Local and Regional Governance Research, University of Cardiff.

Geraldine Lievesley is senior lecturer in politics at Manchester Metropolitan University. Her research focuses on Latin American and Cuban politics. She is a member of the Society for Latin American Studies and the Cuba Research Forum. Recent books include the co-edited *In the Hands of Women: Paradigms of Citizenship* (2006) and *The Cuban Revolution: Past, Present and Future Perspectives* (2004).

Steve Ludlam is a senior lecturer in politics at the University of Sheffield. His past research was mainly on British labour politics, but he now focuses on Cuba. He is a member of the Society for Latin American Studies and the Cuba Research Forum. He co-edits the MUP series Critical Labour Studies. Recent co-edited books include *Labour, the State, Social Movements and the Challenge of Neoliberal Globalization* (2007) and *Governing as New Labour* (2004).

Sara C. Motta lectures at the London School of Economics, where she completed her PhD on contemporary Chilean politics in 2005. Among her publications are articles in *Bulletin of Latin American Studies* and *Political Studies*.

Javier Ozorio is a PhD candidate and professor at the National University of Cuyo. He also teaches in other universities in Latin America, such as the Universidad Autónoma de Mexico. His area of expertise is the sociology of knowledge, politics and social history. His most recent publication is *Marx and the State: Social Determinations of the Thinking of Karl Marx* (Universidad Autónoma de Mexico).

Patricio Silva is Professor of Modern Latin American History at the University of Leiden. His research is focused on democratization and the technocratization of politics in Chile. His recent publications include *The Soldier and the State in South America: Essays in Civil–Military Relations* (edited, 2001) and *In the Name of Reason: Technocrats and Politics in Chile* (2008).

Ernesto Vivares is a teaching fellow at the Department of Economics and International Development at the University of Bath. In 2008 he was awarded his PhD at the University of Sheffield. He teaches and researches world politics, conflict and development, and Latin American social and political economy.

Bibliography

ALBA (n.d.) *ALBA in the Caribbean*, Caracas: Ministerio de Estado para la Integración y Comercio Exterior.

Albó, X. (1987) 'MNRistas to Kataristas', in S. Stern (ed.), *Resistance, Rebellion and Consciousness in the Andean Peasant World*, Madison: University of Wisconsin Press.

Albro, R. (2005) 'The indigenous in the plural in Bolivian oppositional politics', *Bulletin of Latin American Research*, 24(4).

Alexander, M. (2005) 'Cuba: governance and social justice. Cuba's transition: lessons from other countries', www.focal.ca/pdf/alexander.pdf (accessed 23 April 2007).

Alianza Unida Nicaragua Triunfa (2006) *Programa del gobierno de reconciliación y unidad nacional*, www.nicaraguatriunfa.com (accessed 18 January 2008).

Altamirano, C. (1977) *Dialéctica de una derrota*, Mexico City: Siglo XXI.

Alvarez, S. E., E. Dagnino and A. Escobar (eds) (1998) *Cultures of Politics, Politics of Cultures: Re-Visioning Latin American Social Movements*, Boulder, CO: Westview Press.

Alvarez, W., M. Martinez and L. Loasiga (2007) 'Conpes "protégé" los CPC', *La Prensa*, 30 November, www.laprensa.com.ni/ (accessed 30 November 2007).

Amnesty International (2001) 'Americas: day of the "disappeared" – where are they?', asiapacific.amnesty.org/library/ (accessed 28 April 2008).

Anderson, R. N. (1996) 'The Quilombo of Palmares: a new overview of a Maroon state in seventeenth-century Brazil', *Journal of Latin American Studies*, 28(3).

Angell, A. (1988) 'Some problems in the interpretation of recent Chilean history', *Bulletin of Latin American Research*, 7(1).

Angell, A. and S. Carstairs (1987) 'The exile question in Chilean politics', *Third World Quarterly*, 9(1).

Angell, A. and C. Reig (2006) 'Change or continuity? The Chilean elections of 2005/2006', *Bulletin of Latin American Research*, 25(4).

Antunes, J. (2008) 'Argentina: truce in three-week agricultural strike', *World Socialist*, www.wsws.org/articles/ (accessed 11 April 2008).

Araújo e Oliveira, J. B. (2004) 'Expansion and inequality in Brazilian education', in C. Brock and S. Schwartzmann (eds), *The Challenges of Education in Brazil*, Oxford: Symposium Books.

Arrate, J. (1983) 'La vía allendista al socialismo', *Análisis*, 64, September.

— (1985) *La fuerza democrática de la idea socialista*, Barcelona: Ediciones Documentas.

— (1987) *Exilio: textos de denuncia y esperanza*, Santiago: Documentas.

Arroliga, L. (2007) '¿Consejos de ciudadanos o del partido FSLN?', *Confidencial*, 535(1), www.confidencial.com.ni (accessed 30 May 2007).

Arruda, M. (2008a) 'Brasil – outro megaprojeto de alto risco social e ambiental: a ferrovia leste–oeste', www.adital.com.br/site/ (accessed 18 January 2008).

— (2008b) 'Crescimento econômico ou desenvolvimento humão e social? Os impasses da atual conjuntura nacional e global', Paper written for the National Assembly of the Comissão Pastoral da Terra, April.

Arzaluz, M. S. (2002) *Participación ciudadana en la gestión urbana de Ecatepec, Tlalnepantla y Nezahualcóyotl (1997–2000)*, Toluca, Mexico: IAPEM.

Avritzer, L. (2005) 'Modes of democratic deliberation: participatory budgeting in Brazil', in B. de Sousa Santos (ed.), *Democratizing Democracy: Beyond the Liberal Canon*, New York: Verso.

Aziz-Nassif, A. (ed.) (2003) *México al inicio del siglo XXI: democracia, ciudadanía y desarrollo*, Mexico: Porrúa-CIESAS.

Azpiazu, D. (ed.) (2002) *Privatizaciones y poder económico: la consolidación de una sociedad excluyente*, Buenos Aires: FLACSO.

Baierle, S. (2002) 'The Porto Alegre Thermidor? Brazil's "Participatory Budget" at the crossroads', in L. Panitch and C. Leys (eds), *Socialist Register 2003: Fighting Identities: Race, Religion and Ethno-Nationalism*, London: Merlin Press.

Baiocchi, G. (2003) 'Radicals in power', in G. Baiocchi (ed.), *Radicals in Power: The Workers' Party (PT) and Experiments in Urban Democracy in Brazil*, London: Zed Books.

Barragán, R. (2006) *Asambleas constituyentes: ciudadanía y elecciones, convenciones y debates (1825–1971)*, La Paz: Muela del Diablo Editores.

Barros, R. (1986), 'The left and democracy', *Telos*, 68.

Barry, T. (2005) 'Mission creep in Latin America – US Southern Command's new security strategy', 11 July, americas.irc-online. org (accessed 15 October 2005).

Basualdo, E. (2001) *Modelo de acumulación y sistema político en Argentina: notas sobre el transformismo argentino durante la valorización financiera (1976–2001)*, Argentina: Universidad Nacional de Quilmes.

— (2002) *Concentración y centralización del capital en la Argentina durante la década del noventa*, Buenos Aires: Editorial Universidad de Quilmes.

— (2003) 'Las reformas structurales y el plan de convertibilidad durante la decada de los noventa: el auge y la crisis de la valorización financiera', *Revista Realidad Economica*, December.

Batista, P. N., Jr (2008) 'Brasil, credor internacional', *Folha de S. Paulo*, 28 February.

Bell Lara, J. (2002) *Globalization and the Cuban Revolution*, Havana: Editorial José Martí.

— (2004) *Cuba: una perspective socialista en la globalización capitalista*, Havana: Editorial de Ciencias Sociales.

Bernstein, E. (1961 [1899]) *Evolutionary Socialism: A Criticism and Affirmation*, New York: Schocken Books.

Bitar, S. (1986) *Chile, Experiment in Democracy*, Philadelphia, PA: Institute for the Study of Human Issues.

Bolaños, A. and S. González (2004) 'El video, respuesta a las acciones legales contra el Grupo Quart: López Obrador', *La Jornada*, 4 March.

Bolivarian Republic of Venezuela

(2006) *Frases II*, Caracas: Ministerio de Comunicación e Informacíon.

— (2007) *Socialismo del siglo xxi: la fuerza de los pequeños*, Caracas: Colección Temas de Hoy.

Bonilla-Molina, L., M. Harnecker and H. El Troudi (2005) *Herramientas para la participación*, Caracas: Ministerio de la Participación Popular.

Borges, A. (2008) 'State government, political competition and education reform: comparative lessons from Brazil', *Bulletin of Latin American Research*, 27(2).

Boron, A. (2005) 'The truth about capitalist democracy', in L. Panitch and C. Leys (eds), *Socialist Register 2006: Telling the Truth*, London: Merlin Press.

Bouzas, R. (2007) 'Algunos comentarios sobre el comercio exterior argentino en una perspectiva de largo plazo', *Revista del CEI Comercio Exterior e Integración*, Buenos Aires: Ministerio de Relaciones Exteriores, Comercio Internacional y Culto.

Branford, S. and B. Kucinski (2003) *Politics Transformed: Lula and the Workers' Party in Brazil*, London: Latin American Bureau.

Branford, S. and J. Rocha (2002) *Cutting the Wire: The Story of the Landless Movement in Brazil*, London: Latin American Bureau.

Bresser Perreira, L. C. (2001) 'The New Left viewed from the South', in A. Giddens (ed.), *The Global Third Way Debate*, Cambridge: Polity Press.

Bulhões, M. and M. Abreu (1992) *A luta dos professores gaúchos – 1979/1991*, Porto Alegre: L&PM.

Bull, M. (2005) 'The limits of the multitude', *New Left Review*, 35, September/October.

Bulmer-Thomas, V. (2003) *The Economic History of Latin America since Independence*, New York: Cambridge University Press.

Bustillo, I. (2007) 'Situación y perspectivas del desarrollo económico y social de América Latina y el Caribe', Unpublished paper, XXXIV Curso de Derecho Internacional Aspectos Jurídicos del Desarrollo Regional, Rio de Janeiro.

Buxton, J. (2000) *The Failure of Political Reform in Venezuela*, Basingstoke: Ashgate.

— (2005) 'Venezuela's contemporary political crisis in historical perspective', *Bulletin of Latin American Research*, 24(3).

— (2006) 'National identity and political violence: the case of Venezuela', in W. Fowler and P. Lambert (eds), *Political Violence and the Construction of National Identity in Latin America*, London: Palgrave.

Caballero, R. and R. Dornbusch (2002) 'The battle for Argentina', Paper, Massachusetts Institute of Technology, econ-www.mit.edu/files/186 (accessed 11 April 2008).

Cabrero, E. (2005) *Acción pública y desarrollo local*, Mexico: Fondo de Cultura Económica.

Cademartori, J. (1998) *Chile el model neoliberal*, Santiago: Ediciones Chile America CESOC.

Callaghan, J. (2000) *The Retreat of Social Democracy*, Manchester: Manchester University Press.

Calloni, S. (2005) *Operación Cóndor: pacto criminal*, Havana: Ciencias Sociales.

Camini, L. (2001) *Educação pública de qualidade social: conquistas e desafios*, Petrópolis: Editora Vozes.

Cammack, P. (2000) 'The resurgence of populism in Latin America',

Bulletin of Latin American Research, 19(2).

— (2004) '"Signs of the times": capitalism, competitiveness, and the new face of empire in Latin America', in L. Panitch and C. Leys (eds), *Socialist Register 2005: The Empire Reloaded*, London: Merlin Press.

Campbell, D. (2006) 'US accused of bid to oust Chávez with secret funds', *Guardian*, 30 August.

Canaan, J. (2002) 'Theorizing pedagogic practices in the contexts of marketization and of September 11, 2001, and its aftermath', *Anthropology & Education Quarterly*, 33(3).

Cannon, B. (2008) 'Class/race polarisation in Venezuela and the electoral success of Hugo Chávez: a break with the past or the song remains the same?', *Third World Quarterly*, 29(4).

Caram León, C. (2005) 'Women's empowerment in Cuba', in J. Bell Lara and R. A. Dello Bueno (eds), *Cuba in the 21st Century: Realities and Perspectives*, Havana: Editorial José Martí.

Carmona Báez, A. (2004) *State Resistance to Globalisation in Cuba*, London: Pluto Press.

Carothers, T. (2002) 'The end of the transition paradigm', *Journal of Democracy*, 13(1).

Carr, B., and S. Ellner (eds) (1993) *The Latin American Left: From the Fall of Allende to Perestroika*, Boulder, CO: Westview Press.

Carroll, R. (2008) 'Intellectuals condemn authoritarian Ortega', *Guardian*, 24 June.

Casas Regueiro, J., A. Pérez Betancourt, B. González Sánchez, J. Cazañas Reyes and R. Lazo (1990) *A problemas viejos soluciones nuevas: el perfeccion-amiento empresarial en el Minfar*, Havana: Editora Política.

Castañeda, J. (1994) *Utopia Unarmed: The Latin American Left after the Cold War*, New York: Vintage.

— (2006) 'Latin America's left turn: a tale of two lefts', *Foreign Affairs*, 85(3).

Castells, M. (1983) *The City and the Grass Roots*, Berkeley: University of California Press.

Castro Ruz, F. (1987) 'History will absolve me', in M. Harnecker, *From Moncada to Victory: Fidel Castro's Political Strategy*, New York: Pathfinder.

— (2005) 'Speech delivered by Dr Fidel Castro Ruz in the *Aula Magna* of the University of Havana, on November 17, 2005', Havana: Republic of Cuba.

— (2007) *Fidel Castro: My Life*, London: Allen Lane.

Castro Ruz, R. (2007a) 'Speech of 26 July 2007, on the 54th anniversary of the assault on the Moncada barracks', Havana: Republic of Cuba.

— (2007b) 'Speech to the National Assembly, 28 December 2007', Havana: Republic of Cuba.

— (2008a) 'Address at the National Assembly, 24 February 2008', Havana: Republic of Cuba.

— (2008b) 'Concluding intervention at the 6th Plenum of the Central Committee of the Communist Party of Cuba', Havana: PCC.

Centeno, M. A. (2004) 'The return of Cuba to Latin America: the end of Cuban exceptionalism?', *Bulletin of Latin American Research*, 23(4).

Chamorro, C. F. (2007) 'El estilo presidencial', *Confidencial*, 522(2/3), www.confidencial.com.ni (accessed 20 February 2007).

Chávez, D. and B. Goldfrank (eds) (2004) *The Left in the City: Partici-*

patory *Local Governments in Latin America*, London: Latin America Bureau.

Chirinos, C. (2008) 'El fantasma de la Cuarta Flota', www.bbcmundo.com (accessed 3 July 2008).

CID-Gallup (2006) 'Nicaragua public opinion survey, #51-5', April–October, www.cidgallup.com (accessed 17 January 2008).

— (2007) 'Encuesta de opinión pública Republica de Nicaragua', January, www.cidgallup.com (accessed 18 January 2007).

Clement, C. (2007) 'Confronting Hugo Chávez: US "democracy promotion" in Latin America', in S. Ellner and M. Tinker Salas (eds), *Venezuela: Hugo Chávez and the Decline of an Exceptional Democracy*, Maryland: Rowman and Littlefield.

Close, D. (1988) *Nicaragua: Politics, Economics and Society*, London: Frances Pinter.

— (1999) *Nicaragua: The Chamorro Years*, Boulder, CO: Lynne Rienner.

Close, D., and K. Deonandan (eds) (2005) *Undoing Democracy: The Politics of Electoral Caudillismo*, Lanham, MD: Lexington Books.

COHA (Council on Hemispheric Affairs) (2006) 'A very mixed message out of Managua: Nicaragua's elections: a national turning point?', 12 December, www.coha.org (accessed 18 January 2008).

Comissão de Educação, Cultura e Desporto (2001) *Education Forum Transcripts, 13–15 September*, Fortaleza: Assembléia Legislativa do Estado do Ceará.

Comissão de Educação, Cultura, Desporto, Ciência e Tecnologia (2003) *Relatório*, Porto Alegre: Assembléia Legislativa.

CONAIE (2008) 'Comisión de comunicación CONAIE-ECUARUNARI, positivo diálogo entre el gobierno y el movimiento indígena con respecto a la construcción del estado plurinacional', 11 March, www.conaie.org/es/ge_comunicados/ (accessed 24 April 2008).

Confidencial (2008) 'Ortega inaugura nueva era de la "contra"', *Confidencial*, 58(3), www.confidencial.com.ni (accessed 8 May 2008).

Constituent Assembly of Ecuador (2007) 'La administración de justicia será mediante el sistema oral', Quito: Constituent Assembly of Ecuador.

Contreras, J. (2006) 'All signs suggest chastened Sandinista firebrand will embrace moderation', *Newsweek*, 25 December 2006–1 January 2007, www.msnbc.msn.com (accessed 28 December 2006).

Cooper, A. and B. Momani (2005) 'Negotiating out of Argentina's financial crisis: segmenting the international creditors', *New Political Economy*, 10(3).

Cornelius, W., T. Eisenstadt and J. Hindley (eds) (1999) *Subnational Politics and Democratization in Mexico*, San Diego: University of California, Center of US-Mexican Studies.

Correa Flores, R. (ed.) (2005) *Construyendo el ALBA: nuestra norte es el sur*, Caracas: Ediciones del 40º Aniversario del Parlamento Latinamerico.

Cortázar, R. (1993) *Política laboral en el Chile democrático: avances y desafíos en los noventa*, Santiago: Dolmen.

CPT (Comissão Pastoral da Terra) (2004) *Conflitos no campo 2003*, Goiânia: CPT.

Crabtree, J. (2000) 'Populisms old and new: the Peruvian case',

Bulletin of Latin American Research, 19(2).

— (2005) *Patterns of Protest: Politics and Social Movements in Bolivia*, London: Latin American Bureau.

— (2006) 'Desempeño económico, desigualdad y legitimidad política', in P. Domingo (ed.), *Bolivia: fin de un ciclo y nuevas perspectivas políticas*, Barcelona: Editores Bellaterra.

Crabtree, J. and L. Whitehead (eds) (2008) *Unresolved Tensions: Bolivia Past and Present*, Pittsburgh, PA, Pittsburgh University Press.

Cruz Sánchez, E. (2007) 'Poder judicial entre los más corruptos', *La Prensa*, 21 January, www.laprensa.com.ni (accessed 21 January 2008).

CTC (2004) *Manual de procedimiento y guía metodológica para la elaboración del convenio colectivo de trabajo y su control: proyecto de colaboración CTC-LO*, Havana: Central de Trabajadores de Cuba.

— (2006) *La actividad ideologíca y política del movimiento sindical*, Havana: Centro de Trabajadores de Cuba.

Cunningham, S. (1999) 'Made in Brazil: Cardoso's critical path from dependency via neoliberal options to the Third Way in the 1990s', *European Review of Latin American and Caribbean Studies*, 67, December.

Cuperes, R. (2003) 'Effective governance in public services: shared challenges for the European left', in M. Browne and P. Diamond (eds), *Rethinking Social Democracy*, London: Policy Network.

Dahl, R. (1971) *Polyarchy*, New Haven, CT: Yale University Press.

Dahse, F. (1979) *Mapa de la extrema riqueza*, Santiago: Editorial Aconcagua Colección Lautaro.

Dal Din, C. (2000) 'La apertura financiera Argentina de los '90. Una visión complementaria de la balanza de pagos', FIEL Documento de Trabajo no. 64.

Dangl, B. (2008) 'Undermining Bolivia: a landscape of Washington intervention', 7 February, upsidedownworld.org (accessed 3 March 2008).

Dávalos Fernández, R. (2006) *United States vs the Cuban Five: A Judicial Cover-up*, Havana: Editorial Capitán San Luis.

Davis, B. (2007) 'Cuban economists envision role for markets in post-Castro era', *Wall Street Journal*, 10 January.

De Ávila, R. V. (2008) *Acúmulo de reservas cambiais = explosão da dívida interna*, www.adufcg.org.br/artigos (accessed 20 June 2008).

De La Torre, C. (1997) 'Populism and democracy: political discourses and cultures in contemporary Ecuador', *Latin American Perspectives*, 24(3).

De Oliveira, S. M. V. (1995) *CPERS-Sindicato 50 anos: compromisso com a cidadania plena*, Porto Alegre: tchê!.

De Sousa Santos, B. (ed.) (2005) *Democratizing Democracy: Beyond the Liberal Canon*, London: Verso.

De Sousa Santos, B. and L. Avritzer (2005) 'Introduction: opening up the canon of democracy', in B. de Sousa Santos (ed.), *Democratizing Democracy: Beyond the Liberal Canon*, London: Verso.

De Vylder, S. (1976) *Allende's Chile: The Political Economy of the Rise and Fall of the Unidad Popular*, Cambridge: Cambridge University Press.

Debray, R. (1967) *Revolution in the Revolution: Armed Struggle and Political Struggle in Latin America*, Harmondsworth: Penguin.

Denis, R. (2006) (interviewed by Raúl Zelik) 'Destruir y reconstruir. El nuevo estado en Venezuela y los movimientos populares', *La Haine*, 20 April, lahaine.org (accessed 20 May 2006).

Denvir, D. and T. Riofrancos (2008) 'Ecuador: CONAIE indigenous movement condemns President Correa', 16 May, upsidedownworld.org (accessed 12 June 2008).

Dilla, H. (1999) 'Comrades and investors: the uncertain transition in Cuba', *Socialist Register 1999*.

Dinges, J. (2004) *The Condor Years: How Pinochet and His Allies Brought Terrorism to Three Continents*, New York: Free Press.

Domingo, P. (2001) 'Party politics, intermediation and representation', in J. Crabtree and L. Whitehead (eds), *Towards Democratic Viability: The Bolivian Experience*, Basingstoke: Palgrave.

Dominguez, F. (2006) 'ALBA: Latin America's anti-imperialist project, 21st century socialism', 21stcenturysocialism.com (accessed 24 April 2008).

Draibe, S. (2004) 'Federal leverage in a decentralized system: education in Brazil', in R. Kaufman and J. Nelson (eds), *Crucial Needs, Weak Incentives*, Washington, DC: Woodrow Wilson Center Press.

Dresser, D. (2007) 'Mexico: Calderón's first 100 days and the future of political opposition', Paper presented at the State of Mexico's Democracy Conference, Macmillan Center, University of Yale.

Dunkerley, J. (1984) *Rebellion in the Veins*, London: Verso.

— (1994) 'Beyond Utopia: the state of the left in Latin America', *New Left Review*, 206.

— (2007) 'Evo Morales, the "Two Bolivias" and the Third Bolivian Revolution', *Journal of Latin American Studies*, 39.

Dye, D. (2004) *Democracy Adrift: Caudillo Politics in Nicaragua*, Brookline, MA: Hemisphere Initiatives.

Dye, D., and D. Close (2005) 'Personalism and economic policy in the Alemán administration', in D. Close and K. Deonandan (eds), *Undoing Democracy: The Politics of Electoral Caudillismo*, Langham, MD: Lexington Books.

Eckstein, S. (2003) *Back from the Future: Cuba under Castro*, New York: Routledge.

ECLAC (Economic Commission for Latin America) (2004) *Social Panorama of Latin America 2004*, Santiago: ECLAC.

— (2007) *Social Panorama of Latin America 2007*, Santiago: ECLAC.

EIU (2008) 'Economist Intelligence Unit, Country Report: Nicaragua, September 2008', portal.eiu (accessed 19 September 2008).

El Clarín (2002) Special issue on *piquetes* at www.clarin.com/diario/especiales (accessed 24 April 2008).

Ellner, S. (1993), 'The changing state of the Latin American left in the recent past', in S. Ellner and B. Carr (eds), *The Latin American Left from the Fall of Allende to Perestroika*, Boulder, CO: Westview Press.

— (2004) 'Leftist goals and the debate over anti-neoliberal strategy in Latin America', *Science and Society*, 68(1).

— (2007) 'Trade union autonomy and the emergence of a new labour movement in Venezuela', in S. Ellner and M. Tinker Salas (eds), *Venezuela: Hugo Chávez and the Decline of an Exceptional Democracy*, Maryland: Rowman and Littlefield.

Envio (2005) 'Ortega and Murillo tie knot … again?', September, www.envio.org.ni (accessed 19 January 2008).

Erickson, D., A. Lord and P. Wolf (2002) *Cuba's Social Services: A Review of Education, Health and Sanitation*, Washington, DC: World Bank.

Espina, G. (2007) 'Beyond polarization: organized Venezuelan women promote their minimum agenda', *Nacla Report on the Americas*, 40(2).

Espina, M., A. Hernández, V. Togores and R. Hernández (2006) 'El consumo: economía, cultura y sociedad', *Temas*, 47.

Esteva, G. (2007) 'The Asamblea Popular de los Pueblos de Oaxaca', *Latin American Perspectives*, 152(34).

Etchemendy, S. (2005) 'Old actors in new markets: transforming the populist/industrial coalition in Argentina, 1989–2001', in S. Levitsky and M. Murillo (eds), *The Politics of Institutional Weakness: Argentine Democracy*, Philadelphia: Pennsylvania University Press.

Evenson, D. (2001) *Workers in Cuba: Unions and Labor Relations*, Detroit, MI: National Lawyers Guild/Maurice and Jane Sugar Law Center for Economic and Social Justice.

— (2006) 'Cubana de Acero: structure and dynamics of a Cuban factory', *OD Practicioner*, 38(4).

EZLN (Ejército Zapatista de Liberación Nacional) (2005) 'Si nos equivocamos acerca del PRD, ofrecemos disculpas, dice Marcos a don Fermín Hernández', *La Jornada*, 8 August.

Fabius, L. (2003) 'Why social democrats must be European', in M. Browne and P. Diamond (eds), *Rethinking Social Democracy*, London: Policy Network.

FBO (Fórum Brasil do Orçamento) (2005) *Superávit Primário*, 3rd edn, May.

Feinman, J. (2008) 'El Peronism no tiene ideología', *INFOBAE*, www.perfil.com (accessed 11 April 2008).

Fernandes, L. (1996) 'From *Foquismo* to *Reformismo*: Castañeda and the Latin American left', *New Left Review*, 215.

Ferriol Muruaga, A., A. González Gutiérrez, D. Quintana Mendoza and V. Pérez Izquierdo (1998) *Cuba: crisis, ajuste y situación social 1990–1996*, Havana: Editorial de Ciencias Sociales.

Flores, A. (2005) *Local Democracy in Modern Mexico*, Bury St Edmunds: Arena Books.

Folha de S. Paulo (2005a) 'Evolução estatística', 30 October.

— (2005b) 'Aumenta e exclusão', 27 December.

— (2008a) 'Mangabeira unger quer levar água da Amazônia para o NE', 17 January.

— (2008b) 'Obras do PAC esbarram em conservaçã da Amazônia', 17 May.

Foweraker, J. (1995) *Theorizing Social Movements*, London: Pluto Press.

Fox, M. (2007) 'Uruguay's Frente Amplio: from revolution to dilution', June, www.upsidedownworld.org (accessed 26 June 2007).

Foxley, A. (1993) *Economía política de la transición*, Santiago: Dolmen.

Franco, M. (2002) *Fases y momento actual de la estructura social Argentina*, Mendoza: Universidad Nacional de Cuyo.

Frank, M. (2005) 'Investors shown

the door after Cuban U-turn',
Financial Times, 6 June.

Freeden, M. (1988) *Ideologies and
Political Theory: A Conceptual
Approach*, Oxford: Clarendon
Press.

Freire, P. (2000) *Pedagogy of the
Oppressed*, New York: Continuum.

Frenkel, R. and M. Rapetti (2007)
'Argentina's monetary and
exchange rate policies after the
convertibility regime collapse',
CEPR Paper, www.cepr.net/index.
php/publications (accessed 25
February 2008).

Fukuyama, F. (1992) *The End of History and the Last Man*, New York:
Free Press.

Galeano, E. (2000) *Upside Down. A
Primer for the Looking Glass World*,
London: Picador.

— (2004) *Memoria del fuego: I. Los
nacimientos, II. Las caras y las
máscaras, III. El siglo del viento*,
Mexico: Siglo XXI Editores.

Galeano, L. (2007) 'CGR tras
frijoles vendidos por CPC', *El
Nuevo Diario*, 13 December, www.
elnuevodiario.com.ni (accessed
13 December 2007).

Galeano, L. and M. Miranda
(2007) 'Reelección presidencial
perpetua', *El Nuevo Diario*, 25
October, www.elnuevodiario.com.
ni (accessed 25 October 2007).

Gamble, A. and T. Wright (eds) (1999)
The New Social Democracy, Oxford:
Blackwell.

Gandin, L. A. and M. W. Apple (2002)
'Can education challenge neoliberalism? The Citizen School
and the struggle for democracy
in Porto Alegre, Brazil', *Arena
Journal*, 19.

García, C. M. (2005) *Propiedad social:
la experiencia cubana*, Havana:
Editora Política.

García, G. (2003) 'Desarrollo

económico local en Zacatecas', in
E. Cabrero (ed.), *Premio y gestión
local: innovación en gobiernos
locales*, Mexico: CIDE-CODEMUN-
Fundación Ford.

García Linera, A. (2006) 'State crisis
and popular power', *New Left
Review*, 37.

— (2007) 'El desencuentro de dos
razones revolucionarias: indian-
ismo y marxismo', *Cuadernos de
Pensamiento Crítico Latinoameri-
cano*, 3.

Garretón, M. A. (1987) *Reconstruir la
política: transición y consolidación
democrática en Chile*, Santiago:
Editorial Andante.

Gerchunoff, P. and H. Aguirre (2004)
'La política económica de Kirchner en la Argentina: varios estilos,
una sola agenda', *Boletín del Real
Instituto Elcano de Estudios Inter-
nacionales y Estratégicos*, 48, June.

Godio, J. (2004) 'The "Argentine
Anomaly": from wealth
through collapse to neo-
developmentalism', *Internationale
Politik und Gesellschaft*, fesportal.
fes.de/pls/portal30/docs (accessed
11 April 2008).

Goldfrank, B. and A. Schneider
(2003) 'Restraining the revolution
or deepening democracy? The
Workers' Party in Rio Grande do
Sul', in G. Baiocchi (ed.), *Radicals
in Power: The Workers' Party (PT)
and Experiments in Urban Democracy in Brazil*, London: Zed Books.

Golinger, E. (2005) *The Chávez
Code: Cracking US Intervention in
Venezuela*, Havana: Editorial José
Martí.

— (2006) *Bush vs. Chávez: Washington's War against Venezuela*,
Caracas: Monte Avila Editores.

— (2007) *The Chavéz Code: Cracking
US Intervention in Venezuela*,
London: Pluto Press.

Gómez, L. (2002) 'Alumbrado público en Acapulco de Juárez, Guerrero', in E. Cabrero (ed.), *Premio y gestión local: innovación en gobiernos locales*, Mexico: CIDE-CODEMUN-Fundación Ford.

Gómez Saraiva, M. (2007) 'Brasil y Argentina: política externa para América Latina en tiempos recientes', *América Latina Hoy. Revista de Ciencias Sociales*, 45, redalyc.uaemex.mx/redalyc (accessed 26 March 2008).

González, E. (2003) *Génesis y desarrollo organizativo del Partido de la Revolución Democrática en Querétaro 1989–1997*, Unpublished MA thesis, Universidad Autónoma de Querétaro.

Gott, R. (2000) *In the Shadow of the Liberator. Hugo Chávez and the Transformation of Venezuela*, London: Verso.

— (2004) *Cuba: A New History*, New Haven, CT: Yale University Press.

— (2007) 'Latin America as a white settler society', *Bulletin of Latin American Research*, 26(2).

Grandin, G. (2006) 'Latin America's new consensus', *The Nation*, 1 May, www.thenation.com (accessed 2 May 2006).

— (2008) 'Losing Latin America: what will the Obama doctrine be like?', 10 June, www.venezuelanalysis.com (accessed 12 June 2008).

Grigsby, W. (2004) '2004 municipal elections: the FSLN-Convergence victory in numbers', *Envio*, November, www.envio.org.ni (accessed 18 January 2008).

Grindle, M. (2004) *Despite the Odds: The Contentious Politics of Education Reform*, Oxford: Princeton University Press.

Grohmann, L. G. M. (2001) 'O processo legislativo no Rio Grande do Sul: 1995 a 1998', in F. Santos (ed.), *O Poder Legislativo nos Estados*, Rio de Janeiro: FGV.

Grugel, J. (2003) 'Democratisation studies globalisation: the coming of age of a paradigm', *British Journal of Politics and International Relations*, 5(2).

— (2007) 'Latin America after the Third Wave', *Government and Opposition*, 42(2).

Grugel, J. and M. Riggirozzi (2007) 'The return of the state in Argentina', *International Affairs*, 83(1).

Guarneros-Meza, V. (2006) *Partnerships and Participation in Mexican Urban Governance: The Experience of "Historic Centres" in Querétaro and San Luis Potosí*, Unpublished PhD thesis, De Montfort University, Leicester.

Guevara, A. (2005) *Chávez: Venezuela and the New Latin America. An Interview with Hugo Chávez*, New York: Ocean Press.

Guzmán, V. and P. Portocarrero (1985) *Dos Veces Mujer*, Lima: Mosca Azul Editores.

Harnecker, M. (2007a) *Rebuilding the Left*, London: Zed Books.

— (2007b) 'Blows and counterblows in Venezuela', in L. Panitch and C. Leys (eds), *Socialist Register 2008: Global Flashpoints: Reactions to Imperialism and Neoliberalism*, London: Merlin Press.

Hatcher, R. (2002) 'Participatory democracy and education: the experience of Porto Alegre and Rio Grande do Sul, Brazil', *Education and Social Justice*, 4(2).

Hawkins, K. (2003) 'Populism in Venezuela: the rise of Chavismo', *Third World Quarterly*, 24(6).

— (2006) 'Dependent civil society: the Circulos Bolivarianos in Venezuela', *Latin American Research Review*, 41(1).

Haya de la Torre, V. R. (1970) *El antimperialismo y el APRA*, Lima: Editorial Amauta.

Held, D. (2003) 'Global social democracy', in A. Giddens (ed.), *The Progressive Manifesto: New Ideas for the Centre-Left*, Cambridge: Polity Press.

Hellinger, D. (1991) *Venezuela: Tarnished Democracy*, Boulder, CO: Westview Press.

Hellinger, D. and S. Ellner (eds) (2003) *Venezuelan Politics in the Chávez Era: Class, Polarization and Conflict*, Boulder, CO: Lynne Rienner.

Hennigan, T. (2008) 'The turbulent priest challenging a dynasty', *The Times*, 18 April.

Hérnandez-Navarro, L. (2006) 'La APPO', *La Jornada*, 21 November, www.lajornada.unam.mx (accessed 21 November 2006).

Herrera Salas, J. M. (2007) 'Ethnicity and revolution: the political economy of racism in Venezuela', in S. Ellner and M. Tinker Salas (eds), *Venezuela: Hugo Chávez and the Decline of an Exceptional Democracy*, Maryland: Rowman and Littlefield.

Hite, C. (2000) *When the Romance Ended: Leaders of the Chilean Left, 1968–1998*, New York: Columbia University Press.

Hoffman, B. and L. Whitehead (2007) *Debating Cuban Exceptionalism*, New York: Palgrave Macmillan.

Holloway, J. and M. Sitrin (2007) 'Against and beyond the state: an interview with John Holloway', www.upsidedownworld.org/ (accessed 15 June 2007).

Hylton, F., and S. Thomson (2007) *Revolutionary Horizons: Past and Present in Bolivian Politics*, London: Verso.

IBGE (Instituto Brasileiro de Geogra-

fia e Estatística) (2007) Quoted in *Folha de S. Paulo*, 17 June.

Ikeda, L. (2007) 'George W. Bush conversó con Bolaños y Ortega', *La Prensa*, 9 January, www.laprensa.com.ni (accessed 9 January 2007).

INEP (2004) *Resultados do Saeb 2003: Brasil e Rio Grande do Sul*, Brasília: Ministério da Educação.

IRC (2003) 'The Buenos Aires Consensus', Silver City, NM: Interhemispheric Resource Center, americas.irc-online.org/ (accessed 13 April 2008).

James, C. L. R. (1980) *The Black Jacobins: Toussaint L'Ouverture and the San Domingo Revolution*, London: Allison & Busby.

Jones, G. and A. Pisa (2000) 'Public–private partnerships for urban land development in Mexico: a victory for hope versus expectation?', *Habitat International*, 24.

Jones, G. and A. Varley (1999) 'The reconquest of the historic centre: urban conservation and gentrification in Puebla, Mexico', *Environment and Planning A*, 31(2).

Juaréz, L. (2007) 'Vargas en desgracia con Ortega', *La Prensa*, 3 August, www.laprensa.com.ni (accessed 3 August 2007).

Kapcia, A. (2000) *Cuba: Island of Dreams*, Oxford: Berg.

— (2008) *Cuba in Revolution: A History since the Fifties*, London: Reaktion Books.

Karl, T. (1987) 'Petroleum and political pacts: the transition to democracy in Venezuela', *Latin American Research Review*, 22(1).

— (1997) *The Paradox of Plenty: Oil Booms and Petro-States*, Berkeley: University of California Press.

Katz, C. (2004) 'Coyuntura, modelo y distribución: las tendencias de la economía Argentina', *Revista Internacional en la Web*, www.

argenpress.info (accessed 11 April 2008).

Kautsky, K. (1981 [1918]) *The Dictatorship of the Proletariat*, New York: Greenwood Press.

Kay, C. (1989) *Latin American Theories of Development and Underdevelopment*, London: Routledge.

Kay, D. (1987) *Chileans in Exile: Private Struggles, Public Lives*, London: Macmillan.

Kennedy, D. (2006) 'Second chance for Nicaragua's Ortega', *BBC News*, 8 November, news.bbc. co.uk (accessed 18 January 2008).

Kirby, P. (2003) *Introduction to Latin America: Twenty-First Century Challenges*, London: Sage.

Klepak, H. (2005) *Cuba's Military 1990–2005: Revolutionary Soldiers during Counter-Revolutionary Times*, New York: Palgrave Macmillan.

Kosacoff, B. (1999) 'El caso argentino', in D. Chudnovsky, B. Kosacoff and A. López (eds), *Las multinacionales latinoamericanas: sus estrategías en un mundo globalizado*, Buenos Aires: Fondo de Cultura Económica.

Krastev, I. (2006) 'New threats to freedom: "democracy's doubles"', *Journal of Democracy*, 17(2).

Kulfas, M. (1999) *Características de la inversión extranjera en Argentina en la decada del noventa*, Buenos Aires: CEP.

— (2001) *El impacto del proceso de fusiones y adquisiciones en la Argentina sobre el mapa de grandes empresas*, Santiago: CEPAL.

Kulfas, M. and M. Schorr (2002) 'Sector industrial: la industria Argentina en el scenario post-convertibilidad', *Revista Realidad Economica*, 190, August/September.

Laclau, E. (1977) *Politics and Ideology in Marxist Thought*, London: New Left Books.

Laclau, E. and C. Mouffe (1985) *Hegemony and Socialist Strategy: Towards a Radical Democratic Party*, London: Verso.

Landau, S. (2004) 'The revolution turns forty', in A. Chomsky, B. Carr and P. M. Smorkaloff (eds), *The Cuba Reader: History, Culture, Politics*, Durham, NC: Duke University Press.

Latinobarómetro (2006) *Latinobarómetro Report 2006*, www. latinobaromentro.org (accessed 15 February 2008).

Lazar, S. (2006) '*El Alto, ciudad rebelde*: organisational bases for revolt', *Bulletin of Latin American Research*, 25(2).

Lenin, V. I. (1970 [1918]) *The Proletarian Revolution and the Renegade Kautsky*, Peking: Foreign Languages Press.

Leogrande, W. M. (2007) 'A poverty of imagination: George W. Bush's policy in Latin America', *Journal of Latin American Studies*, 39.

Levačić, R. and P. Downes (2004) *Formula Funding of Schools, Decentralization and Corruption: A comparative analysis*, Paris: International Institute for Education Planning.

Levy, D., K. Bruhn and E. Zabadúa (2001) *Mexico: The Struggles for Democratic Development*, Berkeley: University of California Press.

Lievesley, G. (1999) *Democracy in Latin America: Mobilization, Power and the Search for a New Politics*, Manchester: Manchester University Press.

— (2004) *The Cuban Revolution: Past, Present and Future Perspectives*, Basingstoke: Palgrave.

— (2006) 'Ideology, gender and citizenship: women in Latin and

Central America and in Cuba', in
S. Buckingham and G. Lievesley
(eds), *In the Hands of Women. Paradigms of Citizenship*, Manchester:
Manchester University Press.

Loasiga Lopez, L. (2008) 'Venezuela
financiará Hambre Cero', *La
Prensa*, 4 January, www.laprensa.
com.ni (accessed 4 January 2008).

Loasiga Lopez, L., Y. Luna and
L. Sanchez Corea (2007) 'Reelección continua y una constituente
tienten al FSLN', *La Prensa*, 16
January, www.laprensa.com.ni
(accessed 16 January 2007).

López, M. (2007) 'La gestión de Kirchner y los tratados bilaterales',
Paper, Centro de Estudios de
Nueva Mayoría, www.nuevamayo-
ria.com (accessed 4 April 2008).

López Maya, M. (2007) 'Venezuela
today: a "participative and pro-
tagonistic" democracy', in L. Pan-
itch and C. Leys (eds), *Socialist
Register 2008: Global Flashpoints:
Reactions to Imperialism and
Neoliberalism*, London: Merlin
Press.

Lousteau, M. (2003) *Hacia un feder-
alismo solidario*, Buenos Aires:
Temas Grupo Editorial.

Loveman, B. (1993) 'The political left
in Chile, 1973–1990', in B. Carr
and S. Ellner (eds), *The Latin
American Left. From the Fall of
Allende to Perestroika*, Boulder,
CO: Westview Press.

Löwy, M. (1981) *The Politics of Combined and Uneven Development*,
London: Verso.

— (2000) 'A Red government in the
south of Brazil', *Monthly Review*,
52(6).

Ludlam, S. (2009) 'The blinkered eye
of the perfect storm: the case of
the Cuban Five and the political
culture of terrorism in Miami,
Florida', in J. Schwartzkopf and

A. Kirchhofer (eds), *Workings of
the Anglosphere*, Trier: Wissen-
schaftliger Verlag.

Luxemberg, R. (1900) *Social Reform
or Revolution?*, London: Merlin
Press.

Lynch, J. (2006) *Simón Bolívar: A Life*,
New York: Yale University Press.

Maia, M. H., S. H. Cruz and S. L.
Vieira (2001) 'Eleições de diretores no Ceará: uma visão geral
do processo', in S. L. Vieira (ed.),
*Eleição de diretores: o que mudou
na escola?*, Brasília: Plano Editora.

Marenco, E. (2008) 'CSJ falla en
combo una de cal y una de arena
para Ortega', *El Nuevo Diario*,
11 January, www.elnuevodiario.
com.ni (accessed 11 January
2008).

Mariátegui, J. C. (1974) *Siete ensayos
de interpretación de la realidad
peruana*, Lima: Editorial Amauta.

Marques, J. L. (1998) *Rio Grande do
Sul: a vitória da esquerda*, Petrópolis: Editora Vozes.

Marquetti Nodarse, H. (2006) 'Le
restructuración del sistema
empresarial en Cuba: tendencias
principales', in O. E. Pérez
Villaneuva (ed.), *Reflexiones sobre
economía cubana*, Havana: Editorial de Ciencias Sociales.

Martí, J. (2007) *Our America*, Melbourne: Ocean Press.

Martinez Baharona, E. (2009) 'The
political kidnapping of the judici-
ary', in D. Close and S. Marti (eds),
*The Sandinistas and Nicaraguan
Politics since 1979*, New York:
Palgrave.

Martínez de Hoz, J. (2008) 'Otra
cortina de humo: mas persecu-
ción', foros.cerolag.com/f-mesa-
de-politica-60/ (accessed 4 April
2008).

Martínez Puentes, S. (2004) *Cuba
beyond Our Dreams: Economy,*

Politics and Unionism in the Material, Moral and Human Work of the Cuban Revolution, Havana: Editorial José Martí.

Marx, K. (1962) 'The eighteenth *Brumaire* of Louis Napoleon', in K. Marx, *Selected Works*, vol. 1, Moscow: Foreign Languages Publishing House.

— (1971) *Manifesto of the Communist Party*, Moscow: Progress Publishers.

— (1974) 'Critique of the Gotha Programme', in D. Fernbach (ed.), *Karl Marx: The First International and After*, Harmondsworth: Penguin.

— (1979) *Capital*, vol. 1, Harmondsworth: Penguin.

Marx, K. and F. Engels (1974) *On Colonialism*, Moscow: Progress Publishers.

McCaughlan, M. (2004) *The Battle of Venezuela*, London: Latin America Bureau.

McKinley, J., Jr, and J. Repolgle (2006) 'Leftist headed to victory in Nicaragua', *New York Times*, 7 November, www.nytimes.com/2006 (accessed 18 January 2008).

Méndez-Ortíz, A. (2005) 'René Bejarano: absuelto por lavado de dinero', *La Jornada*, 6 July, www.jornada.unam.mx/ (accessed 16 March 2007).

Mendonça de Barros, L. C. (2008) 'A política industrial do governo de Lula', *Folha de S. Paulo*, 16 May.

Mesa-Lago, C. (2004) 'Experiences in the Americas with Social Security pensions and their reform: lessons for workers and unions', *Labour Education*, 121, April, New York: International Labour Organization.

Mettenheim, K. (1995) *The Brazilian Voter: Mass Politics in Democratic Transition, 1974–1986*, London: University of Pittsburgh Press.

Mideplan (Ministerio de Planificación y Cooperación) (2008) 'Lucha contra la pobreza y reforma previsional destacan a Chile en foro internacional', www.mideplan.cl (accessed 17 March 2008).

Miguel, L. F. (2008) 'Political representation and gender in Brazil: quotas for women and their impact', *Bulletin of Latin American Research*, 27(2).

Miller, N. (1999) *In the Shadow of the State*, London: Verso.

Ministerio de Comunicaión e Información (2006) *Ley de Consejos Comunales*, Caracas: Colección Textos Legislativos.

Mohanty, C. (2003) *Feminisms without Borders: Decolonizing Theory, Practising Solidarity*, Durham, NC, and London: Duke University Press.

Mommer, B. (2003) 'Subversive oil', in D. Hellinger and S. Ellner (eds), *Venezuelan Politics*, Boulder, CO: Lynne Rienner.

Monasterios, K., P. Stefanoni and H. Do Alto (2007) *Reinventando la nación en Bolivia*, La Paz: CLACSO Editores and Plural.

Monreal, P. (2006) 'La globalización y los dilemas de las trayectorias económicas de Cuba: Matriz Bolivariano, industrialización y desarrollo', in O. E. Pérez Villaneuva (ed.), *Reflexiones sobre economía cubana*, Havana: Editorial de Ciencias Sociales.

Mora, M. (2007) 'Zapatista anti-capitalist politics and the "other campaign": learning from the struggle for indigenous rights and autonomy', *Latin American Perspectives*, 153(34).

Morales, J. (2001) 'Economic vulnerability in Bolivia', in J. Crabtree and L. Whitehead (eds), *Towards*

Democratic Viability: The Bolivian Experience, Basingstoke: Palgrave.

Morales, M. (2005) 'Los gobiernos locales y los partidos políticos', *Gestión y Política Pública*, 14(2).

Morales Cartaya, A. (2001) 'Palabras finales', *Gaceta Laboral*, 2.

— (2005) 'Cómo alcanzar el alto desemeño del capital humano en las entidades', *Gaceta Laboral*, 11.

Moreno, M. (2006) *Emergencia del paradigma de gobernabilidad en América Latina*, Unpublished PhD thesis, Leiden University.

Morley, M. and C. McGillion (2002) *Unfinished Business: America and Cuba after the Cold War, 1989–2001*, Cambridge: Cambridge University Press.

Morris, E. (2007) 'How exceptional is the Cuban economy?', in B. Hoffman and L. Whitehead (eds), *Debating Cuban Exceptionalism*, New York: Palgrave Macmillan.

— (2008) 'Cuba and Venezuela', at www.londonmet.ac.uk/research-units/cuba/past-events/buxton-and-morris.cfm (accessed 3 June 2008).

Moser, P. (2006) 'Old rebel finds new cause', *Globe and Mail*, 7 November, www.theglobeandmail.com (accessed 18 January 2008).

Motta, S. (2006) 'Utopias re-imagined: a reply to Panizza', *Political Studies*, 54(4).

— (2008) 'New ways of making and living politics: the Movimiento de Trabajadores Desocupados de Solano and the "Movement of Movements"', *Bulletin of Latin American Research*, 27(2).

MST (2008) 'About Brazil's Landless Workers Movement', www.mst brazil.org (accessed 24 April 2008).

Muhr, T. (2008) 'Nicaragua re-visited: from neo-liberal "ungovernability" to the Bolivarian Alternative for the Peoples of Our America (ALBA)', *Globalisation, Societies and Education*, 6(2).

Munck, R. (1990) 'Farewell to socialism? A comment on recent debates', *Latin American Perspectives*, 65(17).

Murillo, R. (2006) 'El voto de la conciencia', *Unida, Nicaragua Triunfa*, www.nicaraguatriunfa. com (accessed 17 January 2008).

Naspolini, A. (2001) 'A reforma da educação básica no Ceará: uma construção coletiva', *Estudos Avançados*, 15(42).

Navarrate, P. (2005) 'A continent at the crossroads', *Red Pepper*, January, www.redpepper.org (accessed 10 February 2005).

Neruda, P. (1984) *Canto general*, Barcelona: Burguera Libro Amigo.

Nova Gonzáles, A. (2006) 'El mercado interno de los alimentos', in O. E. Pérez Villaneuva (ed.), *Reflexiones sobre economía cubana*, Havana: Editorial de Ciencias Sociales.

Novelli, M. (2007) 'Sintraemcali and social movement unionism: trade union resistance to neoliberal globalisation in Colombia', in A. Gamble, S. Ludlam, A. Taylor and S. Wood (eds), *Labour, the State, Social Movements and the Challenge of Neo-liberal Globalisation*, Manchester: Manchester University Press.

Nueva Izquierda (2007) 'Línea política – documento base', www. nuevaizquierda.org.mx (accessed 26 February 2007).

O'Donnell, G. (1994) 'Delegative democracy', *Journal of Democracy*, 5(1).

— (1996) 'Poverty and inequality in Latin America: some reflections', Kellogg Institute for International Studies Working Paper no. 225, July, www.nd.edu/~kellogg/

publications (accessed 24 April 2008).

O'Donnell, G., P. C. Schmitter and L. Whitehead (eds) (1986) *Transitions from Authoritarian Rule*, Baltimore, MD: Johns Hopkins University Press.

O'Shaughnessy, H. (2007) 'Are we keeping up with Latin America?', 2007 Annual Lecture of the Society for Latin American Studies, www.slas.org.uk/about/docs (accessed 3 June 2008).

O'Toole, G. (2003) 'A new nationalism for a new era: the political ideology of Mexican neoliberalism', *Bulletin of Latin American Research*, 22(3).

Observador Económico (2007) '¿2007–2008: un nuevo comienzo o más de lo mismo?', 31 December.

Olivares, I. (2008) '¿Quien controlará fondo petrolero?', *Confidencial*, 1(6), www.confidencial.com.ni (accessed 21 January 2008).

Oppenheim Hecht, L. (1993) *Politics in Chile: Democracy, Authoritarianism, and the Search for Development*, Boulder, CO: Westview Press.

Osava, M. (2007) 'Brazil: no consensus on success of land reform', Inter-Press Service, 22 March.

Panizza, F. (2005) 'Unarmed utopia revisited: the resurgence of left-of-centre politics in Latin America', *Political Studies*, 53(4).

— (2006) 'La marea rosa', Análise de conjuntura observatorio político Sul-Americano no. 8, August, Rio de Janeiro: Instituto Universitario de Pesquisas do Río de Janeiro IUPERJ/UCAM.

Pantoja, A. (2007) 'Consejos avanzados de nuevo sistema político', *El Nuevo Diario*, 15 February, www.elnuevodiario.com.ni (accessed 15 February 2007).

Paulson, J. (2000) 'Peasant struggles

and international solidarity: the case of Chiapas', in L. Panitch and C. Leys (eds), *Socialist Register 2001: Working Classes, Global Realities*, London: Merlin Press.

Pearce, J. (1982) *Under the Eagle: US Intervention in Central America and the Caribbean*, London: Latin American Bureau.

— (2004) 'Collective action or public participation? Complementary or contradictory democratisation strategies in Latin America', *Bulletin of Latin American Research*, 23(4).

Perez Baltadano, A. (2009) 'Nicaraguan political culture and the FSLN: from utopianism to pragmatism', in D. Close and S. Marti (eds), *The Sandinistas and Nicaraguan Politics since 1979*, New York: Palgrave.

Pérez Lara, A. (2005) 'Articulación social-clasista y nuevos actores sociales en América Latina', in G. Valdés Gutiérrez (ed.), *Pradigmas emancipatorios en América Latina*, Havana: Editorial Academia.

Pérez Navarro, L. (2008) 'Nuevo sistema de pagos por resultados', *Granma*, 11 June.

Petras, J. (1988) 'State, regime and the democratization muddle', *Latin American Studies Association Forum*, 18(4).

— (1990) 'The metamorphosis of Latin America's intellectuals', *Latin American Perspectives*, 17, Spring.

— (1997) 'Latin America: the resurgence of the left', *New Left Review*, 223.

— (1999) *The Left Strikes Back*, Oxford: Westview.

— (2006) 'Is Latin America really turning left?', www.venezuelanalysis.com (accessed 5 July 2006).

— (2007a) 'Latin America – four competing blocs of power', petras. lahaine.org (accessed 7 May 2008).

— (2007b) 'Latin America's changing mosaic: movements in flux and center-left governments in power', petras.lahaine.org (accessed 7 May 2008).

Petras, J. and F. I. Leiva (1994) *Democracy and Poverty in Chile: The Limits to Electoral Politics*, Boulder, CO: Westview Press.

Petras, J. and H. Veltmeyer (2005) *Social Movements and State Power: Argentina, Brazil, Bolivia, Ecuador*, London: Pluto Press.

Pierson, C. (2001) *Hard Choices: Social Democracy in the 21st Century*, Cambridge: Polity.

Pizarro, C., D. Raczynski and J. Vial (eds) (1995) *Políticas económicas y sociales en el Chile democrático*, Santiago: CIEPLAN/UNICEF.

PNUD (2005) *La economía más allá del gas*, La Paz: Programa de las Naciones Unidas para el Desarrollo.

— (2007) *El estado del estado en Bolivia*, La Paz: Programa de las Naciones Unidas para el Desarrollo.

Political Database of the Americas (2008) pdba.georgetown.edu (accessed 18 January 2008).

Porras, F. (2005) *Broadening Understandings of Governance: The Case of Mexican Local Government*, Unpublished PhD thesis, University of Warwick, Coventry.

Portes, A. and K. Hoffman (2003) 'Latin American class structures: their composition and change during the neoliberal era', *Latin American Research Review*, 38(1).

Prado, F., S. Seleme and C. Peña (2007) *Poder y elites en Santa Cruz*, Santa Cruz: Cordaid and Cedure.

Prud'homme, J. F. (1997) 'El PRD:

su vida interna y sus elecciones estratégicas', Occasional Paper no. 39, Mexico: Centro de Investigación y Docencia Económicas.

Przeworski, A. (1985) *Capitalism and Social Democracy*, Cambridge: Cambridge University Press.

Raby, D. (2006a) *Democracy and Revolution in Latin America and Socialism Today*, London: Pluto Press.

— (2006b) 'Venezuela: the myths of James Petras', December, www.venezuelanalysis.com (accessed 21 December 2006).

Ramírez-Saiz, J. M. (1998) 'Tendencias de la alternancia política y de la transición democrática en los ayuntamientos del area metropolitana de Guadalajara', in J. M. Ramírez-Saiz (ed.), *¿Cómo Gobiernan Guadalajara? Demandas Ciudadanas y Respuestas de los Ayuntamientos*, Mexico: Porrúa-IIS/UNAM-Universidad de Guadalajara.

— (2003) 'Organizaciones cívicas, democracia y sistema político', in A. Aziz-Nassif (ed), *México al inicio del siglo XX1: democracia, ciudadanía y desarrollo*, Mexico: Pirrúa-CIESAS.

Rands, M. (2008) 'Os dois brasis', *Folha de S. Paulo*, 24 February.

Rapoport, M. (2002) *Tiempos de crisis, vientos de cambio: Argentina y el poder global*, Cali: Grupo Editorial Norma.

Reed, A. (2006) 'Nicaraguans favour abortion in some cases', www.angus-reid.com (accessed 16 January 2008).

Regalado, R. (2007) *Latin America at the Crossroads. Domination, Crisis, Popular Movements and Political Alternatives*, Melbourne: Ocean Press.

Reid, M. (2007) *Forgotten Continent:*

The Battle for Latin America's Soul, London: Yale University Press.

Rénique, G. and D. Poole (2008) 'The Oaxaca commune: struggling for autonomy and dignity', *NACLA Report on the Americas*, 41(3).

Republic of Cuba (1992) *Constitución de la República de Cuba*, Havana: Editora Política.

Retamar, R. F. (2000) *Todo Calibán*, Havana: Editorial Letras Cubanas.

Ricupero, R. (2004) 'UNCTAD past and present: our next forty years', 12th Raúl Prebisch Lecture, Geneva, 12 September, cep.cl/UNRISD/References/UNCTAD/ (accessed 11 April 2008).

Ríos Tobar, M. (2007) 'Chilean feminism and social democracy from the democratic transition to Bachelet', *NACLA Report on the Americas*, 40(2).

Roberts, K. (2002) 'Social inequalities without class cleavages in Latin America's neoliberal era', *Studies in Comparative International Development*, 36(4).

Robinson, W. I. (1995) 'Pushing polyarchy: the US–Cuba case and the Third World', *Third World Quarterly*, 16(4).

— (2007) 'Transformative possibilities in Latin America', in L. Panitch and C. Leys (eds), *Socialist Register 2008: Global Flashpoints: Reactions to Imperialism and Neoliberalism*, London: Merlin Press.

Rocha, J. (2002) 'Lula win raises hopes in Brazil', *NACLA Newsletter*, December.

Rochlin, J. (1997) *Redefining Mexican 'Security': Society, State and Region under NAFTA*, Boulder, CO: Lynne Rienner.

Rodríguez, V., P. Ward and E. Cabrero (1999) *New Federalism and State Government in Mexico: Bringing the State Back In*, Austin: University of Texas.

Rodríguez Elizondo, J. (1990) *Las crisis de las izquierdas en América Latina*, Caracas: Editorial Nueva Sociedad.

Rodríguez-Acosta, C. and A. Rosenbaum (2005) 'Local government and the governance of metropolitan areas in Latin America', *Public Administration and Development*, 25.

Rogers, T. (2007) 'Ortega balances Venezuelan aid, IMF', *Nica Times*, 27 April–3 May, www.nicatimes.net (accessed 7 May 2007).

— (2008) 'Nicaraguan opposition resists Chavez's expanding "revolution"', *Christian Science Monitor*, 3 January, www.csmonitor.com (accessed 3 January 2008).

Rosen, F. (2007) 'Breaking with the past: a 40th anniversary interview with Margarita López-Maya', *NACLA Report on the Americas*, 40(3).

Rueschemeyer, D., E. H. Stephens and J. D. Stephens (1992) *Capitalist Development and Democracy*, Chicago: University of Chicago Press.

Rugama, M. (2008) 'Campesina apenada por querer vender chancha', *El Nuevo Diario*, 2 January, www.elnuevodiario.com.ni (accessed 3 January 2008).

Ruiz, L. (2006) *Francisco Wuytack: la revolución de la conciencia*, Caracas: Fundación Editorial el Perro y la Rana.

Russel, R. and J. G. Tokatlian (2003) *El lugar de Brasil en la política exterior Argentina*, Buenos Aires: Fondo de Cultura Económica.

Sabo, E. (2007) 'Education reforms make the grade', *Nica Times*, 8–14 June, www.nictimes.net (accessed 16 June 2007).

Sader, E. (2005) 'Taking Lula's measure', *New Left Review*, 33.
— (2008) 'The weakest link? Neoliberalism in Latin America', *New Left Review*, 52.
Salazar, M. (2008) 'Peru: indigenous organizations aim for the presidency', 29 May, www.upsidedownworld.org (accessed 6 June 2008).
Sanchez Corea, L. and O. Enriquez (2007) 'Alcalde Marenco reta a Murillo', *La Prensa*, 10 June, www.laprensa.com.ni (accessed 10 June 2007).
Sandbrook, R., M. Edelman, P. Heller and J. Teichman (2007) *Social Democracy in the Global Periphery: Origins, Challenges, Prospects*, Cambridge: Cambridge University Press.
Saney, I. (2004) *Cuba: A Revolution in Motion*, London: Zed Books.
Santín, L. and M. Tapia (2006) 'Cabildo infantil: Acapulco, Guerrero', in T. Guillén, P. López and P. Rojo (eds), *Premio y gestión local: municipio y buen gobierno*, Mexico: CIDE.
Sarmiento, D. F. (1998) *Facundo: Or Civilization and Barbarism*, Harmondsworth: Penguin.
Sassoon, D. (1996) *One Hundred Years of Socialism: The West European Left in the Twentieth Century*, London: I.B.Tauris.
Schmidtke, O. (ed.) (2002) *The Third Way Transformation of Social Democracy*, Aldershot: Ashgate.
Schneider, B. R. (1998) 'The material bases of technocracy: investor confidence and neo-liberalism in Latin America', in M. A. Centeno and P. Silva (eds), *The Politics of Expertise in Latin America*, London: Macmillan.
Schnookal, D. and M. Muñiz (eds) (1999) *José Martí Reader: Writings on the Americas*, Melbourne: Ocean Press.
Schwartzmann, S. (2003) 'The challenges of education of Brazil', Working Paper CBS-38-2003, Oxford: Oxford University Centre for Brazilian Studies.
Shank, A. (2008) 'El Salvador: The UDW interview with FMLN presidential candidate Mauricio Funes', 12 May, www.upsidedownworld.org (accessed 12 June 2008).
Shuster, F. (2005) 'Izquierda política y movimientos sociales en la Argentina contemporánea', in C. Garavito, P. S. Barret and D. Chávez (eds), *La nueva izquierda en América Latina*, Bogotá/Barcelona: Grupo Editorial Norma.
Sigmund, P. E. (1977) *The Overthrow of Allende and the Politics of Chile, 1964–1976*, Pittsburgh, PA: University of Pittsburgh Press.
Silva, P. (1993) 'Social democracy, neoliberalism, and ideological change in the Chilean socialist movement, 1973–1992', *Nordic Journal of Latin American Studies*, 23(1/2).
— (2008) *In the Name of Reason: Technocrats and Politics in Chile*, University Park, PA: Penn State University Press.
Sivak, M. (2007) *Santa Cruz: una tésis: el conflicto regional en Bolivia (2003–2006)*, La Paz: Plural.
Skelcher, C., N. Mathur and M. Smith (2005) 'The public governance of collaborative spaces: discourse, design and democracy', *Public Administration*, 83(3).
Smith, W. S. (1987) *The Closest of Enemies: A Personal and Diplomatic Account of US–Cuban Relations since 1959*, New York: Norton.
Soberón Valdés, F. (2005) *6to período ordinario de sesiones de la sexta legislatura de la asamblea nacional*

del poder popular, Havana: Republic of Cuba.

Spronk, S. (2008) 'After the water wars in Bolivia: the struggle for a "social-public" alternative', 29 April, www.upsidedownworld. org (accessed 12 June 2008).

Spronk, S. and J. R. Webber (2007) 'Struggles against accumulation by dispossession in Bolivia: the political economy of natural resource contention', *Latin American Perspectives*, 153(34).

Stahler-Sholk, R., H. E. Vanden and D. Kuecker (2007) 'Globalizing resistance: the new politics of social movements in Latin America', *Latin American Perspectives*, 34(2).

Stédile, P. (2003) 'Three directions in Brazil', *ZMag*, October, www. zmag.org (accessed 10 January 2004).

— (2004) 'Brazil's landless battalions: the *Sem Terra* movement', in T. Mertes (ed.), *A Movement of Movements: Is Another World Really Possible?*, London: Verso.

— (2007) 'The class struggles in Brazil: the perspective of the MST', in L. Panitch and C. Leys (eds), *Socialist Register 2008: Global Flashpoints: Reactions to Imperialism and Neoliberalism*, London: Merlin Press.

Stokes, D. (2006) '"Iron fists in iron gloves": the political economy of US terrorocracy promotion in Colombia', *British Journal of Politics and International Relations*, 8(3).

Stolowicz, S. (2004) 'The Latin American left: between governability and change', in D. Chavez and B. Goldfrank (eds), *The Left in the City: Participatory Local Governments in Latin America*, London: Latin America Bureau.

Suárez Salazar, L. (1997) *¿Aislamiento o reinserción en un mundo cambiado?*, Havana: Editorial de Ciencias Sociales.

Svampa, M. (2007) 'Las fronteras del gobierno de Kirchner: entre la consolidación de lo viejo y las aspiraciones de lo nuevo', *CDC*, 24, www.scielo.org.ve.

Swords, A. C. S. (2007) 'Neo-Zapatista network politics: transforming democracy and development', *Latin American Perspectives*, 153(34).

Swyngedouw, E. (2005) 'Governance innovation and the citizen: the Janus face of governance-beyond-the-state', *Urban Studies*, 42(11).

Taylor, M. (2006) *From Pinochet to the 'Third Way': Neoliberalism and Social Transformation in Chile*, London: Pluto Press.

Thomas, H. (1971) *Cuba or the Pursuit of Freedom*, London: Eyre & Spottiswoode.

Thomson, A. (2008) 'Mexico City looks for food crisis solution in families' backyards and roof terraces', *Financial Times*, 28 June.

Torrado, S. (2004) *La herencia del ajuste: cambios en la sociedad y la familia*, Buenos Aires: Capital Intelectual.

Tulchin, J. S. and A. Varas (eds) (1991) *From Dictatorship to Democracy: Rebuilding Political Consensus in Chile*, Boulder, CO: Lynne Rienner.

Tunnerman Bernheim, C. (2007) 'El laberinto jurídico de los CP', *El Nuevo Diario*, 4 December, www. elnuevodiario.com.ni (accessed 5 December 2007).

Unasur (2008) *Tratado constitutivo de la unión de naciones suramericanas*, www.comunidadandina. org/unasur/tratado_constitutivo. htm (accessed 4 June 2008).

UNDP (2004a) *Democracy in Latin America: Towards a Citizen's Democracy*, New York: UN Development Programme.

— (2004b) *Democracy in Latin America: Towards a Citizen's Democracy: Statistical Compendium*, New York: UN Development Programme.

UNICEF (2008) 'At a Glance: Nicaragua', www.unicef.org/infoby country/nicaragua.html (accessed 21 September 2008).

United Nations (2006) *Full Employment and Decent Work for All: Regional Highlights*, Geneva: United Nations.

US Department of State (2004) *Commission for Assistance to a Free Cuba: Report to the President, May 2004*, Washington, DC: US Department of State.

— (2006) *Commission for Assistance to a Free Cuba: Report to the President, July 2006*, Washington, DC: US Department of State.

Valdés, J. G. (1995) *Pinochet's Economists: The Chicago School in Chile*, Cambridge: Cambridge University Press.

Valdés Mesa, S. (2008) 'Más allá el salario', *Bohemia*, 22 April.

Valente, M. (2008) 'Argentina: farm strike exposes Fernández's weak flank', 31 March, www. upsidedownworld.org (accessed 7 April 2008).

Valenzuela, A. (1978) *The Breakdown of Democratic Regimes: Chile*, Baltimore, MD: Johns Hopkins University Press.

Valenzuela, J. S. (1992) 'Democratic consolidation in post-transitional settings: notion, process, and facilitating conditions', in S. Mainwaring, G. O'Donnell and J. S. Valenzuela (eds), *Issues in Democratic Consolidation: The New South*

American Democracies in Comparative Perspective, Notre Dame, IN: University of Notre Dame Press.

Van Cott, D. (2003) 'From exclusion to inclusion: Bolivia's 2002 elections', *Journal of Latin American Studies*, 35(4).

Vanden, H. E. (2007) 'Social movements, hegemony, and new forms of resistance', *Latin American Perspectives*, 153(34).

Vargas, V. (1982) 'El movimiento feminista en el Perú', Mimeo, Lima.

Vargas Llosa, M. (n.d.) 'Alturas de Macchu Picchu: sube a nacer conmigo hermano (los jaivas)', www.youtube.com/watch? v=QZ8C0Y21OVY (accessed 22 March 2008).

Vidal, E. M. and I. S. de Farias (2005) 'SAEB no Ceará: o desafio de definer o foco na aprendizagem', in *Gestão para o sucesso escolar*, Fortaleza: Edições SEDUC.

Vieira, S. L. (2005) 'Financiamento e gestão da educação pública', *Gestão escolar, recursos financeiros e patrimoniais*, Fortaleza: SEDUC.

Vieira, S. L. and I. S. de Farias (2002) *História da educação no Ceará: sobre promessas, fatos e feitos*, Fortaleza: Edições Demócrito Rocha.

Vilariño Ruiz, E. (1997) *Cuba: reforma y modernización socialista*, Havana: Editorial de Ciencias Sociales.

Vilas, C. M. (1997) 'Participation, inequality and the whereabouts of democracy', in C. M. Vilas, D. A. Chalmers, K. Hite, S. B. Martin, K. Piester and M. Segarra (eds), *The New Politics of Inequality in Latin America: Rethinking Participation and Representation*, New York: Oxford University Press.

Wainwright, H. (2005) 'Lula's lament', *Red Pepper*, October, www.redpepper.org (accessed 15 November 2005).

Waylen, G. (1996) 'Democratization, feminism and the state in Chile: the establishment of SERNAM', in S. M. Rai and G. Lievesley (eds), *Women and the State. International Perspectives*, London: Taylor & Francis.

Weisbrot, M. (2001) 'Don't cry for the IMF, Argentina', www.commondreams.org.

Weisbrot, M. and D. Baker (2002) 'What happened to Argentina?', Briefing Papers, Washington, DC: Center for Economic and Policy Research.

Weisbrot, M. and L. Sandoval (2007) 'Argentina's economic recovery: policy choices and implications', CEPR Paper, www.cepr.net/index.php/publications/reports/ (accessed 11 April 2008).

Whitehead, L. (2001) 'The emergence of democracy in Bolivia', in J. Crabtree and L. Whitehead (eds), *Towards Democratic Viability: The Bolivian Experience*, Basingstoke: Palgrave.

— (2007) 'On Cuban political exceptionalism', in B. Hoffman and L. Whitehead (2007), *Debating Cuban Exceptionalism*, New York: Palgrave Macmillan.

Wilkinson, S. (2008) 'US Cuba policy after Bush: succession or transition?', *International Journal of Cuban Studies*, 1(1).

Williamson, E. (1993) *The Penguin History of Latin America*, Harmondsworth: Penguin.

Wilpert, G. (2007) *Changing Venezuela by Taking Power: The History and Policies of the Chávez Government*, London: Verso.

Wolfensohn, J. (1999) 'A proposal for a comprehensive development framework. A World Bank document, January 21 1999', Washington, DC: World Bank.

World Bank (2003) 'Strategies for poverty reduction in Ceará: the challenges of inclusive modernization', Report no. 24500, BR, 10 April, Washington, DC: World Bank.

Yashar, D. (2005) *Contesting Citizenship: the Rise of Indigenous Movements and the Post-liberal Challenge*, Cambridge: Cambridge University Press.

Zegada, M., Y. Tórrez and G. Cámara (2008) *Movimientos sociales en tiempos de poder*, La Paz: Centro Cuarto Intermedio.

Zibechi, R. (2005) 'New challenges for radical social movements', *NACLA Report on the Americas*, 38(5).

— (2007) '5th Congress of Brazil's Landless Movement: creating the basis for a new world?', 24 August, wwwupsidedownworld.org (accessed 7 April 2008).

— (2008) 'The Latin American right: finding a place in the world', *NACLA*, 41(1).

Index